Western Echoes of the
Harlem Renaissance

Western Echoes of the Harlem Renaissance

The Life and Writings of Anita Scott Coleman

Edited by
Cynthia Davis and Verner D. Mitchell

University of Oklahoma Press : Norman

Also Edited by Cynthia Davis and Verner D. Mitchell

Where the Wild Grape Grows: Selected Writings, 1930–1950, by
   Dorothy West (Amherst, 2005)

Library of Congress Cataloging-in-Publication Data

Western echoes of the Harlem Renaissance : the life and writings of
Anita Scott Coleman / edited by Cynthia Davis and Verner D. Mitchell
      p.   cm.
   Includes bibliographical references.
   ISBN 978-0-8061-3956-2 (hardcover : alk. paper)
   ISBN 978-0-8061-3975-3 (pbk. : alk. paper
   1. Coleman, Anita Scott. 2. Authors, American—20th century—
Biography. 3. African American authors—Biography. 4. African
Americans—Biography. 5. Harlem Renaissance. I. Davis, Cynthia J.,
1964– II. Mitchell, Verner D., 1957–
   PS3505.O2774Z95 2008
   813'.52—dc22
   [B]
                                                    2008009094

The paper in this book meets the guidelines for permanence and
durability of the Committee on Production Guidelines for Book
Longevity of the Council on Library Resources. ∞

1   2   3   4   5   6   7   8   9   10

To the memory of Anita Scott Coleman

Contents

List of Illustrations   xi

Preface   xiii

Acknowledgments   xix

Chronology   xxi

Introduction: Anita Scott Coleman in the Southwest   3

Part I: Stories

The Brat   75

Three Dogs and a Rabbit   85

El Tisico   94

The Little Grey House   98

Cross Crossings Cautiously   109

Jack Arrives   112

Bambino Grimke   118

Bambino: Star Boarder   129

Rich Man, Poor Man   139

Pot Luck: A Story True to Life   147

Two Old Women A-Shopping Go!
    A Story of Man, Marriage and Poverty   157

The Mechanical Toy   163

Love for Hire 171

. . . G'Long, Old White Man's Gal . . . 174

Phoebe and Peter up North 181

Phoebe Goes to a Lecture 188

Part II: Poems

Hands 195

Impressions from a Family Album 197

Portraiture 201

Idle Wonder 202

The Shining Parlor 203

Black Faces 204

America Negra 205

Baptism 208

Words, Words, Words 210

This, Then, Is Courage 211

The Colorist 212

Humility 213

The Pool 214

Steps to Transcendence 215

A Tale and a Moral 217

The Treasure-Trove of Andy Kane 218

Mystery 219

This Knowledge Springs 220

Freedom Is A-Borning Still 221

Awareness 223

Peace Talk 225

Peace Item 226

The Land Where Silk Came From 227

Peace Is a Little Bird 228

Whence Cometh Strength 229

Travel-Log 231

Veils That Blow 232

From a Trolley Window   233
Proposal   234
What Choice?   235
Lasting Impression   236
She Was Not Wise   237
Inspiration   238
Black Baby   239
Adventure   241
A Year Is Not Long   242
Parenthood   243
Life Is a See-Saw   245
The Good Tomorrow   247
I Am Glad for Tears   248
Boarding Home for Children   249
How Glad I Am   252
November   253
Lamps   254
Dry Bones   255
Barter   256
Tribute   257
Routine   258
Decision   259
The Dust of the Streets   260
Respective Flight   261
Modes   262
Definition   263
Prima Donna Musing   264
She Is Not Proud   265
On Hearing Four White Men Singing Spirituals   266
Audition   267
Folksong   268
Theme with Variations   269

Part III: Essays

Unfinished Masterpieces   275
Arizona and New Mexico—The Land of Esperanza   280

Appendix I. Stories by Anita Scott Coleman
   Not Included in This Volume   287
Appendix II. The Family of Anita Scott Coleman:
   A Genealogical Chart   288–289
Notes   291
Works Cited   297

Illustrations

Anita Scott Coleman as an infant in Guaymas, Mexico   47

Scott family in Mexico   48

Mary Ann Stokes Scott in Mexico   49

Mary Ann Stokes Scott and her daughter Anita, ca. 1907   50

African American troops, or "Buffalo Soldiers"   51

William Henry Scott and his Masonic brothers in
Silver City, New Mexico, ca. 1910   52

Coleman's brother, William Ulysses Scott, in military uniform   53

Coleman's sister-in-law, Ida Gonzalez, on the ranch, ca. 1915   54

Sisters-in-law Anita Scott and Ida Gonzalez Scott
on the ranch, ca. 1915   55

Anita "Annie" Scott, reading at the ranch, ca. 1915   56

Ruth Ann Scott in Silver City, New Mexico, ca. 1932   57

Anita Coleman and her children on the ranch, ca. 1925   58

Crisis award winners, February 1927   59

Coleman's first Los Angeles residence   60

The Citizens' Band, ca. 1910   61

Negro History Club, Los Angeles, 1937   62

Harold Coleman and classmates, Jefferson High School,
ca. 1942   63

Army boxing team during World War II, ca. 1943   64

Spencer Scott Coleman, November 1952   65
"Daddy Jim" Coleman in his printing shop, Los Angeles,
    ca. 1940   66
Daddy Jim returning from the library, Los Angeles, ca. 1940   67
Coleman and children going to church, Los Angeles   68
Coleman surrounded by family members and foster
    children, 1948   69
Coleman, her husband, and her sister-in-law Willianna Hicks,
    at the Hollywood Bowl, Los Angeles, ca. 1948   70
Coleman's final residence, Los Angeles   71
Coleman's grandchildren, July 2006   72

Unless otherwise noted, all photographs are from the Anita Scott Coleman family collection.

Preface

When my five offspring finish with their graduations and what-
not, I shall settle down comfortably, while my husband stands
by to fend off peddlers, solicitors and agents, muzzle the telephone,
put out the cat, tie up the dog and supply me with ice cream,
preferably strawberry sundaes . . . and I shall, I shall write!
Anita Scott Coleman, *Pittsburgh Courier* 13 July 1940

Anita Scott Coleman (1890–1960), born in Mexico of African
American parents, enjoyed a contemporary reputation as one of the
most distinctive and prolific of the Harlem Renaissance writers. Despite
the distance between Harlem and her homes in Silver City, New
Mexico, and later Los Angeles, Coleman published numerous short
stories, essays, articles, and poems in the important race journals of
uplift and social change (the *Crisis*, the *Messenger*, the *Competitor*, and
Opportunity); in African American newspapers such as the *Pittsburgh
Courier*, the *Nashville Clarion*, the *Southwest Review*, and the *Chicago
Defender*; and in the black women's publication *Half-Century Magazine*. Coleman's name "cropped up frequently on literary prize short-
lists," alongside Zora Neale Hurston, Countee Cullen, Marita Bonner,
Langston Hughes, and Claude McKay (Lutz and Ashton 25). In
1928, at the zenith of the Harlem Renaissance, the *Messenger* hailed
Coleman as "one of the best of the Negro writers and a winner of
many prizes for short stories" ("Unfortunate" 111).

In Los Angeles, where she lived from 1926 to her death in 1960, Coleman was certainly aware of fellow writers at work there, including Langston Hughes, Loren Miller, Arna Bontemps, and Wallace Thurman, all of whom visited or lived in the "Harlem of the West" (Glasrud and Champion 77).[1] She would also have known of Charles S. Johnson's visit in 1927 to Los Angeles, where he surveyed labor conditions and organized a group of prominent "race men and women" into a writers' group called the Ink Slingers. The poetry of Hughes and the civil rights activism of Miller influenced this group, which included the playwright Garland Anderson (Tyler 35).[2] During these same years, she corresponded with Countee Cullen, whom she came to know in his capacity as assistant editor for *Opportunity*.

The *Crisis* and *Opportunity* were widely circulated Harlem Renaissance journals. Based in New York and underwritten by biracial civil rights organizations, the magazines provided a forum for African American artists through literary contests, public awards ceremonies, and publication. Beginning in the fall of 1925 with her second submission to the *Crisis*, Coleman won five *Opportunity* and *Crisis* awards. Literary scholars, historians, economists, and sociologists all recognize the Harlem Renaissance as an intense period of innovative and original work by African Americans in poetry, prose, drama, visual arts, and music. In addition to Coleman, contributors to the movement included the painters Aaron Douglas and Hale Woodruff, musicians Louis Armstrong and Alberta Hunter, and writers Zora Neale Hurston and Langston Hughes. Arnold Rampersad calls the Harlem Renaissance "that dramatic upsurge of creativity in literature, music, and art within black America that reached its zenith in the second half of the 1920s" (Rampersad, "Introduction" ix).

In March 1925, in what many consider a landmark event of the Harlem Renaissance, the Rhodes Scholar, philosopher, and literary critic Alain Locke gathered a virtual "Who's Who among black American artists, intellectuals, and scholars into an anthology illustrated by the Austrian artist Winold Reiss and the African American Aaron Douglas" (Rampersad, "Introduction" xiii). The anthology, *The New Negro*, published by the prominent New York firm of Albert and Charles Boni, included the work of Rudolph Fisher, Jean Toomer, Zora Neale Hurston, Bruce Nugent, Eric Walrond, Countee Cullen, Claude McKay, James Weldon Johnson, Langston Hughes, Arna

Bontemps, Georgia Douglas Johnson, Anne Spencer, and Helene Johnson. Not only does the volume celebrate artistic achievement, it also opposes "the long history of the vilification of black American and African culture. . . . Although the anthology deliberately avoids racial polemics, it raises a clear note of protest against assumptions about blacks in influential racist works" (Rampersad, "Introduction" xv). Unfortunately, as Rampersad points out, "the Crash of 1929 and the ensuing Depression . . . effectively destroyed the Harlem Renaissance" ("Introduction" xix).

Almost all of the writers published in the *Crisis* and *Opportunity* and *The New Negro* anthology, with the exception of Langston Hughes, faded into oblivion in the 1950s. Only in the past several decades have scholars made concerted efforts to recover the work of these individuals. A case in point is Helene Johnson, whose oeuvre was recovered and edited by Verner Mitchell in *This Waiting for Love* (2000). Johnson is now taught extensively as a twentieth-century American woman poet. Like the writings of her peers Helene Johnson, Dorothy West, Willa Cather, and Zora Neale Hurston, Anita Scott Coleman's work is too important, too vibrant to be buried in her relatives' closets.

In the past ten years, Coleman's work has been reprinted in at least a dozen anthologies, including *Harlem's Glory* (1996), *The Opportunity Reader* (1999), *The African American West* (2000), and *Ebony Rising* (2004).[3] Such attention to her work confirms the widespread interest in teaching Coleman, but neither a cohesive collection of her writing nor a biography of her life and work exists. Although minimal research has been done on Coleman, several recent academic publications affirm the quality of her work.[4]

This volume aims to recover her literary legacy. In making available Coleman's finest stories, essays, and poems, we hope to provide a hitherto unavailable perspective on the life and work of a unique and accomplished, though relatively unknown, twentieth-century African American woman writer. We thus concur with feminist critics Sandra Gilbert and Susan Gubar, who maintain that "only in recent years have scholars begun 'to excavate and dig' in a general effort to recover the lives and works of forgotten or neglected 'women worthy of praise'" (Gilbert and Gubar x).[5] A number of the stories and poems have never been reprinted. Several first appeared in important African

American publications such as the *Half-Century Magazine* and the *Bronzeman*, copies of which are now very difficult to find.

Like her mentor, W. E. B. DuBois, Coleman explores issues of concern to the African American community, including power relationships and discrimination in the workplace; structural racism; interracial and intraracial prejudice; passing; lynching; the underemployment of skilled men; hegemonic standards of beauty; the adjustment of rural Southerners to the urban North; and the dangers of materialism and consumerism. Coleman's work is also important because it depicts an African American family who, over three generations, moved from western Florida to Mexico to New Mexico and finally to South Central Los Angeles. The history of the Scott-Colemans, in their search for opportunity and freedom, thus reflects major patterns of African American geography and migration. Since Coleman draws on the family saga for her stories, essays, and poems, her work provides a unique record of black life in the West and the Southwest. While her oeuvre, in its exploration of regionalism, nature, ethnic diversity, American history, women's issues, and social justice, might be grouped with such southwestern classics as Helen Hunt Jackson's *Ramona* and Cather's *Death Comes for the Archbishop*, Anita Scott Coleman is one of the very few African American southwestern women writers of her generation.

There has been some confusion about Coleman's published work. Her only book of poetry, *Reason for Singing*, appeared in 1948. Coleman's children's book, *The Singing Bells*, was published posthumously in 1961. Occasionally she wrote stories under various pseudonyms, including her mother's maiden name, Anne Stokes, as well as the family names William Henry and Elizabeth Stokes.[6] This fact apparently led several critics to attribute to Coleman a volume of verse titled *Small Wisdom* (1937), written by a woman named Elizabeth Stapleton Stokes. In a collection of African American women's poetry, *Shadowed Dreams: Women's Poetry of the Harlem Renaissance*, Maureen Honey includes twenty-two "Coleman" poems, half of which are the work of Stapleton Stokes. Like Mary E. Young, Sondra Kathryn Wilson, Bruce A. Glasrud, and Laurie Champion, Honey repeats Ann Shockley's 1988 claim that "under her pseudonym Elizabeth Stapleton Stokes," Coleman published her inaugural poetry collection

Small Wisdom (Glasrud and Champion 77, 80; Honey 33; Shockley 449; Wilson *Messenger Reader* 410; Young 271).

We were skeptical about the assertion that Coleman had written *Small Wisdom* after noting significant differences between that book and *Reason for Singing* in language, style, tone, imagery, structure, subject matter, and theme. For instance, the former contains a number of sonnets, while the poems in *Reason for Singing* are written in a free, Whitmanesque verse form. *Small Wisdom* contains no vernacular language, nor any references to African American identity, issues, culture, or history. While the speaker in a poem should not be conflated with the writer, certain personal poems in *Small Wisdom*, such as one in which the speaker regrets never having had a daughter, did not seem to reflect Coleman's family of two girls and three boys. Perhaps most significantly, none of the poems published by Coleman in anthologies and journals during the 1920s and 30s appeared in *Small Wisdom*, which was published in 1937. A few thematic similarities do exist, such as reflections on nature, world peace, childhood, and spirituality. The authors of both works are also solidly grounded in the canon of English and American literature. In the final analysis, however, the differences so outstripped the commonalities, that we decided to conduct further research to confirm the claims of our predecessors.[7]

Another research concern to us was the oft-repeated, and erroneous, assertion that Coleman's father was a Cuban who fought for the Union and purchased her mother as a slave.[8] The chronology of this claim simply did not make sense. As we ascertained from census records and family interviews, Coleman's mother, Mary Ann Stokes, was born in 1869 and thus could never have been a slave. Mary Stokes came from a farming family near Tallahassee, Florida, and received at least an eighth grade education. We also determined that Coleman's father, William Henry Scott, was born in Virginia in 1864, which would have made him a very young husband and Union soldier.[9] Scott did, however, serve ten years in the U.S. Army in the 1880s as a "Buffalo Soldier," or Indian scout.[10]

Although much of this information, later corroborated in official sources, was forthcoming from the large and cooperative Scott-Coleman family in Silver City, New Mexico, and Los Angeles, earlier scholars did not interview Coleman's relatives. Nor did they examine street directories, death indexes, cemetery records, or census reports; instead, the errors of previous researchers were simply repeated. Such an approach is, of course, rather deplorable, especially at a time when accurate recovery work is so crucial to African American literary studies.

We have organized this volume into four parts. Our opening essay provides an overview of Coleman's writing, her place in the literary canon, her literary influences, and her nuanced membership in the Southwest's African American middle class. The other three parts of the book consist of sixteen short stories, five dozen poems, and two essays published in journals, newspapers, and anthologies during the twenties, thirties, and forties, as well as selections from Coleman's 1948 volume of verse *Reason for Singing*. Because many of the poems function, in part, as ruminations on themes or issues later developed into stories, we group this work thematically; such an organization should also make the poems and stories more accessible to students.

The purpose of our book, then, is not only to set the record straight and to make Coleman's writing and biography available to scholars but also to illuminate her unique socioeconomic and cultural position as a black woman from the Southwest. We have tried to provide correct and accessible information about Coleman and her family and to contextualize her as a Western voice of the Harlem Renaissance. We hope this book will appeal to a broad readership and that scholars of Western intellectual history, the Harlem Renaissance, and women's studies, as well as the general public, will find it interesting and informative. To this end, we ground our work in careful research, but avoid the convoluted, overly arcane language occasionally found in academic treatises.

Acknowledgments

This book would not have been possible without the generosity, kindness, and scholarship of a number of very important persons. First, we would like to thank the family of Anita Scott Coleman: Anita Green, Lisa Coleman, Jeanette Thompson, Cindy Henderson, Ida Caffey, Douglas Jackson, and David Jackson, all of whom generously shared with us memories, photographs, and memorabilia of their family, and whose enthusiasm for and pleasure in the project was matched only by our own.

The unsung heroes of academic research are, of course, librarians, and we were fortunate in working with some of the very best. We gratefully acknowledge Kathryn Stolpe, Miller Library, Western New Mexico University; Shannon McQueen, African American Museum and Library at Oakland (California); Perida Mitchell, Thomas County (Georgia) Public Library; Pat Bennett, Silver City (New Mexico) Museum; Paula Phillips and Wayne Key, McWherter Library, University of Memphis; Ruth Shoge and Cynthia Sutton, Miller Library, Washington College, (Chestertown, Maryland) for extending faculty borrowing privileges; and Bob West, State Library of Florida. Terry Humble, historian of Silver City, New Mexico, provided valuable insights on the community as Coleman would have known it. Paul M. Beall of the Martin County (Florida) Genealogical Society graciously provided a copy of the Elizabeth Stapleton Stokes obituary. We are particularly grateful to the University of Memphis Faculty Research Grant Fund for its generous research funding.

Our colleague DoVeanna Fulton read numerous drafts of the manuscript and gave prompt, thoughtful feedback. Leander Barnhill helped to locate Coleman's heirs and was a reassuring voice of wit and warmth. Michael Willard, P. Gabrielle Foreman, Kevin Mulroy, and Dace Taube helped immensely with the research, as did our research assistants Jennifer Weber, Edward Robinson, Kelly Burchfield, and Sara Hoover. Martha Shaw and Reginald Holmes opened their homes to us, chauffeured us around Los Angeles, took photographs of Coleman's family, and were models of generosity and friendship. Barry Barr and Jim Messersmith of "Tallulah's" in Rock Hall, Maryland, provided encouragement, and an ideal environment in which to write.

We would also like to thank Alice Stanton of the University of Oklahoma Press for her help in scheduling and facilitating the various components of the project. Ray Lambert provided outstanding copyediting assistance. We are also deeply indebted to our sponsoring editor, Matthew Bokovoy. Thank you, Matt, for your unwavering enthusiasm and wise counsel. This book would not have been possible without your vision and support.

Finally, for their inspiration and many acts of kindness, we thank our families and friends: most especially our parents, without whose example and support none of it would have been possible; our children and their generations, Renee, Matthew, Jared, and Courtney; and as always, Robert and Veronica, to whom this book is offered with love.

Anita Scott Coleman Chronology

May 12, 1887	Parents, Mary Ann Stokes, of Tallahassee, Florida, and William Henry Scott, a Virginian, marry in Wheeler, Texas.
May 24, 1888	Birth of brother William Ulysses in Tallahassee.
1889	Her father, a corporal assigned to Troop K, 9th Regiment, U.S. Calvary, retires from the U.S. Army (at San Carlos, Arizona Territory), after ten years of service.
November 27, 1890	Anita Scott Coleman (ASC) born in Guaymas, Sonora, Mexico.
1893	Family, which includes ASC and her five-year-old brother William, moves to Silver City, New Mexico.
May 1909	ASC graduates from New Mexico Normal School in Silver City, now Western New Mexico University. Works as a school teacher.
January 6, 1912	New Mexico becomes the forty-seventh state.
February 14, 1912	Arizona becomes the forty-eighth state.
October 16, 1916	ASC marries James Harold Coleman, a printer and photographer originally from Virginia.
August 11, 1917	Brother William serves in the U.S. Army in France during World War I, initially in the Medical Department, 523rd Engineers.

September 6, 1917	Daughter Willianna, named for James Coleman's mother, is born in Silver City.
February 1919	ASC publishes her first story, "Phoebe and Peter up North," in the *Half-Century Magazine*.
July 16, 1919	William, now assigned to the Medical Department, 1st Provisional Company, Fort Bliss, Texas, is discharged from the Army. He receives the World War I Victory Medal and the World War I Victory Lapel Button.
September 21, 1919	Son James Scott Coleman is born.
March 7, 1921	Daughter Mary Elizabeth is born.
September 8, 1922	Son Spencer Scott Coleman is born.
Spring 1924	Husband James Harold Coleman moves to Los Angeles, seeking employment and educational opportunities for their children.
1925	ASC writes scenarios for Pathé films.
August 1925	Short story "Three Dogs and A Rabbit" wins a third prize in the inaugural annual literary contest sponsored by the *Crisis*. "Remarks Upon Three Things as They Are," a second story, wins an honorable mention.
September 30, 1925	Father William Henry dies in Silver City.
May 1926	Personal experience essay, "The Dark Horse," wins a second prize in *Opportunity* magazine's annual literary contest.
September 1926	After finding employment as a typesetter in a printing shop, James Coleman purchases a house and sends for the family. ASC moves with her children and mother from their New Mexico ranch to California. The family lives at 5402 Hooper Avenue, in South Central Los Angeles.
October 1926	"Unfinished Masterpieces" wins a second prize in the essay division of the Amy Spingarn Contest in Literature and Art, sponsored by the *Crisis*. "Flaming Flame" receives an honorable mention in the short story division.
June 25, 1928	Son Harold S. is born in Los Angeles.

1930	ASC attends Mount Zion Baptist Church, Fiftieth Street and Hooper Avenue, Los Angeles, Rev. Frank H. Prentice, pastor.
1931	Husband James employed as manager of the African American newspaper *New Age Dispatch.*
March 15, 1931	Death of mother, Mary Ann Scott, in Los Angeles. ASC accompanies the body to Silver City, where her brother, who still resides in New Mexico, meets her at the train station. Mary is interred in Memory Lane Cemetery, adjacent to her husband.
Ca. 1934	Brother William, his wife Ida Gonzalez Scott, and four of their children—Ulysses, Walter, Robert, and Ruth Ann—relocate from Silver City to Los Angeles. The two older daughters, Mary and Esther, are already in the city living with ASC.
1936	Brother William works for R. E. Robson Farm Service, Baldwin Park, California. He resides at 1029 East Thirty-fourth St., Los Angeles.
1938	James Coleman works as a printer for S. L. Walker Co. The family now lives at 1208 East Thirty-fourth Street, Los Angeles.
February 1, 1939	Daughter Willianna "Billie" Coleman, a Spanish major and member of the Alpha Kappa Alpha sorority, receives her A.B. from the University of California at Los Angeles (UCLA).
May 1940	"Baptism" wins first prize in the Robert Browning Poetry Contest, sponsored by the University of Redlands and open to all California poets.
June 15, 1940	Billie receives an M.A. in Spanish from UCLA.
1941	ASC boards children in her home.
1942	ASC helps found the Mount Zion Baptist Church "Young Matrons" Circle, for which

	she serves as assistant counselor. Billie is organist for the church's senior choir.
1943	Sons James and Spencer serve in the U.S. Army in Europe during World War II. Both are members of the Headquarters 780th Military Police Battalion.
1948	ASC publishes a volume of poems, *Reason for Singing*.
September 13, 1950	Daughter Willianna Coleman Washington dies in Los Angeles at age thirty-three.
September 24, 1950	Husband James Coleman dies in Los Angeles.
December 23, 1950	Youngest child, Harold Scott Coleman, dies in Los Angeles.
1951	ASC lives with her son-in-law, Russell Washington, at 203 W. Fifty-second Street, Los Angeles, to help care for her grandchildren, James, Spencer, and Anita Washington.
1952	After her son-in-law's death, ASC and the three children live with her daughter, Mary Elizabeth Jackson, at 2722 Kenwood Avenue, Los Angeles.
March 27, 1960	ASC dies of ovarian cancer at age sixty-nine in Los Angeles and is buried two days later in a "companion" grave with her husband at Evergreen Cemetery, section J, lot 1776.
1961	*The Singing Bells*, a children's book, is published posthumously by Nashville's Broadman Press.
February 22, 1975	Brother William dies in Los Angeles.

Western Echoes of the
Harlem Renaissance

Introduction: Anita Scott Coleman
in the Southwest

In new country,
They have tilled the soil of an alien land.

Anita Scott Coleman, "Hands," 1948

FLORIDA, MEXICO, AND NEW MEXICO: 1835–1926

In Anita Scott Coleman's story "El Tisico" (1920), an African American family—mother, father, and baby boy—waits in "a little mud city" in northern Mexico for the Atchison, Topeka, and Santa Fe Railway to carry them back across the border. The year is 1893, and the family is terrified lest their baby die in Mexico, since they would be unable to bury him in the United States. In reality, Coleman herself was the sick child, suffering from pneumonia, who made the journey with her parents and older brother, William Ulysses (Caffey). The family's destination, Nogales, was the border town on the railway line from Guaymas where they had lived for the past five years.

"El Tisico" (the title refers to a character who is ill with tuberculosis) is a double-framed story, and the second narrator, a white railroad man who witnessed the events of thirty years earlier, recalls the fictional family's urgency to reach the United States and the magical way in which the "daredevil" engineer makes the train fly through space and time, going "faster than a whirligig in a Texas cyclone." When one compares the actual event with the text, the biblical trope of the

Nativity is evident. The narrator recounts a "miraculous" event witnessed many years earlier, and supernatural elements occur in a story of family homecoming. In keeping with the trope, Coleman changes the sex and age of the baby and reduces the size of the actual family to three.

When the story returns to the present (1920), Coleman weaves the Nativity trope into a discussion of patriotism by several white railroad men. Coleman's father worked on the Santa Fe Railway, and the convincing dialogue in the story reflects her careful observation of his coworkers. The men are listening to a Red Cross benefit performance by three black musicians. The vocalist is clearly a disabled and unemployed veteran; his powerful baritone, according to one of the railroad men, would be "worth a million headed under different color." The banjo player, to whom the title of the story refers, has tuberculosis. This disease was of particular concern to the African American community at the time; some black public health physicians warned the disease could "seal the fate of our race" (Hutchinson 103).[1]

While "El Tisico" ostensibly celebrates patriotism, racial harmony, and cooperation on the railroad, the text actually dramatizes W. E. B. DuBois's strong criticism, the year before, of the treatment of black veterans.[2] Coleman may also have been thinking of her brother William, who served in France and who had difficulty finding work after his discharge in 1919. In fact, the Red Cross, to whom the musicians donate their proceeds, had only begun accepting black nurses in 1918. Coleman's condemnation of structural racism thus links her to contemporaries Jessie Fauset, Dorothy West, and Marita Bonner, all of whom avoid polemics, yet "enter current debate through a sustained interrogation of the underlying ideologies and conditions which support public policies of discrimination" (C. Allen 14).

Given such policies, it is not surprising that the issue of where an African American family should locate its physical, moral, and spiritual "place" or home becomes an important theme in Coleman's oeuvre. The home space functions as a refuge from injustice, misunderstanding, and discrimination in the work of a number of black women writers, including Pauline Hopkins's novel *Contending Forces* (1900), Alice Dunbar-Nelson's story "Hope Deferred" (1914), and West's *The Living Is Easy* (1948). Coleman first explores the theme in the "Peter and Phoebe up North" series published in the *Half-Century Magazine* (1919–20). She develops the idea further in "Jack Arrives" (1920), "The Little Grey House" (1922), "Three Dogs and a Rabbit" (1926), "Silk Stockings" (1926), and "The Brat" (1926). In "Two Old Women A-Shopping Go! A Story of Man, Marriage and Poverty" (1933), as in all of these texts, home is not a restrictive space or a domestic prison for women, or even an escape from racist reality, but a site of agency for the African American family. Home thus functions as both a response to and a goal of migration and diaspora; indeed, Coleman's work foregrounds her own family's history as they journey from Florida to Mexico, to New Mexico, and finally to California in search of spiritual fulfillment and economic opportunity.

JOHN AND FRANCES STOKES IN TALLAHASSEE, FLORIDA: 1835–1869

Coleman's maternal grandparents were John Stokes, a blacksmith, farmer, and minister, born in Virginia in 1835, and Frances Stokes, a mulatto slave born in Leon County (Tallahassee), Florida, the same year.[3] John Stokes may have escaped bondage and sought freedom in north Florida among the Seminoles, or he could have enlisted in the Union Army and migrated to Florida after the Civil War, as did a number of white and black veterans.[4] Several of Coleman's poems offer further clues to her grandparents' history.

"Impressions from a Family Album" (1930) suggests that her grandfather resisted slavery even as a young child. The poem's narrator, looking at a daguerreotype "struck" when "Grand-Pap was very old," repeats Grand-Pap's recollections of his childhood: "he was allus kept / To wait 'pon ol' Marse Tom." Although his duties—shooing flies, fetching pipes, and mixing mint juleps—were light, he also describes Marse Tom's brutal, irrational whippings that were all the more heinous since Grand-Pap's beautiful mother was probably Marse Tom's mistress, and he the child of that union. Grand-Pap asserts his own resistance as he recalls "all the times he said:— / 'Thank-ee,' and cussed ol' Marster . . . / Underneath his breaf." Coleman thus illustrates ways in which the experiences of slavery, absent in public documents, are remembered and handed down through family narratives.[5]

The North Florida birthplace of Coleman's grandmother, Frances Stokes, her designation in the census as mulatto, and her photograph, all indicate that she was of mixed, probably Seminole, ancestry, a theme Coleman addresses in "America Negra" (1948).[6] The title of this Whitmanesque poem about America's multiethnic origins employs the Spanish construction of a noun followed by an adjective and should be translated "Black America." The poem foregrounds both black-Seminole liaisons and the tribe's history of dispossession and forced migration: "I am Africa . . . / stealing forth to meet / A lover in the everglades, / Chief Heartache." While the poem notes the movement, migration, and intermingling of both Seminole and southwestern Indians, as well as Celts, Anglo-Saxons, Europeans, and Asians, the overarching image, as indicated in the poem's title, is Africa and its quintessential place in American history.

Coleman's poem "Hands," like "America Negra" and "El Tisico," weaves together family history, the theme of home and migration, and biblical allusion to explore important issues in African American history. The cadenced language and five repetitions of "they" suggest Psalm 23. Coleman recalls John Stokes's occupation as a blacksmith in the words "iron-wrought"; his hands are "padded hard in calloused flesh" in order to "rescind the spring of steel." Her grandfather's "old black working-man's hands" cleared land and "wielded an ax felling trees," and he provided a safe homestead for the family. The labor of Anita's grandmother and mother is compassionately recalled: "wash-tub hands, / Curled like claws from clutching and squeezing." Moving through the generations, Coleman alludes, again in biblical phrasing, to issues her father may have encountered while settling in Mexico: "they have tilled the soil of an alien land / They have builded a house in an unfriendly habitat."

The poem concludes with a reference to the youngest generation and affirms that labor, migration, discrimination, and injustice cannot repress the family's innate artistic ability. The description of young women with "slender," "lovely," and "dusky" hands, recalls the Song of Solomon and probably refers to Anita's daughters, both of whom were musical and played the piano: "fluttering over ivory keys / Like a raven's wings / Beating their way . . . / Mounting higher."[7]

John and Frances Stokes raised eight children in Tallahassee. Most of the original African American residents of the area had arrived in bondage from Virginia, the Carolinas, and Georgia, although several free black Floridian families lived in the area, including Mr. Proctor, a builder, whose homes are now historic Tallahassee landmarks ("Blacks Played"). Even before the Civil War, a black physician, Dr. Gunn, treated patients of both races from his office on College Street. After the war, several of the Stokes' contemporaries became successful farmers, including the Gardner brothers, Simpson Coswell, Peter Copeland, and Ichabod Barrows ("Blacks Played"). John Stokes, like many African American men who were literate, became a minister in addition to his other occupations. Frances worked as a laundress, one of the only occupations open to black and mulatto women in Leon County (Rogers 157).[8]

MARY ANN AND WILLIAM SCOTT: 1869–1889

Frances Stokes bore eight children including Mary Ann, Coleman's mother, born in 1869. Higher education for African American youth in Tallahassee was nonexistent, but "black churches took the lead in educating black children . . . [since] even as late as the turn of the century, blacks were only permitted to attend school three months out of the year" ("Blacks Played"). Despite the truncated school year and crowded, poorly equipped classrooms, literacy was clearly a family priority since Mary still attended school in 1880.[9] Two of Mary's siblings became farmers and two worked as servants.[10] Mary entered domestic service in 1885 and met her husband, William Henry Scott, shortly thereafter.

Scott, a tall, dark-skinned man with an impressive handlebar moustache, hailed from Virginia, although his father was originally from the British West Indies and his mother from New York. Scott enlisted in the U.S. Army in 1879 and served with the 9th Cavalry throughout the Southwest. Coleman reports that her father was an Indian scout, and in 1883 forty African American scouts were assigned to Fort Elliott, Texas; Scott was probably part of that contingent. He and Mary Stokes married in 1887 in nearby Wheeler, the county seat of the Texas Panhandle.[11] While William Scott fulfilled his military service, Mary Stokes Scott, designated a "camp follower," worked as a laundress.[12] In 1888, she returned to her family in Tallahassee and gave birth to their son, William Ulysses.[13]

Scott's career as a scout and Buffalo Soldier, as all black troops after the Civil War came to be called, was also linked to the history of Florida's Black Seminoles. These individuals were the original Seminole-Negro Indian Scouts, although by Scott's time African Americans from other regions of the country had joined the Indian Scouts. The Black Seminoles, or Seminole Maroons, who were technically slaves of both the Seminoles and their original owners, took tribal leadership roles in the Seminole Wars, and their reputation as warriors was well known.[14]

Some of the strongest resistance came from the Maroons in the Second Seminole War, a fact that led the U.S. government, in a strategy of divide and conquer, to free the group: the Maroons "had chosen promises of freedom and removal over further resistance and had separated from the Indians in order to achieve this goal" (Mulroy 33). Many of the Black Seminoles were then hired by the U.S. Army as government agents, guides, interpreters, and negotiators between the United States and various Indian tribes. Skilled warriors and trackers who knew the territory and spoke Spanish and English, the Seminole Maroons, according to a trooper of the 9th Cavalry, "were the best body of scouts, trailers and Indian fighters ever engaged . . . along the border" (Mulroy 117).

As Indian raids decreased, the scouts guarded wagon trains and railroads from outlaws, worked as explorers, mappers, surveyors, translators, escorts and guides, and built forts and roads. In 1914, the Army disbanded the scouts and the Department of the Interior refused their request for deeded land; thus "these men ended their military careers largely unknown and unrecognized, disappearing into the shadows of western history" (Ravage 49). Coleman, however, asserts in "Arizona and New Mexico—The Land of Esperanza" the presence of both the Buffalo Soldiers and the Maroon Scouts in the West, claiming that "Negroes have fought and struggled over all the vast stretches . . . [of] one-time Indian Territory, the Panhandle, New Mexico and Arizona. . . . [These] honorably discharged Indian war fighter[s] . . . thought . . . that 'here' was as good as 'way back there' to settle down and rest after [a] long arduous campaign" ("Esperanza"). Although Coleman does not say so, she is clearly thinking of William Scott as she writes these words.

Scott retired from the military in 1889, and the family moved to Guaymas in the northern Mexican state of Sonora. Here, Mary's life was easier; she employed a Mexican maid to assist her, and her son William Ulysses, who had an excellent ear for languages, often translated for his mother (Caffey).

It is unclear why the family chose Guaymas, or what work Scott pursued there. A photograph taken at this time of Anita, William Ulysses, and their parents, shows a smartly dressed family looking into the camera with expressions of confident well-being.

Scott may have heard of Guaymas during his army service; the city figured in American history in 1781 when forty-four emigrants, twenty-six of whom were black and mulatto, made the thousand-mile journey by foot to what would become Los Angeles. Guaymas was occupied during the Mexican-American War by the U.S. Navy, and in 1853 William Walker attempted to establish his own empire there, before decamping for Nicaragua. Despite such colonialist depredations, Mexico had always welcomed African Americans. Since the Mexican War of Independence (1810–21), blacks worked there as miners, ranchers, farmers, entrepreneurs, artisans, musicians, fishermen, stevedores, soldiers, and explorers (Vincent 273). Mexico's first congress specifically forbade discrimination and any mention of race in government records or documents (Vincent 272). Among the many African Americans who sought economic opportunity in Mexico was James Hughes, the father of Langston Hughes.

THE SCOTT FAMILY IN SILVER CITY, NEW MEXICO

According to family lore, Anita's fragile health precipitated the Scotts' departure from Guaymas, a journey she later described in "El Tisico" (Caffey). The family settled in Silver City, New Mexico, near Fort Bayard, where many African American troops saw military service. Obituary and census reports confirm Coleman's assertion that a number of Buffalo Soldiers, Indian Scouts, and Civil War veterans retired there. Silver City was the end of the line of a spur of the Santa Fe Railway where William Scott found employment. Scott also claimed 160 acres of land through the Homestead Act. The ranch house that he established was home to Anita, her husband

James Coleman, and their first four children until 1926 (Caffey; D. Jackson).

Coleman's story "The Little Grey House" probably describes the careful planning and design that went into the family's home. Coleman's oldest daughter, Willianna, wrote about the "very, very happy family" in the "small gray house" on the ranch: "Honeysuckle twined its foliage about the door. A path outlined by vari-coloured rocks led to the welcome shade of blooming paradise trees" (W. Coleman 1). From the windows, the family could see "Lone Mountain with its ever-changing colors"; nearby were rock formations known as Indian Head and Kneeling Nun (W. Coleman 8). Across a sandy arroyo through which flash floods rushed in the rainy season, the railroad tracks stretched toward town. Coleman uses the flooded arroyo for a dramatic scene of rescue in the story "Love Wins."

Clearly, Coleman envisions the ranch and her father when she notes "the intrepid, stalwart Negro home seeker [who] forms a small yet valiant army in the land of esperanza [hope]" ("Esperanza"). As Coleman points out in the same essay on the African American presence in New Mexico and Arizona, the race has contributed to the region's development since the time of the first Spanish explorers ("Esperanza"). Through the years, several African Americans distinguished themselves as linguists and translators of Native American languages. In 1823, Edward Rose worked as a fur trader and interpreter for the Missouri Fur Company (Richardson 1). James Beckwourth, also an interpreter as well as a scout and explorer, discovered Beckwourth Pass in the Sierra Nevada mountains and owned a hotel in Santa Fe in 1846 (Richardson 1). Albuquerque included several notable residents such as Lt. Henry O. Flipper, the first black West Point graduate and a civil and mining engineer, and the diplomat Ralph Bunche (Richardson 4). According to Coleman, however, "the greatest outstanding feature of the Negro population . . . in New Mexico" is the existence of "two exclusively Negro towns: Blackdom, sixteen miles south of Roswell and situated in the Chavis County oil area and Vado . . . a score of miles below Las Cruces" ("Esperanza").

Blackdom was founded in 1911 by Francis Boyer, a graduate of Morehouse College. Boyer and one of his students, Daniel Keys, walked to New Mexico from Georgia, where Boyer taught at the

Pelham Industrial Normal School. The two established a town of forty acres and publicized it throughout Texas and Oklahoma (Richardson 56). When Coleman described Blackdom in 1926, it boasted 300 residents, 50,000 acres of homesteaded land, a Baptist church, a school house, and a post office ("Esperanza"). The women of Blackdom were famous for their cooking, and on Emancipation Day, the town always invited "the white folks out for a big feed," after which "the Negroes challenged the white men to a baseball game" which the former always won (Richardson 56). Today the neighboring towns, Dexter and Greenfield, still exist, but Blackdom, crushed by the Dust Bowl and the Depression, is a ghost town (Richardson 56).

Francis Boyer left Blackdom before its demise and founded Vado, a cotton-growing community in the Mesilla Valley that Coleman describes as "jammed against the State's scenic highway, plodding its way to the high road of success" ("Esperanza"). Despite threats by the Ku Klux Klan, the Southern black settlers held their ground and created a thriving center of cotton agriculture (Richardson 90). Coleman evidently knew the area as her mother and her daughter Willianna made a car trip around 1923 to picturesque Las Cruces. Willianna loved "the small, romantic city of Las Cruces . . . known in song and story for its Spanish and Indian history" (W. Coleman 7).

Silver City, where the Scott family settled, is situated in the foothills of the Pinos Altos Range, close to the Santa Fe Railway. It was originally a shipping point for ore and livestock; Anita's brother William Ulysses remembered trainloads of silver ore being delivered to the smelting works where "fires roared and men were busy all day and all night" (Work Projects Administration; W. Coleman 5). Unlike other New Mexico towns that evolved from transient mining camps, Silver City was settled by civic-minded Easterners who intended to stay, drawn by the weather, the fertile land, and the suitability of the soil for manufacturing building brick (Alexander 15). The city's shade trees were admired by visitors, and "every property holder" was urged to "set out new trees" (*Southwest Sentinel* [hereafter *SS*] 22 Sept. 1885). Coleman notes the area's "limitless" mineral resources, "great stretches of timbered land[,] . . . vast stretches of grass grown plains [for] the cattle industry[, and] recently completed dams for the conservation of a bounteous water supply" ("Esperanza").

The climate was beneficial for those like Anita who suffered from pulmonary ailments, and Silver City supported three sanatoriums, including the largest one in the country. An announcement of the opening of the Africo-Tubercular Sanatorium in 1910 noted that "an institution of this kind has long been needed by the colored people, a large percentage of whom are afflicted by tubercular trouble" (*Independent Enterprise* 27 Dec. 1910). Silver City historian Terry Humble maintains that the sanatoriums were not segregated, but "taking the cure" was an expensive proposition so poorer whites and blacks lived in boarding houses and hoped that what Coleman calls the "health-giving 'ozone' and revivifying sunlight" would cure them ("Esperanza"). The Africo-Tubercular Sanatorium did not prosper, and by 1926, according to Coleman, Silver City offered "no especial provision . . . for the Negro health-seeker," with the exception of the Veterans Hospital at Fort Bayard ("Esperanza"). She adds, however, that such an establishment would be an entrepreneurial opportunity.[15] Ironically, considering Coleman's interest in this subject, two of her children were to die of lung-related illnesses.[16]

Judging from Coleman's writing, Silver City welcomed the Scott family. "The joyous freedom of the West" offered "for every man be he white or black . . . a bigger and a better chance, that is not encountered elsewhere in these United States" ("Esperanza"). When the Scotts arrived, the African American community included recent migrants from Missouri, Alabama, Virginia, and Tennessee, as well as long-time residents George Parker, George Williams, J. Crockett Givens, William Garrett, and William McNeal, to whom the newspapers respectfully referred as "colored pioneers."[17] The small black population lived where they chose without restrictions (Caffey). African Americans worked as teamsters, lumber pilers, stock tenders, bakers, cooks, janitors, housekeepers, dishwashers, whitewashers, and laborers.[18] Farmers from the Southern states grew cotton in the Maricopa and Mesilla valleys; Coleman notes that "farming, more than all . . . other industries, swings wide its gates and cordially welcomes the Negro" ("Esperanza").

African Americans in Silver City participated fully in civic life. Coleman's father was an active member of the local Prince Hall Masonic Lodge. The lodge organized religious, benevolent, and social functions; it drew a number of its members from nearby Fort Bayard.

A photograph shows William Scott and nine of his Masonic brothers dressed in full regalia. Scott's lodge may have included P. Livingston, George Parker, and Jim Burgess; these prominent businessmen arranged the community's participation in the memorial service for General U. S. Grant. They announced that African American families would make up any shortfall in the funds that had been collected to finance the ceremony (*SS* 8 Aug. 1885).

Professional and business men with whom the Scotts would have been acquainted included a preacher, a justice of the peace, two barbers, a "restauranteur," a miner, and the proprietor of a "confectionary and reading room."[19] George Williams, a rancher, owned "a nice bunch of cattle which he ranges near Hudson's Hotsprings"; he was "the only colored member of the Grant County Stock Association" (*SS* 6 Mar. 1885). Williams, who came to Silver City before the Civil War, made his money mining gold in Mogollon County (Richardson 2). Judge J. Crockett Givens, also a mine owner, served as a justice of the peace and was "one of the best-known colored men in the southwest." He had come to Fort Bayard in 1880 "being a member of the colored cavalry stationed at the Post." When he died in 1915, his obituary was on the front page of the local newspaper (*Independent Enterprise* 30 Apr. 1915). George Parker, another Civil War veteran who Coleman describes as "the gamest bear hunter who ever followed a trail [and] a lucky prospector [who] amassed a fortune in mines," was "a much respected citizen" who left "considerable real estate to his wife" ("Esperanza"; *SS* 27 Jan. 1903).

The city's female pioneers included Mrs. Ida Givens, wife of Judge Givens, and Mrs. Emma Ruddle, "one of the best known colored residents of Silver City," whose wedding ceremony in the Catholic church was announced in the newspaper (*SS* 13 Dec. 1901; 15 Mar. 1927). Women who worked outside the home did so as midwives, servants, cooks, laundresses, and janitors. Mrs. Louise Grigsby was a midwife who "has attended many ladies in this city and is highly esteemed by all who know her" (*SS* 10 Jan. 1896).

Coleman's essay on the region captures the Wild West flavor of her hometown. Although never as famous as Dodge or Tombstone, Silver City in the 1890s would have witnessed cattle rustling, gambling, gunfights, semilegal prostitution, train robberies by outlaws like the Black Jack Gang, and the last of the Apache raids (Alexander 6; *SS*

26 Jan. 1898). Silver City's most notorious resident was Billy the Kid, who arrived with his mother shortly before she died of tuberculosis. As Coleman notes, American history, in its persistent attempt to eradicate the black presence in the West, not only ignores the participation of blacks in law enforcement, but edits out their connection with legendary American outlaws. In fact, the victim who precipitated Billy's flight from Silver City was a black man, and two African Americans rode with the posse that eventually killed him ("Esperanza"; Richardson 2). Blacks were actively involved in law enforcement. George Parker was a friend of Silver City's famous sheriff, Harvey Whitehill, and Coleman may have been referring to Parker, a "crack shot," when she noted that black men "have accompanied posses in the capture of dangerous bandits" (Humble; "Esperanza").

Coleman occasionally mentions cowboys and ranch hands in her work, but she notes that "very few black men have ridden beneath the stars, singing cowboy chants to still the restless herds." In reality, however, about 25 percent "of the 35,000 men who went up the trail from Texas with herds during the heroic age of the cattle industry, 1866–1895 . . . were Negroes" (Porter 347). Since William Scott worked on the railroad, he may have known of Matthew "Bones" Hooks, a cowboy who later became a Pullman porter on the Santa Fe line. Hooks once laid aside his Pullman jacket and cap "to mount and break an outlaw [horse] which no one had been able to ride, while his train stood in the station" (Porter 353). The Sutton brothers, Will and Joe, were also famous as "riders of bad horses" in Clayton, New Mexico, near the Oklahoma border, where they broke horses for many ranchers (Richardson 62). Discrimination certainly existed on the trail, although according to Porter, "paradoxically, the race prejudice which prevented more than a very few Negro cowhands from rising to the status of foreman or trail boss may have spurred able and ambitious Negroes into taking up land, acquiring cattle, and setting up as independent ranchers" (Porter 9). Bazz Smaulding and his sons, for example, owned a large ranch near Clayton and were prominent members of the black community in New Mexico (Richardson 63).

The cultural life the Scotts enjoyed in Silver City was not extensive, but touring musical groups and the talented soldiers at Fort Bayard provided some diversion for the community. The Fisk Jubilee Singers occasionally performed to sold-out crowds at the opera house (*SS* 8 May 1895). The troops at Fort Bayard also offered concerts. A visitor to the fort reported that she had "listened to a squad of colored troopers who are well up on plantation melodies" (Kenner 16). The soldiers' skills at telling stories, singing, and performing "on the mouth organ or the banjo" helped to pass time at the fort and kept up morale on long winter marches (Kenner 17). When a black soldier played reveille, or even solemn taps at the fort, he often improvised on the trumpet, to the delight of his listeners (Kenner 16). The military routine was occasionally relieved at other forts, and probably at Fort Bayard also, when the soldiers of the 9th and 10th Cavalry sponsored formal balls to which the community was invited.[20]

Coleman and her family would also have enjoyed watching "photo-plays," or moving pictures. In 1908 film companies discovered the beneficial climate and shooting conditions in the West; Pathé, the French company for which Coleman later wrote scripts, established itself in Edendale, California, in 1911. The following year, three units of the Power Company were on location in New Mexico (Bordwell, Staiger, and Thompson 122).

The 9th Cavalry and other all-black regiments were favorite cinematic subjects of Thomas Edison, and the Scott family would probably have watched the popular documentaries on black soldiers (Cripps, *Slow* 12). Early film editors had not mastered the techniques of cutting and splicing that later created demeaning stereotypes of blacks. *The Ninth Negro Cavalry Watering Horses* (1890) shows the dignity and skill of African American soldiers. In the film, the audience sees "crisp armed black men outside their prescribed 'place.' Black troopers in smart order pass before a fixed camera shooting at a cloudless sky broken by a single tall pine" (Cripps, *Slow* 12). Coleman may well have seen the film and remembered the tall pine; she uses the same image in her poem "Portraiture," an ode to the tenacity and dignity of black men.

CHILDHOOD AND FAMILY LIFE

Coleman never wrote directly about herself and left no journals and very few letters. One can, however, extrapolate from her stories a picture of her life with her family on the Scott ranch. Anita was the cherished daughter of a strong, loving, progressive father and an affectionate mother. In "Rich Man, Poor Man" (1920), Drusilla Evans' father is "so big . . . he towered above every other man in the community . . . and so shrewd and industrious . . . that the Evans ranch and the Bar-Crescent-E brand was as widely known as other longer standing . . . outfits." Similarly, in "The Little Grey House," Opal Kent has a "dear[,] . . . kind, indulgent dad." Opal recalls how "the lines of care faded from his face" as he sat in the late afternoon sun, watching her prepare dinner. Coleman seems to have enjoyed an unusually close relationship with her parents, with whom she lived until their deaths.

According to family members, Coleman enjoyed a privileged childhood under her mother's watchful eye (Caffey; Green). While other children might "wallow at will in the dusty street," Anita, "in stiffly-starched gingham and ribbon bows in her hair . . . spent her time among the flower-beds, playing 'a'leery' with her rubber ball, or mimicking grown-ups with her dolls and tea set" (". . . G'Long, Old White Man's Gal . . ."). In turn, Coleman provided the same meticulous attention to her own children; her daughter Willianna started kindergarten in "a frilly white dress and spotless white soxs and shiny black shoes" (W. Coleman 4).

Throughout her childhood, Anita enjoyed horseback riding and other activities on the ranch. Around the age of twelve she fell from a horse and sustained a serious injury that doctors feared would render her unable to bear children (Caffey). Her solicitous father provided a horse and buggy in which her brother drove her the three miles to school every day. William Ulysses later told his family that Anita's fragile health was a topic of discussion in the family, and that his sister spent much of her time at home, reading and writing (Caffey). In a photograph taken when she was about sixteen, Anita, immaculately dressed in white, sits in a gazebo, engrossed in a book, with the ranch water tower in the background.

Despite her health issues, Coleman was outgoing and enjoyed people, especially children (Caffey). She had a good sense of humor, and she loved laughter and music. Anita was known in the family for singing around the house; often she chose sentimental hymns like "The Old Rugged Cross," but she also liked the blues. Her favorite was W. C. Handy's "St. Louis Blues" (Henderson et al.).

Although the ranch was on the outskirts of Silver City, life was not dull, for William Scott was an affable, generous host, rather like Daniel Evans in "Rich Man, Poor Man" and Timothy Phipps in "Three Dogs and a Rabbit." Scott enjoyed entertaining his guests with "long drawn-out tales of Indian War days" and his adventures on the railroad ("Rich Man, Poor Man"). On a more serious note, he and his friends discussed religion, politics, and, most importantly, the "Race Question [which was] discussed again and again and over and over" ("Rich Man, Poor Man"). The references in Coleman's texts to notorious "race haters" like Mississippi senator James K. Vardaman and South Carolina senator Benjamin Tillman show that she listened carefully to the political discussions in her home. Her father often used irony and "true American humor" to diminish such enemies of the race and Anita would join in the laughter at "their piteously self-belittling antics" ("Rich Man, Poor Man"). Later, Anita employed her father's use of irony as a way to treat issues of racism and discrimination in her work.

Since he worked on the railroad, William Scott would have brought home the regional black newspapers that circulated among railway workers. The family undoubtedly subscribed to journals of race uplift such as the *Crisis*, in which DuBois's outspoken editorials protested injustice to black men and took President Woodrow Wilson to task for abandoning his African American constituency.[21] As a "race man," Scott protected his children, but he also made them aware of the harsh realities of American life. Anita would have seen "the red headlines of some paper herald some atrocity done a Negro—always some unknown, far-off Negro, but the little band of black men gathered in the . . . parlor were wont to discuss it . . . in subdued and sorrowful voices" ("Rich Man"). Later, in stories like "Cross Crossings Carefully" and "The Brat," Coleman would address the lynchings and race riots about which her family and friends read and spoke. As a sensitive young woman living in a remote area, Anita undoubtedly benefited from a father like William Scott. Scott contributed to her voice and self-confidence as an artist, and he inspired her sympathy toward and admiration of black men, which is a hallmark of her work.

In addition to what she learned at home, Anita furthered her education at the high school attached to the New Mexico Normal School; she, William Ulysses, and William's future wife, Ida Gonzalez, all graduated from the high school. Although some schools in New Mexico, such as those in Albuquerque, were beginning to be segregated, high schools attached to state tertiary institutions were not. Upon graduation, "Annie Scott," as she was then known, matriculated at the Normal School, and in 1909 she was one of a graduating class of seven. She was well liked and her classmates knew of her interest in writing. The first public reference to Coleman's literary career is the class poem published in the yearbook: "Annie, so good in the Literature class / Found out in geometry, it was hard to pass" (*The Normalite* 23).

Despite her own positive educational experience, Coleman would have known of the discrimination suffered by three of her contemporaries in Albuquerque. In 1907 Yola Black, Frances Ellsworth, and Anedia Jasper were seniors at Albuquerque High. Since "some of the students did not want to graduate with the three colored girls" the principal, J. A. Miller, "took the girls in his buggy and registered them at the Albuquerque Normal School which had college preparatory courses. Mr. Miller lost his job because of this and there were no colored students in the high school." The incident precipitated the formation of Albuquerque's NAACP, to which Coleman refers in her essay on New Mexico. Eventually, the NAACP blocked the segregation of Albuquerque's schools, and Yola Black became the first African American graduate of the Albuquerque Normal School (Richardson 47; "Esperanza").

In 1908, Coleman and a classmate at New Mexico Normal School asked Elisabeth Nichols, one of their teachers, to write to Booker T. Washington about the possibility of teaching jobs in the nation's capital. Coleman kept Washington's reply, on Tuskegee letterhead, in which he regrets that "there would be little likelihood of their being able to secure positions in the Washington schools." Washington does suggest that the young women take the civil service examination for teachers in the "Islands." He also encourages them to apply to schools directed by Tuskegee graduates such as Hungerford Normal in Eatonville, Florida, and institutions in Utica, Michigan; Denmark, South Carolina; and Topeka, Kansas (Washington).

Photographs of Coleman at this time show a slim, well-dressed young woman with strong, firm features and her father's dark complexion. She had high cheekbones, heavy-lidded eyes, and a warm, rather shy, expression. Her parents encouraged her self-esteem and taught her to be proud of her race and to value character and spirituality over physical attributes, qualities she passed on to her children, grandchildren, and foster children (Green). Most of Coleman's female protagonists share her own quiet confidence and sense of self-worth. Mercy Kent in ". . . G'Long, Old White Man's Gal . . ." has "blunt" features, a "swart" complexion, and "kinky" hair, but she refuses to lighten her skin or press her hair. Mercy is "roly-poly," unlike her slim, light-skinned mother, although her "trim ankles and small feet [catch] the eye almost forcibly." Both blacks and whites resent Mercy's advantages and superior education but "she look[s] at them impersonally from wide-set eyes with a cool tolerant stare that ruffled them."

Coleman, perhaps influenced by the independent black women in the work of Pauline Hopkins, created a fictional model that contrasts sharply with that of some contemporaries in the Harlem Renaissance. Unlike the tragic, dissatisfied, or demoralized young women in the work of Paul Dunbar, Dorothy West, and Wallace Thurman, Coleman's characters are undaunted by hegemonic standards of beauty to which they do not conform and are blessed with strong, protective, and intelligent families. Unlike Coleman, Dunbar in *The Sport of the Gods*, Thurman in *The Blacker the Berry* and "Cordelia the Crude," and West in *The Living Is Easy* and "Hannah Byde" depict dysfunctional black families and women who are virtually destroyed by economic discrimination and by interracial and intraracial prejudice.

Although she probably experienced at first hand Dunbar's and Thurman's concerns about the lack of respectable jobs for young black women, Coleman offers a solution in the woman's choice to pull together with her man and to establish a secure family unit based on mutual respect, sacrifice, and entrepreneurial endeavor. In fact, Anita may have considered leaving the area and teaching in Washington, D.C., when she recognized how limited were her opportunities, despite her education, even in relatively open-minded Silver City. Coleman eventually did obtain a local teaching job, which she later said was the best possible career for her. Variations on the dilemma of the educated young African American woman and the tenuous economic resources of the black community appear in stories like "Pot Luck" (1920).

Anne Borden, the protagonist of "Pot Luck" is charming, well educated, and well mannered. Her single mother, herself a pampered woman until her husband's sudden death, worked as a laundress to give Anne every possible advantage. When her mother dies suddenly, Anne is like "a dusky, fairy-like creature in the middle of a highway." Like Emma Lou in *The Blacker the Berry*, Anne looks for a job but "the shops nearby were closed to her because of her color. Theatre-goers would scoff at buying tickets from such a dusky maiden" ("Pot Luck"). She is also too dark to be hired as a telephone operator. Like many Coleman protagonists, Anne is musical and has a good voice but she is not talented enough to go on stage. Her only option is glorified domestic work as a "governess" for a wealthy family.

ANITA SCOTT AND JAMES HAROLD COLEMAN

In "Pot Luck" Anne is singing in the walled garden of her employers' home when Jim Moore, a man with "deep, deep . . . gentle eyes," hears her, and "roguishly chime[s] in with a deep-throated whistle." Upon encountering each other across the wall, Anne and Jim exclaim simultaneously, "It's you! . . . as though this their first meeting [is] but the renewal of an age-long friendship" ("Pot Luck"). Coleman emphasizes the very different social status of the couple: Jim is a gardener who works "in the mud"; he is "a sordid little imp" who nevertheless manages to "intrigue a queen in her court" ("Pot Luck"). Anne, in being willing to take "pot luck" and chance her future with Jim, is rewarded with stability and love.

Significantly, Coleman names the couple in the story after herself and her husband, James Harold Coleman. The initial encounter of the fictional pair does, in fact, resemble their meeting: Anita saw James walking down the street one day "and just decided he was the man she was going to marry" (Green). Their relationship inspired a number of stories in which a privileged woman wisely, if unconventionally, chooses a man of sterling character but of lesser status. The positive male-female relationships in "Silk Stockings," "Pot Luck," "The Little Grey House," and "Bambino Grimke" all originate in such intuitive, spontaneous, life-altering decisions as the one Anita apparently made upon seeing James. Like the couple in "Two Old Women," they may have courted for some years while James solidified his economic prospects. In October 1916, they married and moved in with Anita's parents on the ranch.

James Coleman was born in Virginia and grew up in Washington, D.C. He was a widower and nineteen years older than Anita, although his smooth medium-brown complexion and boyish appearance belied his age (Green). His mother and sister were both named Willianna, and that was the name he and Anita gave to their first child, born in 1917. Coleman was a skilled printer and photographer who may have gone west to work as a chauffeur for a wealthy family, as does John Condon in "Rich Man, Poor Man." Perhaps, like Condon, James was disillusioned with New Mexico and wanted to return east.

In the story "Rich Man, Poor Man," Drusilla's family is "aghast" at the idea of her marrying a "poor nobody" and moving east, and they try unsuccessfully to dissuade her. Anita and James, however, apparently acceded to her family's wish that they remain in Silver City, where they lived for the first ten years of their marriage. In 1924, however, James Coleman moved to Los Angeles, where, after about a year, his family joined him (W. Coleman 8). Anita's father had died on the ranch in the year that James was away, and Mary Scott accompanied her daughter and grandchildren on the train journey to Los Angeles. Anita never again lived on the ranch. William Ulysses and his wife Ida oversaw the property, and, at William Scott's behest, the family kept up with the taxes. In the 1960s Silver City took the ranch as public domain (the family was paid for the property) and created Scott Park; today a marker commemorates William Scott's original 160-acre homestead (Caffey).

In "Two Old Women A-Shopping Go! A Story of Man, Marriage and Poverty," Nell delays her marriage to Horace because he hasn't saved enough money. She takes pride in her social position and observes rather patronizingly that "black men really had tougher sledding than black women." Nell realizes, however, that racism also undermines her own life: despite her intelligence, she holds a poorly paid clerical job. She endures a long commute, presumably because of restricted neighborhoods, and a hostile supervisor. One day, she overhears two elderly ladies bemoaning the materialism of young black women: "What's more, us wimens can make men folks what us choose to. . . . Us 'tis what makes 'em or breaks 'ems." Inspired by the women's words, Nell quits her job and she and Horace strike

out for the ranch he has purchased. Home is thus a site of empower-
ment for both men and women, and a shared entrepreneurial venture
is a form of resistance to racism.

In the same way that Coleman's father and grandfather seem to
have inspired Coleman's older black male characters, so her husband
appears to be the model for the younger generation who are sensitive,
intelligent, and skilled. Unfortunately, they are also frustrated in
their attempts to establish themselves professionally. Just as James
found it difficult to find work in his chosen field until the family
moved to Los Angeles, so discrimination prevents Jack from being
an architect ("Jack Arrives"); John Condon from being a baker ("Rich
Man, Poor Man"); Sam Timons from being a welder ("Cross Crossings
Carefully"); William Williams from being a writer ("Unfinished Masterpieces"); the baritone in the "Black Trio" from achieving national
success ("El Tisico"); and Horace and Robert from making enough
money to get married ("Two Old Women"; "Bambino Grimke").
Sometimes, even if a man is employed, as in "Silk Stockings," his
natural goodness and generosity are repressed by the demoralizing
effects of casual racism: John Silas Light "revered all women. . . . He
hated to see women carrying bundles, or cranking cars, he always
wanted to assist them; and because often he could not . . . because
of color . . . he was rapidly becoming soured . . . just as time and
heat turns sweet milk to clabber."

Coleman's literary treatment of black men thus differs significantly
from that of Maya Angelou, Alice Walker, Ntozake Shange, and Gayl
Jones, in whose works, according to Edward Jackson, "positive images
of black males are the exception rather than the rule" (E. Jackson
22). Coleman's characters do not vent anger and frustration at racism
and underemployment on their women. Nor are they the passive,
defeated dreamers found in the work of Dorothy West.[22] Rather,
Coleman's men are complex, nuanced, and believable, like Hopkins's
Ruell in *Of One Blood* or Hurston's Teacake in *Their Eyes Were
Watching God*. Instead of being gendered or racialized stereotypes,
Coleman's men behave in a variety of ways. Some actions are relatively innocuous, such as insisting their wives straighten their hair to
conform to a new urban lifestyle ("Phoebe and Peter up North") or
flirting with older women for monetary gain ("Bambino Grimke").

Even Coleman's negative male characters are never silly caricatures. The positive males are sincere individuals who work hard and
apply principles of logic and analysis to solve their problems, as Jack
does when he enters a design contest but does not disclose his race
until he wins the prize ("Jack Arrives"). The tension in Coleman's stories
arises from the reader's connection to sympathetic male characters
who must find their way out of unjust and discriminatory situations.

WRITING AND PUBLISHING: THE HARLEM
RENAISSANCE AND THE MAGAZINE YEARS

Coleman wrote and published during a vibrant period in African
American letters. Because of her family's interest in race uplift, her
father's job with the Santa Fe Railway, and the circulation of black
journals among railway workers, she was aware of publishing opportunities in the black press throughout the United States. Despite her
geographical distance from Harlem, she took advantage of the frequent
literary contests and the invitations to submit work to these publications. Coleman also paid close attention to the work of her contemporaries, particularly those with whom she shared public recognition.
In 1926, for example, she won second prize for an essay, "The Dark
Horse," and her photograph appeared in the June issue of *Opportunity*
with Arna Bontemps, F. H. Wilson, and Waring Cuney. That year,
she also won second prize for her essay "Unfinished Masterpieces";
her picture was on the same page in the *Crisis* with Loren Miller, who
won first prize for his essay, and Countee Cullen, who took second
prize in poetry; other winners included Bontemps (poetry); Eulalie
Spence (plays); and Aaron Douglas (art). The previous year, "Three
Dogs and a Rabbit" won third prize in the *Crisis* contest, although
H. G. Wells (who judged the short-story contest along with Sinclair
Lewis, Charles Chesnutt, and Mary White Ovington) placed it second,
after Rudolph Fisher's "High Yaller." Under the pseudonym Elizabeth
Stokes, Coleman was listed in the *Crisis* (Oct. 1925) along with Fisher,
Cullen, Marita Bonner, Langston Hughes, and Frank Horne. Cole-
man's thematic concerns and her experiments with form, voice, and
narrative in stories such as "The Brat" and "Three Dogs and a Rabbit"
show her awareness of the work done by her contemporaries.

Coleman was not the only western writer to submit her work to the New York contests; the lure of Harlem attracted writers from all over the country. In addition to writers from the East Coast, contestants hailed from Colorado, Kansas, Texas, Arizona, Oklahoma, and California. In both 1925 and 1926, the *Crisis* contest received almost 600 entries; in 1927, only half as many entries appeared, but to W. E. B. DuBois, the editor of the journal, reading them was "a joy and inspiration" ("Postscript" 312).[23]

Most of the African American newspapers with which Coleman would have been familiar and in which she later published were based in large cities like New York, Chicago, and Pittsburgh, but even Albuquerque boasted two black papers in the early twenties. The *Southwest Review*, in which Coleman published some articles, was published by S. W. Henry and took a strong stance against discrimination ("Esperanza"). The *Southwest Plaindealer*, owned by S. T. Richards, a former teacher and Pullman porter, envisioned its audience as "a progressive group of liberal citizens" who "put forth a campaign to the Negro voters to get away from cleavage to the Republican Party" (Richardson 51).[24]

Most readers know Coleman's stories, essays, and poems from the major Harlem Renaissance journals, as she published frequently in the *Crisis*, the *Messenger*, and *Opportunity* between 1925 and 1938. Much of her work also appeared in lesser-known African American periodicals, although these pieces have never been collected. Harlem's the *Looking Glass*, self-described as "the picture newspaper for intelligent and thoughtful people" (16 Dec. 1925), published her quasi–science fiction tale "The Mechanical Toy" in 1925. The story appeared next to Wallace Thurman's weekly literary column.

Coleman contributed eight stories between 1919 and 1922 to the *Half-Century Magazine*, a women's magazine from Chicago whose purpose was to "prepare Afro-American women for a place in urban social landscapes" (Rooks 4). Published by a wealthy cosmetics manufacturer, Anthony Overton, and edited by Katherine Williams-Irvin, the magazine described itself as a "colored magazine for home and homemaker" (Fultz 100).[25] The magazine published "the best stories by leading colored writers," and urged readers to submit their own efforts (Rooks 4). Among the best known of these stories was James Weldon Johnson's *The Autobiography of an Ex-Colored Man*, *which the magazine serialized* between November 1919 and December 1920. Columns on etiquette, fashion, domestic science, and home decorating assisted recent Southern migrants to make the "correct" aesthetic choices (Rooks 4). Coleman's Phoebe and Peter series was perfectly tailored for the magazine; readers loved the stories and requested more adventures of upwardly mobile Peter, his pretty country wife, Phoebe, and her feisty best friend, Mayme. Although the characters were rural Southerners, they expressed themselves in proper English, instead of in stereotyped dialect.

In 1930 and 1931, Coleman published two light-hearted and witty stories about a Jazz Age adventurer named Bambino Grimke in the *Bronzeman*, another magazine from Chicago. Robert Cole, the president of Metropolitan Mutual Assurance Company, underwrote the periodical which "featured light fiction, gossip, sports, fashion, and business news" (Weems 6). The *Bronzeman* appealed to a diverse audience and was the first to publish the work of Chester Himes. Coleman's creation, Bambino Grimke, is a band leader, a ladies' man, and a general trickster who gets into a number of scrapes. His intentions are always good and usually, as in his schemes to provide decent accommodations for his jazz band on the road, stem from his resistance to racism and discrimination.

One of the challenges for African American writers during the mid-century was the need to constantly find new venues as popular magazines often lasted only a few years. In 1920, Coleman published "Pot Luck" in the *Competitor*, a short-lived but ambitious Pittsburgh journal published by Robert Vann, who was also the editor of the *Pittsburgh Courier*.[26] Vann's magazine took an assimilationist perspective and strove to attract an educated, upwardly mobile readership. A broad array of articles on black life included detailed sports coverage; the magazine emphasized "social, cultural, and business concerns over political commentary" (Fultz 101). In 1928, Coleman published three stories in *Black and White Chronicle*, a short-lived weekly from Akron, Ohio, founded by Mary Holmes, and another story in the militant *Nashville Clarion*. The *Clarion* supported a number of civil disobedience actions throughout its history including the Nashville streetcar boycott in 1905 and the Fisk University students' strike in 1925. By the end of the thirties, however, most of the African American magazines in which Coleman published had disappeared. Between 1940 and 1943, she published several stories in the large national news-papers, the *Pittsburgh Courier* and the *Chicago Defender*. Until the present volume, most of the stories from these periodicals have never been anthologized or republished.

LITERARY STYLE AND INFLUENCES

Coleman's work draws on a number of sources. First, she closely follows the current debates on African American literature, art, music, and politics. Like her contemporaries, she explores themes and issues of concern to the black community, such as job discrimination and racial violence. Coleman clearly models her work on that of prominent black artists and intellectuals such as Pauline Hopkins, Charles W. Chesnutt, W. E. B. DuBois, Langston Hughes, and James Weldon Johnson. Coleman is also well versed in the British and American literary canon, as she demonstrates in thematic, aesthetic, and stylistic references to the work of Walt Whitman, Emily Dickinson, Charles Dickens, Charlotte and Emily Brontë, and William Shakespeare. She often enriches her work with biblical tropes, references, and allusions. The popular culture of the West, specifically western and African American humor and storytelling, are evident in her fiction and poetry. Finally, she uses the syntax and techniques of film in much of her work.

Not surprisingly, considering that he personally read and critiqued Coleman's submissions to the *Crisis* contests, W. E. B. DuBois became an important influence on the content and style of her work. Although she apparently admired Booker T. Washington during her college years, her stories about the underemployment of skilled black men indicate that she perceived the flaws in the Tuskegee model. She would undoubtedly have read the 1914 editorial in the *Crisis* in which DuBois asserts that vocational training will never achieve Washington's aims since there was never any intention on the part of white industry to hire black graduates of trade schools.[27] In several of her stories, Coleman dramatizes DuBois's critique of the Tuskegee model and the pointlessness of vocational training given the structural inequities in hiring practices.

In addition to his political and philosophical influence on her work, DuBois also shaped Coleman's style. Like her mentor, she often

adopts an ironic, mock-heroic tone that includes allegory and apos-
trophes to the reader, as well as extended metaphors, repetition,
sophisticated vocabulary and syntax, archaic constructions, and the
personification of abstract qualities. For example, in *The Souls of Black
Folk*, DuBois personifies and allegorizes the American "problem" of
the color line: "And there in the King's Highway sat and sits a figure
veiled and bowed" (35). Similarly, in "Pot Luck," Coleman describes
Life as "a capricious woman who delights to twist away the thread
with which man weaves the tapestry of his existence."

Like DuBois and James Weldon Johnson, Coleman experiments
with the fragmented consciousness of a protagonist and reveals a
modernist preoccupation with heteroglossia and multiple perspec-
tives, a technique particularly well suited to film. In "Bambino: Star
Boarder" Coleman simultaneously presents the opposing thoughts
of three characters: "She thought: The perfect darling, of course he
might stay. He thought: Indeed not! My fine fellow, this home was
built for two. Bambino was thinking: Go slow, Bo, slow . . . 'cause
now, any little move yo' make might be a bad move." Coleman's
best stories like "The Brat," "Three Dogs and a Rabbit," and "El
Tisico" accomplish deft shifts in narrative voice among men, women,
blacks, and whites. As Glasrud and Champion point out, "one of
the strengths of Coleman's fiction is her use of innovative technical
strategies. . . . She uses the second person to talk directly to the
reader . . . and challenges the reader to find [the moral of the story]"
("Anita" 79). Coleman's work thus "suggests through self-reflexive
narrative that fiction exposes a conceptual truth not found in factual
truth" (79).

James Weldon Johnson's novel *The Autobiography of an Ex-Colored
Man* (1912), which is, as Baker points out, "a fictional rendering of
The Souls of Black Folk," informs Coleman's stories about passing,
"Three Dogs and a Rabbit" and "The Brat" (Baker 22). That Coleman read Johnson's work is evident, as her early stories and Johnson's
novel appeared in some of the same issues of *the Half-Century Magazine*, occasionally on the same page. Like Johnson, she explores passing
as subversion and posits race as a social and economic construct.
Coleman's preoccupation with alienation and isolation, the psychic
costs of passing, gives her work a particularly modernist affiliation.
"The Brat" borrows Johnson's trope of African American music as a

"symbolic projection of a double consciousness" (Baker 21). Both Coleman's and Johnson's protagonists agonize between embracing black culture through music and using music to disguise their origins. Music thus functions in Coleman's text as both an escape from and a marker of race.

The frame story of "The Brat" opens in the home of Aggie, an affluent, apparently white woman. While a storm rages outside, Aggie listens to "America's world-famed tenor," David Kane, sing "I Hear You Calling Me." Her favorite record plays "over and over, tenderly, hauntingly." Outside, in counterpoint to Kane's music, the wind is "shrieking and howling like runaway fury" while "the rain [is] pounding like fifty drummers, each bent on out-drumming his mate." Coleman thus codes the story's African American subtext through acts of resistance such as drumming and running away.

Allusions to Shakespeare's *Macbeth* and to the poetry of Emily Dickinson give further texture to the story. Coleman suggests Dickinson's poem "Wild Nights" by opening "The Brat" with the words "A wild night." Like the protagonist of Dickinson's poem, Aggie is a solitary woman engaged in an erotic fantasy. The abrupt punctuation of her fragmented thoughts recall the similar structure of the poem ("Wild Nights—Wild Nights! / Were I with thee / Wild nights would be / Our luxury").[28] Both poem and storm contextualize Aggie's isolation and her obsession with Kane's voice. Coleman thus sets the stage for a fairy tale of race, shape-shifting, and metamorphosis. It is, as Aggie reflects, "a night for surprises!"

Jennie, an elderly black woman, appears suddenly, pounding on the door like "a genii from Aladdin's lamp." Her knock, "clattering, banging, biff-booming, biff-booming" is almost indistinguishable from "the drum-beats of the rain"; it further establishes the African American subtext. The door pounding also recalls the porter's scene in *Macbeth* which warns that an unnatural act has been committed within doors. Aggie welcomes her guest and, in another allusion to *Macbeth*, dresses her in "borrowed robes": Jennie accepts "a warm robe, padded silken mules and woolen hose." In giving Jennie her own clothes, Aggie begins to relinquish her apparent "white" identity and to embrace Jennie as a "mother."

In the second frame of the story, Jennie tells a tragic tale of her unwanted, mixed-race child and a terrible race riot. Listening to Jennie,

Aggie feels that her voice has "a haunting quality, a resonance . . . that vaguely stirred some chord, a memory though indefinable." Jennie's only friend, Biddy, whom she assumes is a light-skinned black woman, is shot in the riot, but manages to bring Jennie's child to her own wealthy parents. When Jennie visits her son months later, she is shocked to discover that "they were white—white folks. White, Miss Aggie, like you." Realizing that Biddy's family thinks the child is their grandson, Jennie "pretend[s] [she] was his old nurse, come to see him." The biblical allusion to Moses and Miriam, and Jennie's sacrifice in giving up her child, underscore the terrible psychic cost of passing.

James Weldon Johnson's thesis of the social construction of race becomes clear when it turns out that David Kane, the famous tenor, is Jennie's son. Like the narrator of *The Autobiography of an Ex-Colored Man*, Kane has made a brilliant career; his dark skin is popularly attributed to "his boyhood home on the western plains"; his "dark, coarse hair in curly ringlets" is rationalized because "curly hair is ofttimes the only outward mark of genius." Listening to him sing, however, Jennie insists: "any fool knows that ain't no white man's voice." Just as the protagonist of Johnson's novel reflects that "I cannot repress the thought that, after all, I have chosen the lesser part, that I have sold my birthright for a mess of pottage" (154) so Kane's secret makes him "lonely, so lonely. His poor heart aches and he can't tell why." Coleman then suggests that Aggie too is passing; after all, the reader only has Jennie's word that Aggie is white, and of course she was mistaken in assuming that her friend Biddy was black. Both Aggie and David Kane, then, choose the white world but at great cost to their psychic integrity and emotional stability.

Western and African American folk traditions also influence Coleman's style. Her irony and sense of humor and her folk background reveal themselves in the poems "On Hearing Four White Men Singing Spirituals," "Idle Wonder," and "The Treasure-Trove of Andy Kane." Listening to her father, his friends, and the family's Mexican ranch hand, Coleman would have heard local legends, tall tales, "lies," and African American stories of clever tricksters. In the improvised "yarns" of cowboys and ranch hands, designed to relieve the boredom of long trail rides, animals talked and behaved like humans, while heroes like James Beckwourth, Kit Carson, and Pecos Bill, outlaws like Billy the Kid, and tricksters like the Mexican Juan Quatorce performed surreal and superhuman deeds.

Coleman undoubtedly heard the railroad tales about John Henry's superhuman strength and the ways in which Bre'r Rabbit signified on larger, stronger adversaries. William Williams in "Unfinished Master-pieces" is the quintessential American trickster who runs away from postbellum slavery in the cotton fields and makes his way west as a hobo and confidence man. Coleman demonstrates that Williams is a true artist who, had circumstances been different, would have expressed his talent for creative writing. Both the western and African American folk traditions veiled serious issues with wit, humor, and exaggera-tion; these elements appear in a number of Coleman's texts including the Bambino Grimke stories and "Three Dogs and a Rabbit," in which the jolly host of the frame story gives no hint of the terror of the hunted man in his tale.

As in the best of Coleman's stories, the narrative structure of "Three Dogs and a Rabbit" is complex and the theme is developed through repetition and variations. The frame device, the central character, the setting, and the surprise ending all recall Charles Chesnutt's story "The Wife of his Youth." Timothy Phipps, like the protagonist of Chesnutt's tale, is an affluent man giving a dinner party. As Phipps carves generous slices of ham for his guests, he downplays his storytelling skill: "this that I'm about to relate isn't much of a story, though you might . . . weave it into a ripping good yarn." Phipps observes that although "The ingredients of story [are] . . . plot[,] . . . characters[,] . . . a setting[,and] . . . love[,] . . . none such [appear] in what I'm a-telling." He then describes two encounters with a beautiful woman, the first under "amazing circum-stances. Circumstances so extraordinary they seem unreal to this day." He next sees her in a crowded courtroom on "the culprit's bench." The petite woman has silvery hair that "crinkled almost to the point of that natural curliness which Negro blood imparts." She has "heavy-lidded eyes . . . which is, as you know, a purely Negro attribute," and a full, ripe mouth. Nevertheless, "that she was any-thing other than a white American was improbable, improbable indeed." She is "the widow of old Colonel Ritton . . . a dauntless, intrepid Indian fighter and pioneer" and the mother of "three notable sons" and "two daughters, feted continuously because of their beauty" who have married into prominent local families.

The second frame is Mrs. Ritton's story. Accused of sheltering a "runaway Negro" pursued by the police, she refuses to divulge the fugitive's location; instead she tells the court that as a young slave girl (the courtroom gasps in disbelief), she made the arduous journey west with her owners. On the trail she protects a frightened rabbit being pursued by her master. Despite her own hunger and the beating received from her master, she hides the animal. The master's son observes the flogging, and although he had always teased and annoyed her, "he changed from that day." The two eventually marry, and Mrs. Ritton's racial identity is absorbed and obliterated in her social position until the day that she sees the fugitive and has a sudden flashback to the events of her youth. Phipps, although he "knew the fugitive was free, and making a rough guess at it, likely to remain so," is over-whelmed by the lovely woman "standing alone in the midst of all those hostile people, tearing apart with such simple words the whole fabric of her life." Even without knowing the surprise ending, one can see how Coleman approaches the theme of passing as a social construct and explores issues of miscegenation and racism in the legal system, all within the framework of a western "tall tale."

Finally, the medium of film clearly shaped Coleman's writing. While writing "Three Dogs" Coleman worked as a script writer for Pathé films; she understood the syntax of film narration, including flashbacks, fast-forwards, dissolves, fades, visual symbols, compressed dialogue, and scenes that are both intimate and dramatic, all of which appear in her work. Coleman remained interested in writing for the media all her life; later she wrote television scripts, including one for Rod Serling's Twilight Zone.[29]

Coleman's work was clearly influenced by the films of Thomas Edison, Oscar Michaux, William Foster, and the all-black Lincoln Productions Company. In 1903 Edison filmed the first version of *Uncle Tom's Cabin* and *The Great Western Train Robbery*. Michaux's films like *The Homesteader* (1919) combined melodrama with western settings and pioneer themes. In *The Symbol of the Unconquered* (1920), a quadroon beauty goes west to claim her dead grandfather's mine (Cripps, "Race" 51). The plots and style of Coleman's texts also suggest connections to the film industry. Her tales of racial uplift recall films by the Lincoln Company such as *The Realization of a Negro's Ambition* (1916), in which an engineer with a degree from Tuskegee loses his job because of prejudice but strikes oil on his father's farm. Lincoln's *The Trooper of Troop K* (1916) documents the 9th Cavalry's bravery and courage in the Battle of Carrizal, an event Coleman describes in her essay on New Mexico (Cripps, "Race" 51; "Esperanza"). "Unfinished Masterpieces" clearly borrows cinematic technique as Coleman urges the reader to travel "backward ho, through the mazes of the past. Stop! 'Why howdy Dora Johns,' darling playmate of my child-years." Coleman transcends time and American geography as she charts the aborted development of two natural artists, a sculptor and a storyteller, both of whom, because of race prejudice, remain "unfinished masterpieces."[30]

Coleman was one of a number of women who found employment writing for silent films at a time when writers were low on the movie studio hierarchy. As was typical, her scripts for Pathé were composed anonymously. Since studios often used as many as twelve writers on a single script, it is likely that she was one of a "stable" of writers who received no credits in the finished film (Bordwell 146).

In 1910, Pathé, a French company, released more movies in the United States than all American companies combined. They produced newsreels, serious anthropological studies, such as "Nanook of the North" (1921), and zany musical comedy shorts with all-black casts, such as "In and Out," "Foul Play," and "Darktown Follies." Despite the fact that by the twenties "the black presence on the screen was overwhelming, at least in the little world of the two-reeler," one cannot assume that Coleman wrote only for black films (Cripps, *Slow* 227). Since she was still living in Silver City, she may have responded to calls for scripts in popular magazines and mailed in her material. While she may have seen announcements in the black journals and magazines in which she published, she could just as easily have responded to calls in the mainstream press, and it is possible that the story editors did not know her race. Coleman describes a similar situation in "Jack Arrives" (1920) when a young black architect wins a contest but does not reveal his race until afterward, confident that his demonstrated talent will supersede any prejudice.

In any case, the advent of sound "ruined race moviemakers [who were] burdened with inventories of silent films, stables of untrained actors, and unwired theatres" (Cripps, "Race" 54). In addition, as film technology advanced, negative images of blacks increased. In slapstick shorts like the Rastus Comedies (1910–11); in lurid tales of tragic mulattos like *The Debt* (1912) and *The Octoroon* (1913); and in D. W. Griffith's many films, stereotypes of the jolly mammy, the silly pickaninny, and the clownish bumpkin were disseminated throughout the country. DuBois and other African American leaders loudly denounced these caricatures, and Coleman too strongly refuted stereotypical images of "funny" blacks in her work, particularly in her essays "Unfinished Masterpieces" and "Esperanza."

THE HORN OF PLENTY: LOS ANGELES 1926–1960

> The very stars of heaven spell Opportunity! Opportunity! For all who care to come and work and work and then work some more to achieve the success that is the reward for efficient work.
>
> Noah D. Thompson, "California: The Horn of Plenty,"
> *Messenger*, July 1924

"Daddy had succumbed to the lure of the Golden West and hied away to Sunny California," wrote Willianna "Billie" Coleman about her father's departure for Los Angeles in 1924 (W. Coleman 8). Anita stayed on the ranch with her parents where she continued writing and "raising children and chickens."[31] By 1926, despite doing ranch chores and mothering four children between the ages of nine and four, Anita had published poetry and fourteen stories and essays in all of the major journals of the Harlem Renaissance. The awards she won for "Three Dogs and a Rabbit" and "Unfinished Masterpieces" testify to her growing literary reputation on the New York scene.[32] Although the ranch clearly provided an atmosphere conducive to her work, Anita apparently acquiesced to her husband's wish to migrate to Los Angeles.

Of course, even before moving to Los Angeles, the Colemans would have known what to expect since the race papers constantly boosted the city's cultural advantages and amenities. In 1913, W. E. B. DuBois visited and wrote an enthusiastic article in the *Crisis*;

photographs showed charming Spanish bungalows and lushly planted gardens that belonged to black families (*Crisis* Aug. 1913: 193). In 1922 Chandler Owen, the publisher of the *Messenger*, claimed that Central Avenue was as sophisticated as New York, "a veritable little Harlem" (Flamming 92).

Among the reasons for the couple's decision was certainly employment. Jobs were scarce in 1926, and it is unclear whether James had been able to work as a printer in Silver City. He may have set his sights on a job at one of Los Angeles's two weekly race newspapers, the *California Eagle*, published by Joseph and Charlotta Bass, and the *New Age Dispatch*, published by Frederick Roberts. All three publishers were well-known "race men and women"; the Basses were in the forefront of antidiscrimination campaigns in housing and employment, and Roberts had been elected to the California legislature in 1918.

Given the progressive environment, James sent for his family in 1926. The group traveled by train and arrived at Fifth Street Station. "Hailing a courteous taxi driver the little family sped through the streets of Los Angeles to the little house on East Fifty Fourth Street, a little green house with a small green lawn in front of it, two blooming rose bushes and geraniums . . . and Daddy's beaming face to welcome them" (W. Coleman 8).[33] By 1927, James had obtained a position as a printer, but life was not easy: "It was the Depression and there was hardly any work. Everyone was on relief, and Harold had a hard time. . . . Men would wait in line to work for fifty cents a day, cleaning the local boxing arena" (Caffey). The situation improved, however, and by 1931 James was the manager of the *New Age Dispatch*.

Another reason for leaving Silver City certainly would have been better educational opportunities. The Coleman children were bright and Anita taught them to read before they entered school. Billie read on a third-grade level at the age of five and skipped kindergarten (W. Coleman 4). Although Anita and her brother had attended integrated schools before World War I, Coleman notes that after "the influx of Negro children to Dona Ana County . . . [they] were not allowed to attend the schools" ("Esperanza"). A state law passed in 1925 mandated separate facilities in areas where blacks had settled, including Vado, Alamogordo, Tucumari, Clovis, Roswell, Artsia, Hobbs, Las Cruces, Carlsbad, and Silver City (Richardson 26; Caffey). In

Albuquerque, the NAACP had organized in 1907 after three students were denied the right to graduate from the public high school. Dr. James Lewis, a member of the NAACP and the proprietor of a tuberculosis sanatorium, went before the state legislature in Santa Fe and argued that New Mexico could not segregate its schools because the state was too poor to afford a dual system (Richardson 45). Due to Lewis's efforts and to the strength of the NAACP chapter, Albuquerque maintained integrated classes, as did Raton, Santa Fe, Las Vegas, and several other communities (Richardson 45). The racial situation in New Mexico was precarious, however, and the Colemans may have feared that, after race riots in Houston in 1917, in Chicago in 1919, and in Tulsa in 1921, it would only worsen.[34]

Education in Los Angeles was a very different proposition. Although a number of "black laws" mandating segregated schools and other exclusions were enacted between 1849 and 1861, public opinion after the Civil War repudiated racist policies. Despite the fact that most Anglo immigrants to California were from the South, by 1880 "a noticeable change took place in the relationship existing between the whites and the Negroes—a change manifested by the admission of Negroes into the public schools, the rise of the Negro business man, and the consideration of the Negro in politics" (Bond 17). For example, Bessie Bruington, the daughter of black pioneers, graduated from the State Normal School (now UCLA) seventh in a class of eight hundred. In 1911 she began teaching at the Holmes Avenue School, located in the African American community south of downtown. Bruington became the first black principal in the Los Angeles school system in 1918 (Bass 10). By 1920, twenty-five African American teachers were employed in the public system. The first black librarian was Miriam Matthews, a contemporary of Anita Coleman and Bessie Bruington. The Matthews had left their home in Pensacola, Florida, in 1907; like Anita's parents, they had moved west in search of better opportunities for their children (Flamming 51, 72).

Once settled in South Central Los Angeles, the Coleman children attended Hooper Avenue Elementary, McKinley Junior High, and Jefferson High School. In the late twenties and early thirties, Jefferson was a racially and ethnically mixed school, although it drew primarily from white working-class families. Student surnames in the graduating class of 1920 indicate that Hispanic, Japanese, Jewish,

Irish, and Italian families lived in the district. Jazz musician Marshall Royal recalls that Jefferson was "very mixed. . . . There were about 20 percent blacks, 5 percent Espanol [*sic*], 2 percent Japanese, 25 percent Italians . . . 20 percent Jewish, and the rest would be just regular Caucasians. . . . They were all in the same classroom and they got along very well" (Flamming 263). Several notable African Americans attended Jefferson including jazz saxophonist Dexter Gordon, actress Dorothy Dandridge (who had attended Hooper Elementary), and choreographer Alvin Ailey. Ambassador Ralph Bunche, the class valedictorian in 1923, had moved to Los Angeles from Albuquerque with his grandmother after the death of his parents. When Harvard accepted Bunche for graduate school, the Women's Auxiliary of the NAACP raised the money for his tuition (Flamming 267). The Colemans had clearly chosen a location where education was a major priority and one in which the African American community was willing to make considerable sacrifices to improve their children's futures.

A third reason for the Colemans' move was probably the fact that home ownership in Los Angeles was a realistic goal for black families. In 1930, despite the Depression, 33.6 percent of all African Americans in Los Angeles owned their own homes, compared to 10.5 percent in Chicago, 15 percent in Detroit, and 5.6 per cent in New York and Boston. Only one in five black families in Denver owned homes, and in San Francisco the number of homeowners was negligible (Bond 56; Bryant et al. 10; Flamming 51). Housing, though attractive, was still restricted, and 70 percent of the city's black population lived in one assembly district near Central Avenue. Here, a janitor or other blue-collar worker could afford one of the "well-built stucco cottage[s] with trim front lawns" located within walking distance of "Brown Broadway" as Central Avenue was called (Bond 68; Bryant 19).

When Langston Hughes visited Loren Miller in Los Angeles in 1932 he thought it "seemed more a miracle than a city, a place where oranges sold for one cent a dozen, ordinary black folks lived in huge houses with 'miles of yards,' and prosperity seemed to reign in spite of the Depression" (Rampersad 236). Hughes was amazed that Miller had found "the swellest apartment in a street of palms and flowers for only $25 a month" (Rampersad 236). Miller was a lawyer and civil rights advocate and a columnist for the *Eagle*. Coleman certainly knew him since they lived about twenty blocks apart, and their pictures had appeared together in the *Crisis* in 1926 when they won the first and second prizes in the essay contest.

Coleman and Miller probably moved in overlapping progressive circles. Anita, who became involved with the peace movement in the forties, belonged to the literary club of the Mount Zion Baptist Church. Miller, a member of the John Reed Club, probably did not care for her writing. He "openly dismissed almost all the writing of the Harlem Renaissance school, including much of Hughes's work, as worthless" (Green; Rampersad 236). When Miller and Hughes returned from a trip to the Soviet Union in 1933, the former gave a talk on his experiences at Second Baptist, the mother church of the Colemans' congregation; it is possible that she and James attended (Flamming 325). Miller's radical politics did not, however, preclude bourgeois comforts; in the early forties Hughes reported to Arna Bontemps that Miller and his wife Juanita had moved to a "beautiful, modern house with a circular staircase and terraced garden" northwest of downtown in the prestigious West Temple District (Nichols 89, 91).

The Colemans' house at 5402 Hooper Avenue was typical of the Central Avenue area: "There are entire streets where the homes are well-kept, the lawns are green, and the families are stable units" (Bond 74). While not as affluent as West Side residents, the Colemans' neighbors comprised business and professional men and several African American pioneer families. Dorothy Dandridge and her mother lived three blocks from the Colemans, and other black show-business people were nearby including the Nicholas brothers, Harold and Fayard (Bogle 36). In the early forties, Chester Himes lived close to Fifty-fourth Street and Hooper Avenue, judging from the precise directions to the neighborhood he provides in *If He Hollers Let Him Go*.

Wealthy black Angelenos preferred to live west of Central Avenue, a neighborhood that Himes locates near Normandie and Twenty-eighth Street: "The houses were well-kept, mostly white stucco or frame . . . California bungalows, averaging from six to ten rooms. . . . The lawns were green and well-trimmed. . . . The air smelled of freshly cut grass and gardenias in bloom" (Himes, *Hollers* 48). On the West Side lived "the only Negro principal in the city, a Y.M.C.A. executive [T. A. Greene], a Methodist bishop, a nationally known architect [Paul R. Williams], a movie actress, several lawyers, a well-known politician, and numerous county and city employees" (Bond 70). Eventually Anita and her family moved to the West Side; her gracious home at 2722 Kenwood Avenue was located in this desirable neighborhood.

In terms of convenience and amenities, however, the Central Avenue community had much to recommend it. According to Flamming, "the intersection of 12th and Central remained the hub of black L.A., but there was a steady move southward, not just among black homeowners but also among key Negro institutions" (263). The original neighborhood included two black newspapers, including the *New Age*, for which Harold Coleman worked, and the 100-room Somerville Hotel (later renamed the Dunbar), which hosted the 1928 NAACP convention. The hotel "housed a pharmacy, barber shop, beauty parlor, and flower shop" (Bryant 9). Hugh Gordon's famous bookshop stocked "the best Negro histories, biographies, literature, and magazines" (Bass 49). The older black churches with their imposing facades were located near Eighth street, including the First African Methodist Episcopal (AME) Church. Biddy Mason, a famous Los Angeles pioneer and entrepreneur, helped organize First AME, the city's very first black church, in 1872. Later First AME led the battle against school segregation (Bass 21). As the population shifted south, "Second Baptist bought land on 24th Street and hired the black architect Paul Williams to design its stately new home"(Flamming 263). The colored YMCA and the Elks Hall built new quarters below Twentieth street. Several movie houses were nearby including the Gaiety and the "sparkling new" Lincoln, "a grand movie palace, complete with an orchestra pit and a broad stage for concerts and theatrical productions" (Flamming 263). At the Lincoln, residents of South Central could have seen a young Dorothy Dandridge and her sister Vivian perform in vaudeville routines (Bogle 31). Other attractions included a roller-skating rink; Robinson's ice cream parlor; and E. G. Johnson's drug store (Flamming 263).

While Anita and Harold probably did not frequent the "dance halls, cabaret clubs . . . [and] speakeasies" along Central Avenue, Coleman apparently knew and wrote about people in the entertainment business who did so (Bryant 10). Some of Coleman's stories feature "sheiks" and "players" like Bambino Grimke, a jazz-band leader who speaks in the latest urban slang. In a letter to her son in the early 1940s, she describes young Angelenos in their zoot suits and big hats, "swaggering down [Crenshaw] Boulevard, in the long coats, trousers zooked to the last minute . . . the 'hottest babies' in town" (A. Coleman, "Letter").

The nightclubs of Central Avenue frequented by Bambino Grimke provided employment for black musicians from all over the country. These included the Apex (later the Club Alabam), where Redd Foxx performed; the Congo; the Quality Café, whose house band included Lionel Hampton; and an after-hours club called Brother's which was "deeply carpeted, overly decorated, lush as an opium den" (Himes, *Collected* 128). Brother's, called Cousin's in Himes's story "A Night of New Roses," was the most popular venue "with the young hip entertainment crowd." The eponymous host was "a black male diva . . . given to wearing flowing robes and a touch of mascara . . . as he floated about greeting his guests" (Bogle 115). Lena Horne was a regular at Brother's, and stars like George Raft, Tyrone Power, Rita Hayworth, Lana Turner, and Betty Grable enjoyed "totally Black clubs" like the Plantation (Bogle 115).

The Colemans enjoyed classical music and frequently attended concerts at the Hollywood Bowl (Green). They may have attended the famous Hollywood Bowl Gospel Extravaganza in 1926 in which "ten choirs from Negro churches competed, drawing huge, integrated audiences" (Flamming 265). A photograph shows a relaxed Anita and Harold Coleman at the Hollywood Bowl with Harold's sister, Willianna, who is dressed more formally in an East Coast tailored suit. Once in Los Angeles, Coleman wrote a number of poems with musical themes; several are about an African American singer who may have been Marian Anderson (Green).

Paradoxically, in moving farther away from the East Coast, Coleman moved closer to the Harlem Renaissance. In 1928, the *Messenger* dubbed her "one of the best of the Negro writers and the winner of many prizes for short stories" (May–June 1928: 111). The same year her son Harold was born. If she was too busy raising children and participating in church activities to socialize with her colleagues and fellow prize winners, she certainly followed their activities in the papers. Arna Bontemps and his family lived a few miles south in Watts which was then a working-class white community (Nichols 91). In 1935,

Langston Hughes was back in Los Angeles, collaborating with Bontemps and living at the Clark Hotel near Central Avenue. Both men looked for work in the film industry, as did Chester Himes (Rampersad 308). Wallace Thurman was in Los Angeles at this time and wrote two films before his early death from tuberculosis (Singh 5). Coleman must have been aware that when Loren Miller invited Hughes to speak at a function sponsored by the Los Angeles Civic League, the YMCA suddenly cancelled the event because of Hughes's "anti-Christ" and "Communist" poem "Goodbye Christ" (Rampersad 309). Zora Neale Hurston arrived in 1941, also hoping to break into film writing. Although their time in Los Angeles overlapped briefly, perhaps the person Coleman would have had most in common with was Eloise Bibb Thompson, a playwright and essayist married to Noah Thompson who worked for both the *Messenger* and *Opportunity*. The couple was part of the literary group called the Ink Slingers that dabbled in literature, though none of the members could rival Coleman's long publishing record.

Changes were occurring in the private and public spheres that affected the Coleman family. By 1939 James Coleman was working for the S. L. Walker Printing Company and the family had moved to 1208 E. Thirty-fourth Street. Willianna, Mary, and their brother James had graduated from Jefferson High School, and Willianna had graduated cum laude from UCLA. Later she obtained a master's degree in Spanish. Once her children grew up, Coleman opened her home to foster children. Several poems written in the forties deal with the innocence of children and with the responsibility of the community to provide love and stability for young people.

As World War II approached Coleman became increasingly interested in the peace movement. Her two older sons, James and Spencer, served in Europe as members of the 780th Military Police Battalion. "Awareness," published in 1948, poignantly captures her grief: "Yet not until / They marshalled my sons, did my / Heart strive with the combat. / 'Twas then I sought the Councilor." An earlier poem uses metaphoric language and the rhythm of a nursery rhyme to convey the urgency of peace: "Peace is a little bird that / Must have her freedom . . . / If she nests, protect her, / If she rests, refresh her, / If she sleeps, 'shoo, shoo' her away / Peace must have her freedom."

In 1943 Coleman summarized her philosophy on writing in a letter to her son Spencer who was stationed in Arizona. "Writing," she says, "is simply transferring to paper all your thoughts and impressions of things coming under observation." She compliments Spencer on his descriptions of "the Sergeant who drank too much" and his hike through the Arizona hills, and explains: "after all, writing is just the same as talking to someone you meet on the street or telling a story at home." With characteristic modesty she adds: "You just want to imagine that it is something hard to do. It is not hard at all." Spencer and James both survived the war and returned home to Los Angeles, where they started families and enjoyed successful lives as a rubber millman and mail carrier, respectively.

Coleman's poetry found critical success throughout the forties. In 1940 her poem "Baptism" won first prize in the California-wide Robert Browning Poetry Contest sponsored by the University of Redlands (Shipley). In 1948, her first book of poetry, *Reason for Singing*, was published by the Decker Press in Prairie City, Illinois. Decker was a prestigious imprint; it published prominent American poets such as Edgar Lee Masters, David Ignatow, Kenneth Patchen, Kenneth Rexroth, and Louis Zukovsky. Decker's international authors included Stéphane Mallarmé and Sor Juana Inés de la Cruz. In 1948, Decker published poetry collections by two other African Americans, Frank Marshall Davis and the eminent scholar John Henrik Clarke. Coleman's book included poems originally published in the race journals twenty years earlier as well as more recent efforts. Her joy at the publication of her book, for which she had worked so long, was marred only by the blinding of James in a printing accident the same year.

Two years later, tragedy struck again. In September she lost her thirty-three-year-old daughter Willianna to tuberculosis and her husband James to heart disease. Two months later, her youngest son Harold died of complications from pneumonia.

Coleman then moved in with Willianna's husband, Russell Washington, to help care for the couple's three children—James, Spencer, and Anita. When Russell died two years later, Coleman began living with her daughter Mary Jackson and her husband, who adopted the three children. Mary Jackson was a teacher and had published a children's book on the California fishing industry. Perhaps as a distraction she encouraged her mother to try her hand at children's literature. Anita began writing a winsome story about a musical family.

In 1960, Anita Scott Coleman died of cancer. Her funeral, a grand celebration of her life, took place at the Mount Zion Baptist Church in Los Angeles, where she had worshipped for over thirty years. She was laid to rest in the Evergreen Cemetery in a companion grave with her husband Harold. Her last book, *The Singing Bells*, was published posthumously in 1961 by Nashville's Broadman Press. Throughout the final difficult years, Coleman found comfort in her family, friends, and church. "'Twas then I learned the ageless truth," she wrote years before, "that we / Through ravages of war and scourge / Through death and trial and times like these / . . . Shall not die, because God lives" ("Awareness").

Although Anita Scott Coleman chose to center her life on family and spirituality, writing was of utmost importance and an essential aspect of her identity. Around 1940 Coleman jotted down a list of wishes and prayers; the first three expressed hopes for her children's success ("Let my Billie teach"), but the fourth stated simply, "Let me have my book of poems published" ("Prayer"). Finding a publisher was difficult and she waited eight more years before *Reason for Singing* appeared. In assessing Coleman's contribution to American literature it is important to note that in spite of domestic demands on her time and the limited venues for black women's writing, her career spanned over forty years, from her first story in the *Half-Century Magazine* in 1919 to *The Singing Bells* in 1961. Between 1919 and 1943 she consistently published an average of two stories or poems a year. Ten stories were printed between 1919 and 1920. By comparison, her contemporary Marita Bonner, who also combined family and writing, published ten stories in eleven years (Allen 12).

Coleman's work resonates on a number of levels. Many of her themes are of particular interest to the black community: race pride, resistance, African American history, oral tradition, and vernacular culture. However, the universality of her work is expressed through stories and poems about ethnic and cultural pluralism, the geography and folklore of the American West, compassion for children and the dispossessed, and a commitment to peace and justice. Stylistically, Coleman is innovative; her work is influenced by the vocabulary and technique of film and by modernist experiments with rhythm, multivocality, and the juxtapositions of time and space. We hope that this volume will enable a new audience to enjoy and appreciate Coleman's unique voice as an African American southwestern woman writer.

Illustrations

Anita Scott Coleman as an infant in Guaymas, Mexico.

Early family portrait of the Scott family in Guaymas, Mexico.

Mary Ann Stokes Scott in Mexico.

Mary Ann Stokes Scott

Anita Scott Coleman

Mary Ann Stokes Scott and her daughter, Anita, ca. 1907.

Some of the African American troops or "Buffalo Soldiers," also known as Indian Scouts, were members of the 9th and 10th Cavalry. Stereograph courtesy of Library of Congress, Prints and Photographs Division, LC-USZ62-57107.

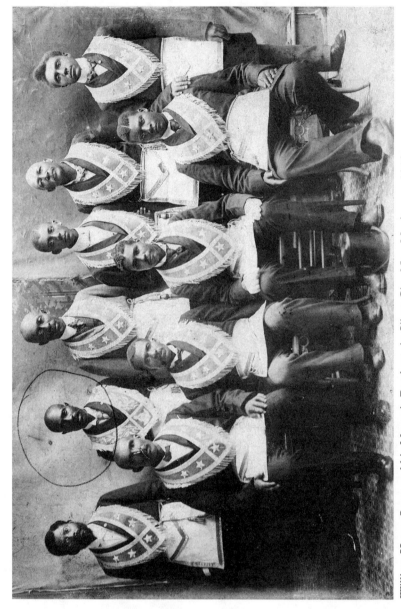

William Henry Scott and his Masonic Brothers, in Silver City, New Mexico, ca. 1910.

Coleman's brother, William Ulysses Scott, in military uniform.

Coleman's sister-in-law, Ida Gonzalez, on the ranch, ca. 1915.

Sisters-in-law Anita Scott and Ida Gonzalez Scott, on the ranch, ca. 1915.

Anita "Annie" Scott, reading at the ranch, ca. 1915.

Ruth Ann Scott in Silver City, New Mexico, ca. 1932.

Coleman and her children on the ranch. Left to right: Mary, Willianna, James, and Spencer, ca. 1925.

THE CRISIS

NEW NEGRO ARTISTS

Cullen   Miller   Dickinson   Coleman   Spence

Crisis award winners, February 1927: Countee Cullen, Loren Miller, Blanche Taylor Dickinson, Anita Scott Coleman, and Eulalie Spence.

Coleman's first Los Angeles residence, 5402 Hooper Avenue, 2006. Courtesy of Reginald C. Holmes.

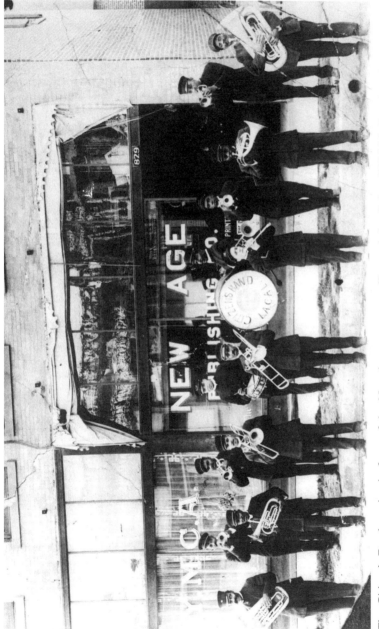

The Citizen's Band, posing in front of the *New Age* newspaper office and the Colored YMCA, Los Angeles, ca. 1910. Coleman's husband, James Harold, worked for the *New Age* as a manager and printer. Courtesy of the African American Museum and Library of Oakland, the Miriam Matthews Collection.

Negro History Club, Los Angeles, 1937. Cousins Willianna (Billie) Coleman, and Esther and Mary Scott.

Harold Coleman (top left) and classmates, Jefferson High School, ca. 1942.

63

Army sergeants Spencer and James Coleman, with their award-winning boxing team during World War II, ca. 1943.

Spencer Scott Coleman, signed "From your black son, Nov. [19]52, Spencer."

"Daddy Jim" Coleman in his printing shop, Los Angeles, ca. 1940.

Daddy Jim returning from the library, Los Angeles, ca. 1940.

Mary

Jin

Spencer

Mama Coleman

Mickey   Jeanie   Anita   Leaving for church

Coleman and children, going to church, 2722 Kenwood Avenue, Los Angeles.

Kenny   Ida Worrill   Barbara Dorsey   Edna   ASC   Billy Dorsey   James R Washington   Micky   Billy
Lorra   Michael Dorsey   Brainard Worrill   Joann Coleman Spencer Washington

Coleman surrounded by family members and foster children, 1948.

Coleman, her husband, and her sister-in-law Willianna Hicks, at the Hollywood Bowl, Los Angeles, ca. 1948.

Coleman's final residence, 2722 Kenwood Avenue, Los Angeles.

71

Coleman's grandchildren: Douglas Jackson, Anita Green, David Jackson, Lisa Coleman, Jeanette Thompson, and Cindy Henderson, Los Angeles, July 2006. Courtesy of Reginald C. Holmes.

Part I

Stories

The Brat

A wild night, a blazing hearth, a rose-lit room, low, sweet music, an over-stuffed armchair and a companion; who can tell a tale of life, as she is—ah, there's charm and warmth a-plenty.

The night was not only wild, it was raving, stark, tearing mad. Rain and wind strove together in a fierce onslaught. The wind shrieking and howling like runaway fury. The rain pounding like fifty drummers, each bent on out-drumming his mate.

My room, rose-lit and cheery, the coziest spot I know. Low music. My favorite record, playing over and over, tenderly, hauntingly. A chair, over-stuffed and comfortable, stretched out its arms, like a mother's wide flung, to embrace me. But— I was companionless. Yet— It is not given unto you or to me to have things at all times.

★　★　★

A knock. A clattering, banging, biff-booming, biff-booming. It had to be, to become distinguishable from the drum-beats of the rain.

What? Who—who? Without on a night like this?

Come in— Come in— Come in.

And in limped old Jennie.

Old Jennie, all twisted and bent with premature age, which wrapped her about like an ill-fitting garment; which wrinkled her skin and whitened her hair, but did not reflect itself in her eyes. Old Jennie's

Messenger Apr. 1926: 105–6, 126.

eyes were marvelous. They sparkled in her wrinkled face like gems—
the gems of youth. Nor did her age lessen her activity. Bent and
lame as she was, she worked amazingly, accomplishing the labors of
three women with speed that was unbelievable. She was a silent
creature, speaking only when speech was imperative and then in the
fewest words. Her voice had a haunting quality, a resonance, a something that vaguely stirred some chord, a memory, though indefinable; like a whiff of fragrance from a forgotten perfume. I have never
seen old Jennie smile. Yet, in her presence there is no trace of gloom,
no hint of sadness. And her eyes so sparkling, so youthful, have often
caused me to idly wonder.

She came upon me now, as surprisingly as a genii from Aladdin's
lamp. Old silent Jennie out of the night and the storm into my rose-
lit room, dripping wet, and to my utter surprise, quite full of words.

"It's only me, Miss Aggie, only me. 'Twas my day up to the Towers,
and the storm— Ain't it the worse you ever saw? Overtook me on
my way home, right here in this neighborhood, where I felt like a rat
a-gettin' drowned, 'til I remembered you and 'lowed how you would
give me shelter 'til the storm pass."

A night for surprises indeed. Old Jennie esteeming me above my
fellows. A pleasing surprise bobbing up to nod at me like daisies on
a hillside. A pleasing, warming, cheering surprise that old Jennie, old
black Jennie, old wash-woman, scrub-woman, ugly, wrinkled, old, old
thing esteemed me above my fellows. Straightway my thoughts turned
to a warm robe, padded silken mules and woolen hose, and they were
surprises for Jennie. Oh, what a night for surprises!

Presently Jennie and I were sitting before my hearth. And such a
blaze was roaring up the chimney.

"How jolly to have you with me, Jennie. How glad I am you thought
of me," said I.

"Humph!" rejoined old Jennie.

We sat there, my old wash-woman and I, a long, long while saying
nothing. Then suddenly, old Jennie spoke:

"Miss Aggie, that music, that music is making me want to tell you
somethin' I ain't never told nobody before. Somethin' no other living
person knows but me. And it's true, true, true; God knows it's true."

She paused and I did not break the silence. I fancied it was not
me she was talking to. She was answering the magic of my rose-lit

room, the glowing warmth, the music, yes, most of all the music. So I remained quiet in my best of chairs and waited.

"I ain't no old, old woman like I seems. The number of my years ain't many. Not many, Miss Aggie, if you just count time. But if you reckons the days I've spent in sorrow and pain and regrets, then I'm old, old, old.

"I was young and wild. So wild and young when the riot occurred. It ain't no call for tellin' dates or naming places, it's just one bitter fact I'm mindful of. As for the riot, there hasn't ever been one so bad since and it weren't never one so bad before. Black folk were butchered and slaughtered right and left, and white folks—Well, the black folks fought back, that's what made it a riot. I was young, but I wasn't too young to be a mother. A wild young thing and a mother.

"My baby. I can see him now, as he was then. Little trusting mite. My baby. He was one year old. 'Twas his birthday, that day of the riot. Baby, my baby, is what I call him now, but then I called him 'the brat'—just that. I had no other name to give him. No love for him was in my heart, and his father wouldn't dast to own him.

"It all comes from my being born what I am and from those a-fore me, and I guess those a-fore them. My ma had so many children her one concern was to name us and parcel us out. We were scattered like a litter of kittens, here, there and everywhere. But it never came my turn to go. Maybe it was because I could sing, and singing I earned money to help keep body and soul together.

"You don't know the bitterness of being poor. It ain't the things you ain't got and the havin' to do without and the needin' and the wantin' that crushes the heart out of you. It's the meanness, the little-ness and the pettiness which poverty breeds. It's the tiny splinter lost in the flesh that festers quickest, and being poor is that-a-way—it festers.

"I could sing. So I was sent out into the street to pick up nickels and dimes a-singin'. Pretty soon I'd learned other ways to wheedle coins from those who were untouched by my voice.

"My voice was God-given. I got proof of that. Even if I did use it to carry me to the devil. To the devil I went faster than a pine knot burns. Gettin' wilder and wilder. Payin' no sort 'er attention to any-body. Proud of my singing, proud of my looks, proud of my wildness. Until the time come, when I didn't have a friend, when I wasn't even fit to sing 'fore folks, when I didn't have a crust of bread to eat nor shoes to stick my feet into. Then a girl called Biddy befriended me and stood by me through all my trouble.

"I had seen her often, when I was too proud to notice her kind. A fair, fair girl she was, with big blue eyes and straw-colored hair. Nobody noticed her looks. 'Cause it is common, a common sight enough to see colored folks as white as white folks, and women to see it the other way 'round, too; 'The brat' was a-goin' to be one or the other of that kind.

"Biddy was a queer one with a reputation for using genteel language and of never being known to cheat. She had a kind of humble O-I-want-to-please-you air about her that made her the laughing stock of the folks in our district. She drank like a fish and I suspect she used something else. It's true, she was a queer one, and to top it all she lived with Black Luke, a big burly man as mean as sin and as black as night. When he was a-mind to, he beat her awful. Then, for weeks and weeks afterwards, he'd be kind to her, showing his teeth like a snarling dog at anyone who dared to so much as speak to her. They loved each other all right, and they stuck together through thick and thin. And they shared their home with me. 'The brat' was born under their roof.

"Biddy loved him from the first. And she nursed him and 'tended him and kept him clean. She coaxed Black Luke to buy him little trinkets and pretty little dresses and socks and shoes. She called him 'Little Brat' like I did; but when she said it, soft and sweet-like, it sounded like a caress—'Little Brat—Little Brat.'

"We lived together all of that awful year and Biddy used to tell us about her folks, always with a sort 'er reverence that made you pity her. She told me their names and where they lived so many, many times. I learned 'em like I did my a. b. c's. Then the day came, when 'the brat' was one year old, that day of the riot, and we grown-ones celebrated the occasion with drink. I was dead drunk, too drunk to know or to care how or why they were a-fightin' out in the street.

Black Luke had one of his mean fits and he was sure one man to fear whenever he had one. It seems most like a bad dream but I'm mighty certain he beat Biddy before he drank himself to sleep sitting upright on the floor with his head leant back 'gainst the wall.

"Yes, that part of it is dim like things seen at twilight, before it goes all dark. What I remember is the thick black pressing gloom that fell on me that day. I don't know yet how the riot started but I know that it was awful. Smoke and fire. Smoke and fire and screams and shouts and pitiful cries for help, help, help. A-hearing God's name blasphemed one minute and next minute a-listening to His Name going up in prayer. Rocks, sticks, bricks and pistol-shots flyin' through the air, and people, men, women, and little children, a-scamperin' back and forth, like frightened mice, and others, men, women, and little children, gone mad with tasting blood, fighting like savage beasts and all the while Biddy and Black Luke and 'the brat' and me huddled like stupid sheep in our room. There was Biddy sitting stiffly in a chair with my 'flesh and blood' in her arms staring, straight ahead, straight before her, just staring. And Black Luke asleep on the floor, with his head a-restin' 'gainst the wall.

"Bang, whiz, thud. A bullet spat over me and found its mark in Black Luke's head. He groaned once, toppled over and was still. Another bullet followed and another and another. Someone stood outside a-firin' until their pistol was empty.

"Biddy said: 'Oh, God—God—God!' Six times just that-a-way. Then she was still too, so still, so still. 'The brat' roused in her arms and whimpered. A tongue of flame licked through our roof. It was awful.

"When the fire had burned half way cross, Biddy got up so calm and yet eager, like a young girl goin' out on a ball-room floor to dance. She wrapped an old shawl 'bout my baby and put on her hat. Then she went to Black Luke's body and knelt beside it. She kissed him a long, long kiss on his cooling lips, and her hand over him, slow-like, tender-like, gentle-like. Then she quit that and went to searching in his pockets, first one and then the other, until she had thrust her hand into everyone. But each time they come out empty. She tore open the front of his shirt, a-feelin' all in there. And still her hands were empty. She began to move her lips, a-praying. And tears streamed down her cheeks. She reached for his hat that had fallen off his head, when he toppled, and began a-feelin' inside it. She pulled out the band, her hands all trembly and a-fumblin' in her eagerness. Presently she drew out money, paper money, I don't know how much; then she began to laugh. A funny, funny laugh with tears streaming down her cheeks. She put the money into her bosom, down in between her corset, and came over to me and said, still laughing a little in that funny, funny way, with tears streaming down her cheeks:

"'Jen, you're such a sot, it does not matter if you are killed—. I wish I could be, too. But the brat, somebody's got to save "the brat." I'm going to take him home. Home. Where he'll be cared for and allowed to grow clean like he ought. He is little. Too little to remember all the dirt he's seen. And with my folks he'll have a chance to be a man. Do you hear, Jennie, girl—a man? That's why I'm going to wade through blood—going through that hell out there, to carry him home. Jennie, listen to me—listen, girl—that's why I'm leaving you— to carry him home—to my own folks—home—'

"She stooped then and give me a quick kiss. I recollects how I rubbed it away, a-thinkin' 'bout that long, long one she'd just given Black Luke, and him dead.

"Young I was and wild and foolish and a sot; so I lay there befuddled with drink while she carried my baby away. For an instant I was glad, glad, glad to be shed of 'the brat' forever. He had cost me dear. Something had gone wrong with my voice since his coming. And nobody, except Biddy, had been kind to me. Only Biddy.

"Then suddenly I realized that Biddy was gone—gone. I seemed to know for the first time what that tongue of flame a-lickin' across the roof over my head meant and that poor Black Luke was a-lyin' dead, almost at my feet; and I heard the screaming outside, and the firing. But all I could think of was, Biddy had gone—Biddy, who was kind to me—Biddy had gone and left me trapped in a burning house, with a dead man. I screamed and screamed. Come back, come back. Biddy, come back! And screaming I ran to the window that had been shattered with bullets.

"I got there in time to see a man aim his gun at Biddy. Saw him pull the trigger. Heard the shot. And as sure as God's in Heaven, it struck Biddy; but Biddy kept on a-goin'. I screamed. It seemed that never, so long as I lived, would I ever quit screaming—screaming—screaming.

"They picked me up from where I had fallen through the window. The fall made me a cripple but it didn't kill me. Why—why—why? When I didn't have a single thing to live for? Why, when other women, pure and good—true wives and loving mothers—were slaughtered that day like pigs in a pen? But it was six months before I could leave the hospital, and when I did my voice was gone completely. Six months before I could even start to get ready to go after 'the brat'—my baby.

"I hadn't ever cared for him or wanted him before. Now my heart ached for him, day and night. I think it was the cool, quiet, cleanness all about me, the easy-steppin' doctors and the pretty lady nurses, and the peacefulness, after that awful, awful day, that changed me. I spent all the long hours a-gettin' well, a-picturin' the way he crinkled his face to smile. How it took all his baby fingers to wrap 'round one of mine. Recallin' one by one his cunnin' baby tricks. And wantin' him so hard, it hurt, like pain.

Well, I set about earning my fare to Biddy's home. And I was bent on being presentable, too. I didn't want Biddy's folks a-shame of me. She had talked so much about 'em, I felt I knew the kind 'er folks they'd be. A-lyin' there in the hospital with so much time to think and a-lookin' back, I saw things I hadn't noticed before and some that I had noticed but never heeded, and it made me feel like my folks would'er been their kind if— Well, you know, I felt that-a-way, a-lyin' there. Plain, honest, decent, and mighty proud-like, 'cause God had let you be so. Such thoughts and one thing and another and the gettin' money to go and a whole year had slipped by.

"It was night when I got there, but I went straight to Biddy's home—straight to Biddy's folks. And oh, my God! Miss Aggie, they were white—white folks. White, Miss Aggie, like you. But I wanted my baby. So I mentioned Biddy's name. It was like a password. They welcomed me and treated me ever and ever so nice. I saw my baby and played with him and kissed him. God knows I didn't keep count of times I kissed him in the little while I had the chance.

"Biddy was dead-shot. Just like I knew. She had lived long enough to put my baby in her mother's arms. And her not knowing, supposed 'the Brat' belonged to Biddy. They were glad to have him—'the Brat,' my baby—because they thought he was a little mite of living flesh, sprung from their own—their daughter, to whom they had been harsh, too strict, too hard. They gloried in the chance they'd been given to make it all up to her, through her child.

"And when I saw how clean my baby was, and how healthy he was and wholesome, and all the things they were doin' for him that I could never do, I pretended I was his old nurse, come to see him, 'cause I had loved his mother before him and couldn't help feelin' interested-like in her child. Oh, I set there, a-tellin' 'em lies and lies and lies, while my heart was breakin', and when I could bear it no more I ups and left—and left 'the brat,' too.

"It's funny how easy a heart can break, as easy as an eggshell, only an eggshell breaks but once and a heart mends—mends to break again. So it was from the first; in another year, after I left 'the brat,' I went back to see him again—'lowing I was his old nurse droppin' in for the sake of his mother.

"I made a lot of that lovin' his mother, 'cause I did love Biddy—I love her yet. She was kind to me when nobody else was. And seeing my baby thrive and grow sweeter every year made me grateful. And I remembered her words: 'Jen, you're such a sot, it does not matter if you are killed.' So I started goin' straight and keepin' straight cause of her wantin' much to have 'the brat' grow clean and wholesome.

"I kept it up, a-goin' back every year. Workin' hard and savin' my money, so's to buy my boy gifts. A-breaking my heart over and over until my boy was twelve years old.

"For a long time his playmates had been a-teasin' him 'bout his 'Ol' black mammy.' Poking fun at him and a-laughin'. He stood it, though, 'til he was twelve years old. That's when my heart broke, its last time. It can never break any more. It's still and dead, 'cause it didn't break to mend, the time my boy refused to see me. Even when Biddy's folks forced him to come shake hands, he wouldn't look at me, wouldn't let me kiss him. And wouldn't take my gifts—not one.

"Like a slap in the face I minded the moment when I'd been mighty glad to be shed of 'the brat' forever. My baby—my baby. I grit my teeth, and I tried to pray, and I ain't never been back no more.

"I work, so's I won't have time to think; but I can't get rid of knowing about my boy. It's queer how fore-knowing a mother's heart can be. And this heart of mine that ain't had nothin' 'cept breaks and breaks, knows when my boy is happy and knows when my boy is sad. He ain't happy now and I'm powerless. He ain't happy and it's me who is to blame—me—who never bothered to mother him when I had the chance; who lay stupid drunk while another woman gave up her life to save him from death or a life far worse.

"I told you 'bout my singin'. Well, my boy sings, too. It's his singin' that's a-turnin' to be his curse. His voice that tells you what he is, is the thing that keeps him bound. He sings like only one of my race can sing, but he sings so fine, so fine, Biddy's race won't let him go.

"His skin is dark and his hair is curly, and his eyes are like mine was in the days when I was young and wild. But they don't betray him none. He's bound—he's bound. Oh, my tears are washed out of my eyes crying for him, but I can't loose his chains.

"It's his singing. He's known in every nook and corner. Children know his name and quit their play to listen to his singin'. Everywhere I go somebody's a-hummin' or whistlin' the songs he sings. Somebody's playin' one of his records—like that one now. Like that one now."

Electrified, I started up, repeating her words like a parrot. Old Jennie sat gazing into the fire. The tense lines of her face, the rigidness of her body, made me think of a marble statue of Truth. A statue come to life, to experience the burning pain of all humanity's pretense and subterfuge and lies.

If she heard my query she gave no heed. So I settled back, in my best of chairs, wonderingly, staring wide-eyed at old Jennie. Staring. Wondering. Tensely aware of music, playing tenderly, hauntingly, "I Hear You Calling Me." My favorite song, sung by my best loved tenor, David Kane, one of America's greatest singers. So young and gifted, of whom America is so arrogantly proud. Proud, that he is no foreigner, come to us from across the sea, but truly ours. A product of America.

Yes, he is dark; but his boyhood home is on the western plains, where unfettered winds blew free, to tan his cheek. True, his dark, coarse hair grows in curly ringlets, but curly hair is ofttimes the only outward mark of genius.

"I hear you calling me,
And oh, the ringing gladness of your voice."

Again old Jennie spoke, harshly, bitterly, her voice laden with poignant sorrow that poured over me a torrent of heart-rending grief.

"Listen, listen, any fool knows that ain't no white man's voice. He's mine, he's mine, he's mine. As true as God's in heaven he's mine, Miss Aggie, he's mine."

The drumming rain and the shrieking wind seemed very far, like some hidden chorus in a play of torture. The music trilled through the rose-lit room:

"You called me when the moon had veiled her
light, Before I went from you into the night."

Once more old Jennie spoke. And her voice was the croon of a mother. "He's like a little bird caged up with lions. He's lonely, so lonely. His poor heart aches and he can't tell why."

And my heart
Still hears the distant music of your voice—I hear you calling me."

Suddenly, with one move of her crippled body, old Jennie leaped from her chair, flinging her arms wide in a hopeless gesture. Whispering words, so pain-seared they scorched:
"Miss Aggie, he bears the call of a race. I tell you his race, and his poor old mother callin', a-callin' him."

⋆   ⋆   ⋆

A log cracked and settled upon the embers, showering sparks almost at our feet. In the brighten glow, while my eyes were full upon her, for a second's fleeting flight, old Jennie's face was the face of David Kane, America's world-famed tenor.

Three Dogs and a Rabbit

"This, that I'm about to relate," said Timothy Phipps, "isn't much of a story, though, you might upon hearing it weave it into a ripping good yarn. I'm not much of a talker or a writer. Now maybe when I'm in my cups or in the last stages of a delirious fever—I might attempt to—write." He tilted his head, with its fringe of rough grey hair, a bit backwards and sidewise and laughed. His laughter seeming to echo—write, write, write.

Tinkling with fine spirits and good humor, he ceased laughing to inquire roguishly: "What, say, are the ingredients of a story? A plot? Ah, yes a plot. Ho! ho! ho! The only plot in this rigmarole, my dear fellows, is running, hard to catch, a sure enough running plot. Characters. To be sure we must have characters: A pretty girl, a brave hero, a villain and love. A setting. Of course there must be a setting, an atmosphere, a coloring. We'll say moonlight and a rippling brook and a night bird singing nocturnal hymns in a forest of love. Love pirouetting in the silvery moonlight, love splashing and singing in a rippling brook. Love trilling and fluting in a bird's song—Love and a pretty girl—Love and a brave hero—Love and a villain made penitent and contrite; because of love. Bye the bye, there is no living person who could not fancy the beginning, imagine the entanglements, conceive the climax, unfold the developments, reveal the solution and picture

Crisis Jan. 1926: 118–22.

the finale, having such material at hand. But," laughed Timothy, "none such—none such in what I'm a-telling."

Shedding his joviality for a more serious mien, he queried—

"Have you ever thought how very few really lovely women one meets in a life time? Our pretty young debutantes are far too sophisticated; while our age-mellowed matrons affect *naiveté*, and our bustling house-wives are too preoccupied with directing the destinies of nations to be attractive in the least.

"Men? Bother the men. We are but animals at best. Alert and crafty, lazy and jovial; just as chance decrees, and monotonously alike in our dependence upon woman. All of us are made or marred by our contacts with women. Whenever chance draws her draperies aside to allow a lovely woman to cross our path, it leaves an ineffaceable mark upon our countenance and traces indelible patterns of refinement upon our character.

"Unfortunately, I am of a critical turn of mind together with a pernicious inclination to believe with the ancient Greeks that an ugly body houses an ugly soul and that loveliness dwells only in beautiful temples.

"Certainly, certainly this inclination has led me into more than one blind alley. Ah, if I could only wield the pen as skillfully as I can this—" He flourished a carving knife, for we were at a table and he was occupied at the moment in carving the *pièce de résistance*. "I would tell the world how untrue my premise is. And what a cruel fallacy outer loveliness ofttimes proves itself to be.

"Despite this, my contrary nature clings like a leech to the belief that beautiful temples are invariably beautiful within.

"And it chanced, I say chanced, since there is the probability that someone not half so lovely might have done the same deed, and had such been the case my belief would have suffered a terrible set-back. It chanced that the loveliest woman I ever saw was the most beautiful.

"I saw her first under amazing circumstances. Circumstances so extraordinary they seem unreal to this day, but I won't linger upon them, because they make another story. My second sight of her was in a crowded court-room and it was then while she sat very primly upon the culprit's bench that I had my first opportunity really to see her.

"She was a little woman. Feel as you like towards all other types, but a little woman has appeal. Especially, a little old woman with silvery hair, and an unnameable air about her, that is like fingers forever playing upon the chords of sweetest memories. All this, and a prettiness beside, a trifle faded of course, but dainty and fragile and lovely—rare, you might say, as a bit of old, old lace. And kindliness overlaying this, to lend a charm to her beauty that jewel or raiment could not render. Her silvery hair crinkled almost to the point of that natural curliness which Negro blood imparts. The kind of curl that no artificial aid so far invented can duplicate. Her eyes were extremely heavy-lidded, which is, as you know, a purely Negro attribute, and her mouth had a fullness, a ripeness, exceedingly—*African.*

"That she was anything other than a white American was improbable, improbable indeed. She, the widow of old Colonel Ritton, deceased, of Westview. As dauntless and intrepid a figure as ever lived to make history for his country. His career as an Indian fighter, pioneer and brave, open opposer of the lawlessness which held sway over the far West in the late sixties is a thing that is pointed to with pride and made much of, by Americans. Three notable sons, high standing in their respective vocations, paid her the homage due the mother of such stalwart, upright men as themselves. Two daughters, feted continuously because of their beauty, were married into families, whose family-tree flourished like the proverbial mustard-seed, unblighted before the world.

"There had to be some reason why a lady of her standing was forced to appear in court. The truth is, it was not because of the greatness of her offense; but because of the unusualness of her misconduct which had raised such a hue and cry; until drastic methods had to be resorted to.

"The charge against her was one of several counts, the plaintiffs being three very stout gentlemen, florid-faced, heavy-jowled, wide-paunched to a man. Each of them diffused a pomposity; which while being imposing managed somehow to be amusing. Their very manner bespoke their grim determination to punish the defendant. Their portly bodies fairly bristled with the strength of this intention. The muscles in their heavy faces worked as though the currents of their thoughts were supplied by volts of wonderment, shocking and bewildering. They charged, first: That the defendant willfully hampered them in the fulfillment of their authorized duty. Second: That the defendant had knowingly aided a criminal to evade the hands of the law, by sheltering the said criminal in or about her premises. Third: That the defendant had spoken untruthfully with intent to deceive by denying all knowledge of said criminal's whereabouts. Fourth: That the concealment of said criminal constituted a tort; the criminal being of so dangerous a character, his being at liberty was a menace to the commonwealth."

Timothy Phipps paused, as he busied himself, serving generous slices of baked ham to his guests. In the act of laying a copious helping upon his own plate, he commenced again, to unreel his yarn.

"There is no joy in life so satisfying, so joyous, as that of having our belief strengthened—to watch iridescent bubbles—our castles in the air—settle, unbroken upon firm old earth. To hear our doubts go singing through the chimneys of oblivion. Ah, that's joy indeed. And it is what I experienced that never-to-be forgotten day in the dinkiest little court-room in the world.

"A rainy spell was holding sway and a penetrating drizzle oozed from the sky as though the clouds were one big jelly-bag hung to drip, drip, drip. I was sogged with depression; what with the weather and the fact that I was marooned in a very hostile section of my native land, it was little wonder that my nerves were jumpy and a soddenness saturated my spirits, even though I knew that the fugitive was free and making a rough guess at it, was to remain so. But an emotion more impelling than curiosity forced me to linger to witness the outcome of old Mrs. Ritton's legal skirmish.

"From a maze of judicial meanderings, these facts were made known.

"The old Ritton house was a big rambling structure built at some period so long ago, the time was forgotten. It was not a place of quick escapes, for no such thing as fleeing fugitives had been thought of, in its planning. Unexpected steps up and steps down made hasty flight hazardous. Unlooked for corners and unaccountable turns called for leisurely progress and long halls with closed doors at their furthest end, opening into other chambers, were hindrances no stranger could shun. All told, the house as it stood was a potent witness against the defendant, each of its numerous narrow-paned windows screeched the fact that none but the initiated could play at hide-and-seek within its walls.

"Many pros and cons were bandied about as to why the run-away Negro had entered Ritton's house. That he had done an unwonted thing went without saying—since hunted things flee to the outposts of Nature, shunning human habitation as one does a pestilence: to the long, long road girt by a clear horizon, where dipping sky meets lifting earth, on, on to the boundless space, away to the forest where wild things hover, or a dash to the mountains to seek out sheltering cave and cavern.

"At first, it was thought that entering the Ritton house was a 'dodge' but subsequent happenings had proven the supposition false. It was quite clear that he had gone in for protection and had found it.

"The claimants carefully explained to the court, how they had chased the Negro down Anthony, up Clements and into Marvin, the street which ran north and south beneath the Ritton-house windows. They were not but a few lengths behind the fugitive—not close enough, you understand, to lay hold upon him; nor so near that they could swear that someone signalled from an open window in the Ritton house. How-be-it, they saw the Negro swerve from the street, dart through the Ritton's gate, dash down the walk, and enter the Ritton house. Less than five minutes afterwards they, themselves, pursued the Negro into the building; to find upon entering it a room so spacious that the several pieces of fine old furniture arranged within it did not dispel an effect of emptiness, while the brilliant light of early afternoon showered upon everything, sparklingly, as if to say, 'No place to hide in here' and over beside an open window old lady Ritton sat very calmly, knitting. And upon being questioned she had strenuously denied that a black man had preceded them into her chamber.

"Finally the point was reached, when the defendant took the stand. And the Lord knows, so much depended, that is, as far as I was concerned, upon what she would or would not say—well, what she said makes my story.

"'Gentlemen, the thing you desire me to tell you, I cannot. Though, I think if I could make you understand a little of my feelings, you will cease—all of you being gentlemen—endeavoring to force me to divulge my secret.

"'You, all of you, have been born so unfettered that you have responded to your every impulse; perhaps it will be hard to realize the gamut of my restraint, when I swear to you, gentlemen, that in all my life, I have experienced no great passion and responded to the urge on only two impulses—two—but two—and these gentleman have become for me a sacred trust.

"'It was years ago when I felt the first impulse and answered it. It has no apparent connection with the present occurrence. Yet, possibly, for no other reason than an old lady's imagining, the memory of the first occasion has leaped across the years to interlace itself with this.

"'Wait, gentlemen. I will tell you all about it. This turbulence has awakened old dreams and old longings and opened the doors of yesteryears in the midst of an old lady's musing; but it is worth all the worry. Yes, 'tis worth it.

"'It is strange what mighty chains are forged by impulses and none of us know the strength that is required to break them. My first impulse wrought me much of happiness—very much happiness, gentlemen. Bear with an old lady's rambling—your Honor, and I shall relate just how it happened.

"'I was ten years old, when my master—

"'Pardon? Yes? Yes, Sirs—My master.

"'I was ten years old; when my master gave up his small holdings in the South and came West with his family, his wife,—my mistress— a daughter and two sons and myself. We traveled what was then the tortuous trail that begins east of the Mississippi and ended in the rolling plains beside the Rio Grande. Our trip lasted a fortnight longer than we expected or had planned for. Once along the way, we were robbed. Again, we were forced to break camp and flee because a warring band of Indians was drawing near. Afterwards, we found to our dismay, that a box of provisions had been forgotten or had been lost. Misfortune kept very close to us throughout our journey, our food was all but gone. There was wild game for the killing, but ammunition was too precious to be squandered in such manner. Master had already given the command that we were to hold in our stomachs and draw in our belts until we reached some point where we could restock our fast dwindling supplies.

"'One day, an hour before sun-down, we struck camp in a very lovely spot—a sloping hill-side covered with dwarf cedars and scrub oaks, a hill-side that undulated and sloped until it merged into a sandy-golden bottomed ravine. We pitched our camp in a sheltered nook in this ravine. The golden sand still warm from the day's sunshine made a luxurious resting place for our weary bodies. Below us, a spring trickled up through the earth and spread like lengths of sheerest silk over the bed of sand.

"'In a little while our camp-fire was sending up curling smoke-wreaths, smoke-blue into the balmy air and a pot of boiling coffee—our very last—added its fragrance to the spice of cedars and the pungency of oaks. Sundown came on, and a great beauty settled over everything. Nature was flaunting that side of herself which she reveals to the wanderer in solitary places: the shy kisses she bestows upon the Mountain's brow and, passion-warmed, glows in flagrant colors of the sunset; the tender embrace with which she wraps the plains and the glistening peace shines again in sparkling stars. Beauty that is serene and beauty that brings peace and calm and happiness and is never found in towns or crowded cities.

"'Our three hounds—faithful brutes that had trailed beside us all the weary miles—sat on their haunches and lifted their heads to send up long and doleful cries into the stillness.

"'"Here—here—" cried Master. "Quit that!—Come, come, we'll take a walk and maybe scare up something to fill the pot tomorrow." He ended by whistling up to the prancing dogs and they were off. Up the hillside they went, the dogs, noses to earth, skulking at Master's heels or plunging into the under-brush on a make-believe scent.

"'I sat in the warm sand, a lonely slave-child, watching Master and the dogs until they reached the hill-top. Almost on the instant, the dogs scared up a rabbit. What a din they made yelping, yip, yap, yap and Master halooing and urging them to the race. The frightened rabbit ran like the wind, a living atom with the speed of a flying arrow. Straight as a shooting star, it sped: until turning suddenly it began bounding back along the way it had come. The ruse worked. The dogs sped past, hot on the trail of the dodging rabbit, many paces forward before they were able to stop short and pick up the scent once more. And the rabbit ran, oh, how he ran tumbling, darting, swirling down the hillside, terror-mad, fright-blind, on he came, the dogs on his trail once more, bounding length over length behind him. One last frantic dash, one desperate leap and the rabbit plunged into my lap. I covered the tiny trembling creature with my hands, just in time, before the great hounds sprang towards me. With great effort I kept them off and managed to conceal my captive in the large old-fashioned pocket of my wide skirt.

"'Master, disgruntled at his dogs and quite ireful—it is no little thing for a hungry man to see a tempting morsel escape him— came up to question me. "That rabbit—that rabbit—which way did it go?"

"'When I replied "Don't know," he became quite angry and beat me. Gentlemen, the scars of that long ago flogging I shall carry to my grave. Our food was nearly gone and it was I, the slave-girl, who knew the lack most sorely. But I did not give the rabbit over to my master.

"She paused a little while and in all my life I never before knew such quiet; you could actually feel the silence.

"'It is strange, strange how far reaching the consequences of an impulse may be. Howard, my master's son, witnessed everything. He had always teased me. His favorite pastime had been to annoy the slave-girl with his pranks, but he changed from that day. That day, when he saw his father beat me. And it was he, Gentlemen, who taught me to forget the scars of serfdom and taught me the joys of freedom. In all truth, Sirs, I am the widow of Colonel Howard Monroe Ritton of Westview.'

"There is no use tying to tell you about that," declared Timothy. "It's an experience as indescribable as it is unforgettable. That little old white-haired woman standing alone in the midst of all those hostile people, tearing apart with such simple words the whole fabric of her life. I think it was her loveliness that held them spell-bound; the power of her beauty, that kept them straining their ears to catch every word she said. As if suddenly awakened to her surroundings, she cleared her throat nervously, and hurriedly concluded her story.

"'The necessity of my being here, Gentlemen, is the outcome of my second impulse, an impulse, Gentlemen, nothing more. Each afternoon I sit in my west chamber beside my sunny windows, there is a whole beautiful row of them, as one can see by passing along the street. I like the sunshine which pours through them of an afternoon, and I like to knit. And I like to watch the passersby. And, I think, Gentlemen, whenever I sit there I can recall more easily the things that are passed, the old friends, the old places, the old loves and the old hurts which, somehow, have no longer the power to bring pain.

"'So I was peering—my eyes are not so good—into the street and I saw a cloud of dust, all of a sudden. I thrust my head a little ways through the window, then, I saw a man running; on looking closer, I saw that he was black.

"'Then a queer thing happened, Gentlemen; the first time in years on years, I remembered the days of my bondage. And curiously, yes, curiously I recalled. Wait. No, I did not recall it. I swear to you, Gentlemen, a picture formed before me; a hilly slope overgrown with trees of scrub oak and dwarf cedars—a golden sand-bottomed ravine and twilight falling upon miles on miles of wind-swept prairie, and peace, sweet and warm and kind; brushing my soul and turning my thoughts towards God. And I heard it, the strident yelps of three strong dogs. I saw it—a tiny furry rabbit running for its life. I tell you—it was real, Gentlemen. And while I looked, it faded—changed— glowed into another picture—the one that was being enacted out in the street. It glimmered back to fancy and flashed again to fact, so swiftly, I could not distinguish which. Then, Sirs, they merged and both were one . . . The black man who was running so wildly was only a little terror-mad rabbit. The three stout gentlemen there, (she pointed, quite like a child toward the fat policemen, while a ripple of laughter floated across the room), and the crowd which followed after, very strangely, Gentlemen, every person in it had the visage of my master. I think I cried out at that, Sirs. Yes. Certainly. I cried—at that.

"'Then the black man was in my presence, inside my sunny west-chamber, and I was forced to act—act quickly—.

"'The picture had to be finished, Gentlemen. The rabbit, no, the man—had to be protected. Thank you, Sirs. That is all.'

"Yes," said Timothy Phipps, pensively. "I was the running black gentleman in the story—" He tilted his head a bit backwards and sideways and laughed. His laughter echoing—joy—joy—joy!

El Tisico

"What is patriotism?" shouted O'Brady, the Irish engineer, as peppery as he was good-natured. He was showing signs of his rising choler faster and faster as the heated argument grew in intensity.

He argued that it was a thing men put before their wives, and Tim held that it couldn't be compared with love-making and women.

"Cut it, boys, and listen to this," broke in Sam Dicks, a grizzled old train-man, who had more yarns in his cranium, than a yellow cur has fleas on a zig-zag trail between his left ear and his hind right leg.

"Fire up," roared the crowd of us.

The debate on patriotism had started between O'Brady and Tim Brixtner in the Santa Fé restroom. It was a typical scene,—the long paper-strewn table occupying the center space, and sturdy sons of America—hard-muscled, blue chinned, steady-nerved, rail-road men—lounging around it. Over in the alcove, upon a raised platform, three colored men, who styled themselves, "The Black Trio," were resting after their creditable performance. They had given us some of the best string music from banjo, mandolin, and guitar, I have ever heard.

One of them, a big, strapping, ebony fellow, minus an arm, had a baritone voice worth a million, headed under different color. He sang "Casey Jones"—not a classic—but take it from me, a great one among our kind. He sure sang it. . . .

"El Tisico" (The Consumptive). *Crisis* Mar. 1920: 252–53.

A colored youngster, whom they carried about with them, had just finished passing the hat. It had been all both hands could do to carry it back to "The Black Trio." I, myself, had flung in five bucks, the price I'd pay, maybe, to go to a swell opera.

The guy who played the banjo was a glowing-eyed, flat-chested fellow with a cough, which he used some frequent.

I lit my pipe, and O'Brady and Brixtner and the rest lit theirs. Sam Dicks was about to begin when the "Trio" showed signs of departing. He left us with, "Wait a bit boys," and went to them. He gave the glad hand to the glowing-eyed, coughing one, with a genuine friendship grip. He came back ready for us.

"In the early nineties I was working with Billy Bartell, the greatest daredevil and the squarest that ever guided a throttle. We made our runs through that portion of the country which is sure God's handi-work, if anything is. It always strikes me as being miraculous to see the tropic weather of old Mex and the temperate weather of our U.S., trying to mix as it does along the border. It gives us a climate you can't beat—but the landscape, sun-baked sand, prairie-dog holes, and cactus with mountains dumped indiscriminately everywhere, all covered by a sky that's a dazzle of blue beauty, is what I call God's handiwork, because it can't be called anything else.

"At one of our stops in one of Mexico's little mud cities, a colored family,—father, mother, and baby—boarded the train. The woman was like one of those little, pearly-grey doves we shoot in New Mexico, from August to November—a little, fluttery thing, all heart and eyes.

"When they got on, their baby was a mere bundle, so no one noticed its illness. But it was soon all aboard that a sick kid was on. He *was* a sick kid, too: so sick that every mother's son on that train felt sorry and wanted to do something.

"The mother's eyes grew brighter and brighter, and the father kept watching his kid and pulling out his big, gold watch. The baby grew worse.

"In some way, as the intimate secrets of our heart sometimes do, it crept out that the family was trying to get over to the U.S. side before the baby died. We still had an eight hour run, and the baby was growing worse, faster than an engine eats up coal.

"The mother's eyes scanned the country for familiar signs. Every time I passed through that coach and saw her, I was minded of the way wounded birds beat their wings on the hard earth in an effort to fly. To all our attempted condolence, she replied with the same words:

"'If he lives until we get home—if he lives till we get home.'

"Billy Bartell always knew who his passengers were. He used to say he didn't believe in hauling whole lots of unknown baggage. So he knew that we carried the sick kid. We passed word to him that the kid was worse, and what his parents were aiming for.

"Well, boys, after that, our train went faster than a whirligig in a Texas cyclone. The landscape—cactus, prairie-dog holes, and mountains, rolled into something compact and smooth as a khaki-colored canvass, and flashed past us like sheets of lightning. We steamed into Nogales. The depot was on the Mexican side, but the coach with the sick kid landed fair and square upon American sod.

"The little colored woman with her baby in her arms, alighted on good old American turf. She turned in acknowledgment to the kindness she had received, to wave her hand at the engine and its engineer, at the coaches and all the passengers, at everything, because she was so glad.

"If the kid died, it would be in America—at home."

Old Dicks paused a moment before querying, "Boys, did you get it?"

"You bet," spoke up Brixtner. "That's patriotism. Now, Pat O'Brady! 'Twasn't no man and woman affair either," he cried, eager to resume their interrupted debate.

"Wait a minute, fellows," pleaded Dicks, "wait."

"I want to know, did the kid live?" somebody asked.

"That's what I want to tell," said Dicks.

"Eh, you Tim! Cut it, cut it. . . ."

"That little banjo picker was the kid whose parents did not want him to die out of sight of the Stars and Stripes."

A long-drawn "phew" fairly split the air,—we were so surprised.

"Yes," said he, "and he has never been well, always sick. He's what the Mexicans call, 'el Tisico'."

"Scat. . . . He isn't much of a prize!"

"What's he done to back up his parents' sentiments?"

"He sure can't fight." These were the words exploded from one to the other.

"Do you know what 'The Black Trio' do with their money?" asked Dicks, pride modulating his voice.

"Well—I—guess-not," drawled someone from among the bunch.

"Every red cent of it is turned in to the American Red Cross—do you get me?" And old Dicks unfolded the evening paper and began to read.

"Be Gad, that's patriotism, too," shouted O'Brady. "Can any son-of-a-gun define it?"

The Little Grey House

It was built of cement, of a lighter hue than most cement houses, so it was dubbed the little grey house.

Somehow, its builders pervaded every inch of its rough exterior with an inviting air. Even before it was finished—and we all know most incompleted houses are so mussy and dreary with daubs of paint and spattered lime and splotches of mud and shavings and blocks of wood and the workmen's tools lying all about—but this was different.

The unfinished windows suggested gauzy curtains and flowering plants. The littered interior with its yawning doorways revealing other unplastered chambers and yet more clutter, gave a cheery promise of clean-swept, cozy rooms. The little squat chimney that lifted its stubby nose into the air from the left-hand corner of its roof hinted with all its might, of the hearth-fire that would soon cast its rosy warmth over the inmates of the little grey house; while the chimney that poked its nose towards the sky at the rear of the roof, was a silent witness of many smokes it would exhale from the cooking of savory meals.

Timothy passed the little grey house every morning on his way to work and every evening on his way home—home to his untidy bachelor apartment, where he, himself, made the bed and cooked the meals and washed the dishes whenever they were washed, that was, when

Half-Century Magazine July–Aug. 1922: 4, 17, 19; Sept.–Oct. 1922: 4, 21

Timothy found his cupboard shelves were bare and his sink over-filled with plates and cups.

He was interested from the first—from the moment he saw the men laying off the site for the little grey house. Every evening he paused to take in what had been accomplished during the day. He inspected the foundation—noted the number of rooms there were to be—guessed boyishly just which would be the bed-room, living-room, and kitchen. He hoped heartily there would be an honest-to-goodness kitchen and none of your new-fangled, fool-notion kitchenettes.

"Even if they eat in the kitchen 'twill be better'n one of those fool kitchenettes," he soliloquized. "For now, what in heck is a home without a kitchen, if 'taint just like a ship without a rudder I'll be blowed." He passed on, his broad good-natured face wreathed in smiles at his own wit.

The little grey house was nearing completion when it happened the first time. At the next street crossing he met her. He remembered that she was just about to take the step up to the sidewalk.

Hillsvale was such an up and down hill little place—that each walk began or ended in a flight of steps—and he had politely stood aside to let her ascend.

She acknowledged the little courtesy with the tiniest scantiest acknowledgement that could be.

Friendly Timothy was made somewhat crest-fallen by her chilly manner, wondered if it was just her scant politeness or more of his "infernal, confounded knack at getting in bad with the ladies."

Leastways the encounter put an end to that day's pleasant musing about the little grey house. It made the boiled and steaming "hot-dogs" and the loaf of home-made bread still warm from the oven, that kind old Mrs. Bloom had given him for his supper, and the butter and the tea and the cabbage, he had prepared so painstakingly that morning, guided by a vivid memory of his mother's cold-slaw into a semblance of that dish, and the baker's blue-berry pie, which he meant to use as the climax of his evening's meal taste, as he said, "Like gol-darned saw-dust in his mouth."

"The truth is," he flayed himself further in comical petulance "you are plump put out because a cross old hen gave you the icy stare. Oh boy, she's got your goat."

He tried reading his evening's paper and found himself glaring menacingly at the front page whereon in great black type announced the sweeping victory of a political candidate, who was especially distasteful to him; he flung the paper from him disgustedly.

He tried smoking, but his cigar—one of the same brand he smoked invariably—was the rankest, vilest weed he ever put in his mouth. It was tossed vehemently into the fire.

He stood up then in the middle of his mussy kitchen and scowled at the littered supper-table and the sink full of dirty dishes, then suddenly rolled up his sleeves and gave battle to the disorder until everything shone tidy and neat. "Be blowed," he said and smiled, almost restored to his usual good nature, "if it don't look like a woman did it." But there . . . he had spoken the unlucky word . . . woman. As he uttered it, his thoughts reverted to the object of that species who was causing all the trouble.

"Who in the deuce is she anyhow?" he exclaimed wrathfully. . . . As there was no one to answer him, he presently went to bed, with a conscience as clean as any man's could be, who had lived forty years in this sin-filled world—re-enforced with a kindly good-nature, and a body keyed to the fatigue point by a full day of hard work soon brought refreshing sleep, accompanied by a dream, which he remembered vaguely, featured a plump little brown woman with a regular apple-dumpling sort of a face. For Timothy was certain that an apple-dumpling browned to a turn, and spiced and sugared to suit an epicure's appetite, was the neatest description for the little woman's soft full cheeks and rounded chin.

Altogether he was pleased with that face; until he remembered the eyes. "My stars," he would say, "some ice! Oh boy!" Only, he recalled through the indistinctness of his dream, those eyes had been soft and tender and he declared wonderingly, as he kicked off the covers and rolled out of bed next morning, "They got his goat."

With another day's work "neatly put over" and the makings of a nifty meal—a juicy steak, a package of potato-chips, a dozen freshly baked rolls all tucked into the curve of his arm; with nothing in the world to worry about; the incident of the evening before almost swept from his mind—Timothy paused almost from habit before the little grey house.

"I'll be blowed, if you ain't the prettiest little box of a house I've seen yet!"

Then beset with the thoughts of his yet-to-be-cooked steak, he hurried on—and there—almost in the same spot approached the woman. Timothy grinned broadly over the coincidence and just as he had done the previous evening stood aside politely as she ascended. And again just to a T she acknowledged the little courtesy with the tiniest, scantiest acknowledgment, so scant, that only an intent—a very intent observer could have discerned it at all.

"Well, one thing's certain, old girl," thought Timothy, "you're sure no killer for looks. I reckon it's the old girl's way of pulling off the high and mighty that's got my goat. Anyhow," he announced quite spiritedly to himself, "I'll be blowed if I don't fry this steak and eat every scrap of it—old haughty one, you're not going to spoil my eats every single night, not on your life."

"I wonder," mused Opal Kent half angrily, who all unknowingly lived in Timothy's mind as the plump little lady with the apple-dumpling face, "who on earth that grinning Jacob of a man can be?"

Opal Kent had never received any marked attention from men, so Timothy's eager politeness was bewildering to her simple soul; and his broad smile, which she so contemptuously termed a grin, exasperated her to the limit and what made it worse, she could not reason why— and his intent scrutiny of her as she passed—it was maddening.

"The horrid, horrid thing!" she exclaimed aloud, then in an undertone which sounded cooingly soft as it wafted away on the breeze:

"But he isn't bad-looking a bit, not a bit."

Opal Kent was one of the jolliest, dearest little women in the world, good-hearted to a fault and responsive as a kitten to kindness and gentle treatment; but at present, she was all out of sorts. She was lonely and homesick—homesick as only a homeless woman can be and she was disheartened. Here she was already past the thirty mile sign in years, and as Timothy himself had concluded, "In no way a killer for looks." All in the world she could do was cook and keep house. Of course, there was her crocheting and tatting and knitting, but no valuation could be put upon that, thought Opal for where in the world could you find a homely old spinster fond of her hearth-fire who couldn't?

Poor lonely Opal; like all disheartened people she belittled her attainments, for her cooking was sheerest witchery and she belonged to those rare women who could, given the stimulation of having near her, those she loved, could convert a bare spot in a desert into a home.

To be sure, of this last attribute, none save old Joseph Kent could testify and since he had died a year ago, his testimony was hopelessly out of the question.

Opal had always kept house for her father. As far back as she could remember she had been the little woman of his household. A distant relative had helped old Joseph raise her to an early age of independence and since then, she had been the little mistress of their home.

"Old Joe Kent" had been a grim, forbidding old man, who repulsed rather than encouraged any friendships for himself and daughter. They had lived a bleak and lonely life, relieved, only by the love they bore each other. Old Kent had uncanny success with his pigs and chickens and by supplying his neighbors' tables with these commodities, earned a livelihood. He looked forward a bit for Opal's sake and insured himself quite heavily and the payment of those premiums had eaten the heart out of his meagre income.

Opal had stinted and economized for every dress and every hat or ribbon she had ever possessed. So plus her cooking and house-keeping was an almost instinctive frugality that saved seemingly valueless things and cunningly contrived them into articles of value. She made cunning baby shoes from a man's old, cast-off hat. She saved the vinegar off the pickles to mix her salad dressings, saved turkey feathers and made her own feather dusters, could take a neatly clean carcass, a grain or two of rice, a cabbage leaf, a celery stalk and turn a savory odor that lingered in your nostrils for a fortnight and a pleasing taste that tickled your palate whenever you recalled it.

Almost simultaneously, with the sad occurrence of her father's death and the coming of the insurance money, old Judge Crowley prepared to move west for his wife's health. And Opal was prevailed upon to accompany them as cook.

"Why not?" reasoned Opal, for who in her little home town cared if she went or remained? It was enough to make one sour to think about it, for no one ever suspected how much Opal Kent longed for friendship and there was none among all her life-long acquaintances who could be called friend.

If someone had suggested to Opal that it was her father's fault, she would have been appalled. She would have repudiated it with every ounce of strength of her being. Her father, her dear, old, kind, indulgent dad! How she missed him! She could see him just as he used to be and it was sweet to remember how the lines of care faded from his face as he sat and watched her bustle about preparing the supper. His favorite place was beside the kitchen door, which faced westward. He always sat full in the golden shaft of sunlight. "It warms like nothing else on earth," had been his phrase. And Opal had come to time the evening meal with the fading of the sunlight from the door. Such had been their life together, replete with the nameless love tokens each had performed for the other, with no word of explanation to add to or distract from their pleasure. "You are like your Ma, girl," had been his one form of endearment, and she perceived that those six words summed up the strength of a love that had lasted unto death and beyond the grave and lived again in all of its wondrous beauty for herself.

The Crowleys had settled in Hillsvale six months ago and Opal Kent suddenly decided to invest her insurance money in a home. Hillsvale would be as good a place as any in which to spend her life, since she had no friends or any tie to bind her elsewhere. And forthwith, she had bought the lots and had the little grey house built.

She would rent it at first, of course, and work on, saving every cent of her money until she had enough to allow her to become mistress of the little grey house in earnest.

Then she would raise chickens. Just supposing, if she had fifty hens and got fifty eggs a day, as the ads in the farm papers guaranteed was the simplest thing to do . . . and she would keep bees, the Government bulletins extolled their virtue to the highest . . . a pleasant and profitable industry . . . and she would have a few bunnies, another profitable and little known money-maker, she wouldn't go into that so deeply, but a few would add variety to her meat supply, providing she could kill and eat them after fondling them, as she knew she would do. They were such cunning creatures with their pink noses forever wiggling and their bright eyes constantly watchful. She would have a nice old tabby cat and a collie pup and maybe after she was known in Hillsvale, little children would come to see her and her pets. She would keep a well-filled cookie jar, and of course there would be honey, and perhaps, oh perhaps, she would be ever and ever so happy as mistress of the little grey house, even though she was alone and friendless and had nothing, nothing with which to challenge the coming lonely years. She was unable to suppress the shudder which came when she thought of that.

Taken from all angles, it is quite true that folks are the masters of their own destiny: only one must admit that catching hold of your own particular bit of destiny is nearly as futile a performance as a kitten swirling around trying to catch his tail. At least it appeared so to Opal all bolstered up with expectations over the little grey house.

The big "FOR RENT" sign which was tacked upon the little grey house as soon as it was finished failed to attract any notice whatever. It seemed that all the house hunters and all the disgruntled renters for once in their lives were happily settled and satisfied. Nobody rented Opal Kent's little place, by no means as soon as she expected and certainly not as soon as she had need for it to be.

The Crowleys, without any hint of their intentions, decided to move elsewhere. Opal, finding herself indefinitely linked to Hillsvale because of the little grey house, could not be induced to move with them.

Opal found another place and though it saved her from becoming stranded in a strange town, she did not like it. Not having learned how, she did not make friends readily and her work was confining, so she became acquainted with no one.

She was timid and self-conscious and oppressed by an overgrowing dread of loneliness, and like most homeless women, she was afraid, just afraid of everything.

"Suppose," ran her thoughts, "I should lose my health, what then? Suppose I do not save enough before I am old. . . ."

She grew more and more reticent and her plump, round face grew overcast with dread and her eyes grew sharp. She watched people, watched the expression of their faces and construed them to portend queer things concerning herself, when for the most part her dumpty little figure passed among the crowds unnoticed. She wondered over Timothy's good-natured smile. "Why does he laugh at me so? Oh, dear, I must be funny, and, oh . . . oh, queer."

The first time Timothy saw the "FOR RENT" sign he stopped and gazed at it incredulously. "Well now," he said, "what nut built a house like that to rent? I was as sure as pop that it was going to be some-body's home—somebody who'd love every inch of it and take care of it and plant flowers around it, and all such as that. Now look at that there sign, 'FOR RENT'; just spoils the whole thing, be blowed if it don't."

He continued to meet Opal. In fact, his interest was divided between the little grey house and these meetings with the plump little woman. Taken together, they afforded Timothy something pleasant with which to wind up his lonely evenings. He would think of the little grey house and wonder who'd rent it, and he would think about the little woman, wondering who she was. No one he questioned seemed to know. At bed time he would turn in and maybe dream that he was Lord and Master of both the little woman and the little grey house.

Then as unexpected as the "FOR RENT" sign had been was the "FOR SALE" sign which Timothy glanced up to see one evening as he passed. In smaller lettering the placard stated, further information secured from PITMAN'S REALTY COMPANY.

It set Timothy to thinking. He was preoccupied when he passed the little dumpty woman.

So for once Opal failed to see him grinning, but with a woman's inconsistence, she found herself wondering what in the world had happened to chase his smiles away.

And if Timothy had not been so absorbed he would have been sure to notice the traces of tears which lingered in the little woman's eyes.

Opal was on her way to the little grey house. She had enjoyed so much to go there when her hopes were high. She had found grim satisfaction in seeing it after she knew that as a business venture it was a hopeless failure. And now, that she had decided to sell it, from necessity, she found a torturing delight in looking upon it.

Yes, the place she had was unendurable. She couldn't stand the contempt and the rude treatment, the family for whom she now worked, seemed to think she was a cook's portion. She would sell the little place and get out of it whatever she could and write the Crowleys that she would join them.

That night, Timothy made up his mind. "Be blowed, if I won't buy it myself. . . ." 'Twas a shame for a house like that go to waste! "Who knows?" he questioned, "I might find me a wife, and even if I don't, 'cause a man's single is no sign he has to live like a pig. Gosh no! I'll set out a lilac bush and some flowers and plant some trees. Anyhow, I'll buy the dinged little place and get it off my mind."

Two days later, Opal Kent went to the realty office and transacted her portion of the business pertaining to the sale of the little grey house. She received her money—nearly as much as the little grey house had cost—minus the commission.

With the money in her possession, her plans changed again. She would stay in Hillsvale and see who had purchased the little grey house.

Timothy Martin stopped that evening to inspect his property thoroughly. He went from room to room, there were five, a nice spacious kitchen with built-in cupboards and cabinets, and one end which made an alcove built almost entirely of glass, a stationary table and chairs stood resplendent, invitingly coaxing one to eat. "Holy Pete!" ejaculated Timothy, "I'll plant honeysuckle to climb all over that there glass . . . and won't it be pretty?" In the other rooms, he found window seats with hinged covers and more built-in cabinets and book cases. "Gosh," he exclaimed, "mighty pretty, but it's just been built for a woman. A woman's the only creature on earth that can care for this sort of trick."

He was nearly through with his round of inspection, when he stopped short, startled by a sound. "Gee," he muttered and listened. Again the sound came. "Be blowed, it sounds like someone crying." Timothy quietly retraced his steps, finding nothing until he entered the kitchen.

And there, in the waning sunlight which poured into the glass-walled alcove beside the table, with her head bowed on her arms, sat the little woman, his plump little apple-dumpling woman, "crying, just crying," thought Timothy, "like a great big baby."

Timothy stood stock still and watched her, watched her with a mingled delight and dismay and consternation; delight to find her there, dismay that she was crying and at the very end of his wits for fear his presence would frighten her away.

What should he do? Then a quivering little voice restored him to senses.

"Oh, it's you—it's you! Did you buy it?"

Timothy sensed that she was speaking of the little grey house, and nodded his head in assent. Then in an eager desire to cheer her up, he began to talk in his cheery booming voice.

"Though, I'll be blowed, Miss, the blame little box was intended for a woman and not for the likes of me. All these here fixings tells you that. Now if I had a wife . . . Say, now, you mustn't cry any more. Just you listen to me. I was saying that if I had a wife to putter around and fix this here trinket of a house like it ought to be fixed . . . I'd be the happiest man alive. Gee, Miss, I'm a demon when it comes to setting out vines and flowers and I'd have the yard out front looking like a bit of fairy land and we'd have chickens in the back and maybe a wee turnip patch."

"And," put in Opal, wholly unaware of the strangeness of it all, "I'd planned to have some bees too and just a handful of bunnies. Oh, don't you like to watch 'em wiggle their noses? . . . and I'd meant to have flowers too, holly-hocks and roses and lark-spurs growing everywhere, and a lilac bush under the bedroom window and honey-suckle and climbing roses over the ones in the dining room and I hadn't quite decided what I'd have over the windows in the living room, perhaps I'd have left 'em bare so's to look out and see folks passing . . ."

"Say you," burst in Timothy excitedly, "did you have this house built?" Thrust back into reality by his question, Opal could not speak, for tears choked back her words and her plump little shoulders heaved piteously.

In the wee interval in which he watched her second outburst, goodhearted, good-natured, forty-year-old bachelor, Timothy made a few swift calculations concerning his weeping companion. That in the main they were correct was not surprising for Timothy earned his livelihood by an ability to size up people. His heart jumped exultingly as he concluded she was not married and never had been. It clutched in pity, as he decided she wept thus because she was lonely and friendless and homeless, for he discerned from her tears that the little box of a house had been built to be her home. It took but a minute for his quick mind to ferret out this . . . then the blunt fashion that had ever been his custom that was the main spring of his "infernal, confounded knack of getting in bad with the ladies," expressed itself blurtingly . . .

"There . . . there . . . there," he punctuated each word with a bearish pat on Opal's heaving shoulder. "What in all heck, you crying about now; didn't I say I wanted a wife . . . ?"

And say what you will, the real mating among humans is like the birds, instinctive and unerring, for presently Opal's plumply rounded face was lifted to receive Timothy's smacking kiss; while the kindly sun, blinking his red-gold eye, like a jocose inebriate, slipped quietly away, out of the glass covered alcove, leaving them, master and mistress, in full possession of the little grey house.

Cross Crossings Cautiously

Sam Timons rarely thought in the abstract. His thoughts as were his affections were marshaled concretely. His affections were rolled into a compact and unbreakable ball which encircled his wife Lettie and his young son Sammy. His thoughts—he did not think much—but such as his thoughts were, they involved this, if he did a good turn for somebody, somebody else would quite naturally do him or his a good turn also.

Usually Sam was a cheerful creature. Work and love; love and work, that, boiled down to brass tacks, is the gist of all life, and Sam possessed both. Even though, at present, he was out of a job.

He walked along the sandy road stirring up miniature dust clouds with every step for his heavy feet shuffled wearily with the burden of his dejected body.

He felt down and out. He was at the end of his rope. One dollar in his pocket. He gripped it in his fingers. All he had. But he could not give up. The ball of his affection, as it were, trundled along before him luring him on. He was "hoofing it" to another town to try again.

"Saw wood . . . clean house, paint barns, chop weeds . . . plow, anything, suh. . . . Just so it's work so's I can earn somethin'. I'm a welder by trade, but they don't hire cullud."

Opportunity June 1920: 177, 189.

Behind him stretched the long, dusty way he had come. Before him a railroad zigzagged his path. As his feet lifted to the incline, he raised his eyes, and met advice from a railroad crossing sign:

CROSS CROSSINGS CAUTIOUSLY

He paused to spell out the words, repeating them painstakingly. Then he went on. A little beyond and across the tracks another huge sign caught his attention.

Soon, he had halted beside this one, letting his eyes sidle up and down and over the gaily painted board. Now he was staring open-mouthed at the glaring yellow lion who crouched to spring, now, at the flashy blond lady pirouetting on a snow white mount. He stood quite still thinking. Wouldn't Lettie and little Sam be wild to see such a show.

"'Lo Mister."
Sam swung around like a heavy plummet loosed from its mooring.
"Gee . . . Mister, you 'fraid of me?"
A little girl hardly more than a baby addressed him. She was regarding him with the straight unabashed gaze of the very innocent and of the very wise.

"I want you to carry me to the circus," she announced, when their mutual survey of one another seemed to her enough.

Sam's eyes were fixed on the web-fine, golden hair escaping from two torn places in the child's hat. Already he had seen that the eyes searching his were blue. . . . He fidgeted. He made a move to go.

"Oh, don't, don't go," beseeched the child. "Mother has to 'tend to a meeting, and father is always busy. There is no one else. Mother said I might if only somebody'd take me. See." She thrust out a little smudgy fist—and opening it, revealed a shiny new fifty-cent piece. "This is mine," she said plaintively. "Can't we go?"

Mrs. Maximus McMarr was a busy woman. She managed to attend fourteen clubs each week, but that excluded any time to manage Claudia, her five-year-old daughter. Claudia's father considered children woman's responsibility. One advantage or disadvantage this sort of bringing up gave Claudia, she always got what she wanted.

Something about her made Sam do her bidding now.

They were half way between the McMarr place and the circus grounds before he thought about what he was doing. He clutched at the dollar in his pocket. He wanted to laugh, guessed he was nervous. Suddenly, he stopped abruptly—there was another dusty country road.

CROSS CROSSINGS CAUTIOUSLY

"Oh do come on," urged the child jerking his hand in an ecstasy of delight and impatience.

Further on a half-grown lad passed them, but stopped and turned to watch them down the road. As the man and the little girl drew out of sight, he faced about and pelted up the road.

The noise of the circus leapt up to meet and welcome Sam and Claudia. The music of the band was sweet to their ears. Sam reveled in it and Claudia's little feet danced over the road. Even the bellowing and roars of the wild animals left them undismayed. It was circus day.

Mrs. McMarr had alighted from a friend's car and remained standing beside it, to talk. Both women observed the runner at the same time. Mrs. McMarr felt her heart skid upward into her throat. Claudia had not appeared. She divined that the messenger tended evil for no other than her precious baby. She made up her mind to swoon even before she received the tidings.

The friend went in search of McMarr who for once allowed himself an interruption. Close-lipped, he tumbled off his harvester and rushed pell-mell across his field.

All afternoon, Claudia had been surfeited with care. One after another had tendered and petted and caressed her. Even her father had been solicitous. She curled up, drowsy and very tired, in the big arm chair.

The rain that had threatened to fall all day suddenly commenced like the tat-a-rat-tat of far-off drums. Claudia was wide awake. She sat up. Remembering. The circus band! The monkeys in their little red coats! Her circus man! Something had happened. What?

The impulse to know surmounted the fear she harbored of her father. She slipped over to his chair. He had been very kind today. Perhaps . . . he wouldn't mind telling her . . . Where her circus man was?

Jack Arrives

Jack Derby was a likeable sort, a good mixer, a dandy talker, and a splendid worker. When he married Clarice Winston every one of his friends declared he was bound to be successful, for who with his trade, his disposition and a pretty little wife could not succeed, was an unanswerable question.

Jack married shortly after finishing his course at the Maxwell Mechanical Arts School. In fact as soon as he finished he secured a position with the firm of Sears, Contractors and Builders. It was a fair position for the head of a newly made family of two; but it would not pay if the family increased, and it would go but a short way towards showing off a successful man. But of course, Jack did not intend to be a stationary piece of furniture in his employer's office. His well wishers kept on saying complimentary things about him while they watched and waited for him to "show 'em."

One, two, three, four years passed over Jack's head as slick as a cowboy's toss of a lasso, and he still drew the same pay check, also to the casual observer, there was no discernible change in his pleasing demeanor. Though of course, everyone knew that now, when he went home at night, a small, pert chap, a saucy miniature of himself, climbed onto his knee and called him Daddy. And a close observer could see that a great deal of his sang froid had disappeared and a

Half-Century Magazine Feb. 1920: 5, 14.

steady gleam pierced the friendly light in his eyes, which plainly showed how continuously he pondered the problem of living.

In fact, his problems were becoming quite unsolvable with the afore-mentioned check. The way Junior paddled out his little boots, the manner in which his knee protruded through divers stockings and ye gods! the way he burst out of his little blue jeans, was certainly one vast problem.

Worrying over problems is a joke at all times, and pondering them is debatable, since nothing on earth ponders more on the job than an ass, so when all is said and done, a fellow must get out and hustle if he really wishes to hear success buzz in his ear. Yet it is funny how the really little things, more or less, throw the die in a man's destiny. In Jack's case it was the sugar bowl.

Clarice, Jack's wife, was a sweet little thing, clever as could be, and as cheery as a sunbeam, but she was forgetful. She had a sort of comical forgetfulness too, for instance, she never forgot Jack's favorite dishes but sometimes she would forget to put the salt into one or the sage in another. And this particular morning her forgetfulness had to do with the sugar bowl.

When Jack and Clarice and Junior sat down to breakfast, Jack reached for the sugar but found the bowl empty. Clarice had forgotten to fill it. Seeing this, she sprang up and darted into the kitchen headed for the sugar can on its shelf. She took it down, but alas, it, also, was empty. She had forgotten to order sugar.

Clarice was a winsome little body and never had she appeared more so than now when she skipped back into the dining room, with the empty sugar bowl in her hand. But for once in his life, Jack overlooked her winsomeness as he spied the still empty receptacle for sugar . . . then the storm broke.

Jack wasn't wholly to blame since his nerves were already strained to the breaking point due to the many sugar restrictions he had undergone in recent years. Yet there was no necessity for his raving throughout the meal because he had no sugar. He declared he was growing poorer every day, couldn't afford an ounce or two of sugar,—the idea—he would quit his job, leave the town, go elsewhere and find decent employment that would afford him a living wage. Now the more he raved and ramped, the more imbued he became with these propositions which sprang as it were from an empty sugar bowl.

Finally the clock struck the hour for him to go. Then as he hurriedly
stooped to kiss Clarice good-bye, the tear drop which trickled along
side her nose fell upon his face and he found that she was crying.
And to be sure, woman-like as soon as Clarice knew that he had
observed it, her tears started afresh. And Jack could not for worlds,
leave his own dear little wifey in tears. Then besides there was Junior,
who had hopped down from his place, climbed into his mother's lap
and poked his head up, just far enough to become entangled in the
embrace Jack was giving Clarice, so there it was, a regular family mixup.

By the time Jack was free to go, the car he should have taken was
gone, no jitney in sight, no time could be lost, and the only thing for
him to do was to foot it. In short, Jack reached the office a full hour
late. Mr. Lashney, the manager, with severity due mostly to surprise,
reprimanded Jack sharply, which Jack resented with an equal sharp-
ness. As you probably know the sequence of such things is either
retreat or fire. And Jack skillfully maneuvered the former.

He rushed home with an air of bravado which he certainly did not
feel. Then little Clarice assumed that pure, unalloyed bravery that all
good women display when their men folk are in need. And together
they reconnoitered their field of attainment, and the inventory of
their resources revealed a paltry bank account, a capital stock of
good health and a reserve fund of good spirits—nothing more.

After this a week was spent in seeing Clarice and Junior comfortably situated and their household goods in storage, and Jack set off
in quest of fortune, success, or if you like—simply a job.

The weeks flew into months and the months spun into a year,
swiftly as a boy's top spinning upon its peg, yet Jack had not found
the position which would put him on his feet. Instead, he found that
his nut-brown face, his black friendly eyes and his big smiling mouth
were more potent than leprosy, in chasing away the jobs which might
have been his.

Every ounce of his old time cheeriness vanished as time after time
the work for which he was fitted was denied him. Finally, he worked
at any and all sorts of odd jobs in one town after another, to get
together the monthly allowance to send to Clarice and Junior.

It was a rainy afternoon, Jack had walked all over the town of
Ferndale looking for work. Even his reserve fund of good spirits had
sprung a leak and began to dribble away, when on passing a news-

stand he spied his favorite trades magazine and stopped to purchase a copy of it. He went back to his dingy little room to pore over the periodical and in so doing, forget the many disappointments the year had held for him.

Jack loved his work next best to his wife and baby. Back of the friendly laughter in his eyes slumbered visions of beautiful creations in wood and stone. His strong long fingers never tired of making sketches of his dreams on paper, and his brain worked indefatigably on foundations and wainscots and windows; "a born architect," was the verdict passed upon him by his old associates in the firm of Sears, Contractors and Builders.

Now his fingers turned the leaves almost caressingly as he read them one after another. Then, what? . . . a whole page devoted to an advertisement of a contest. His perfunctory glancing changed as he read in keen interest and when he had finished, he closed the book and looked out from his window over the house-tops off into space where smoky rain-clouds huddled against the sky like downy chicks and the glow of a dream darkened his eyes.

Jack's ambition led to a far off pinnacle where-on he would be able to establish himself as an architect—when people would come from far and near to have him plan their homes and cities would bid him come to plan their public buildings—then, ah then, his bread and butter secure, he would build as he chose and in long years to come, others would look upon his work and see not mere bricks and stones, but the beautiful soul of an artist, for in all of his work he would weave one of his lovely dreams. And that which he had read caused his ambition to right-about face and marshal his dreams together. Again he scanned the page:

$10,000.00
TO BE GIVEN FOR SOMETHING DIFFERENT
$10,000.00
—

To Any One
SUBMITTING PLANS FOR A BUNGALOW
which meets the approval of
MRS. WAGNER ANHAUSER
—

CONTEST OPEN TO ALL

—

Send Sketch and Plans for Bungalow to
HALLOWELL & HALLOWELL

—

Contest Closes January 1st, 1920

Jack held his breath. Could he dare to hope and even then Hope's dancing fires were in his eyes.

In a further perusal of the magazine, Jack saw a brief write-up of Mrs. Wagner Anhauser, a lady of vast wealth, a direct descendent of the famous composer and the equally famous brewer, and Jack smiled as he whimsically thought how the artistic and commercial nature of Mrs. Wagner Anhauser was revealing itself in this blatant method of securing a home. Nevertheless if he could only pluck the substantial, tempting morsel she was holding out—ah if—and again Jack held his breath.

The afternoon drizzle had changed into snow and the ground was covered with a thick slush when Jack set out again. He went to a telegraph office and sent a message:

"Clarice, dear, send blue-print of dream house at once.

JACK."

Even before Jack and Clarice married they had amused themselves planning the kind of bungalow they would build when "dreams came true." After they were married and had found out numerous little kinks in housekeeping, Jack had playfully added corners and cupboards and cabinets and rooms and always with his instinct for beauty uppermost, until now their "dream house," as they called, was a little marvel of beauty and convenience. And this, Jack decided to send to Hallowell & Hallowell.

He had only a short time to wait for the outcome of the contest and while he waited he remained in his little dingy room and to make ends meet he went to work with a bullying contractor, the clod hopper kind, who contracts to erect a building and afterwards portions the work out to any and as many jack-legged carpenters and bricklayers as he can obtain cheaply. To be sure, an ordeal for Jack, but most of his work was in the open. It was in that delightful season of the year when a golden haze suspends itself like a veil from earth to sky; when the evening's layer of snow or the night's hoar frost is vanished by a warm noon-day sun. A time to dream and hope.

It was the end of a dreamy day in March and Jack was somewhat uneasy about Clarice and Junior. When he received his last letter from them, Junior was ill and several days had passed without any other further word. He was horribly tired. The workmen had loitered more than usual and their boss had given full vent to his angry bellowing. He entered his little room wearily and switched on a light. Then his eyes fell upon two letters lying together on a table. His kind-hearted landlady had placed them there. One was from Clarice and the other bore the firm address of Hallowell and Hallowell in the upper right hand corner. This he tore open with feverish haste and read the words which leapt and danced as the paper trembled in his nervous hands. The air in the dingy little room seemed to throb as his intense emotion vibrated through it.

He stood there silent, staring. Then he spoke aloud, "At last, at last!" With that he shook himself and straightened. Then he wheeled about the room in an ecstasy of happiness. Finally, he stopped before his little sheet iron heater which was quite cheerily aglow and spoke.

"Well, well, old boy, this is one on 'em. Why you old black cuss, you've put one over fair and square. Yes siree, and I'll be darned, just the same as if your dad burned hide was white." Then in comical surprise at his own stupidity his voice changed to say, "Drat it, you simp, why don't you get ready for home?" With these words he began to toss his things together preparing for that event. As he worked his mind sang busily with plans for the future and strangely too, not a single plan had to do with wonderful architectural feats, not one, but all were of a trusting, winsome woman and a bonny little boy and a cheery fire on a cozy hearth.

Now and then he laughed—not the hearty, exultant laughter of him who wins, but the softened throaty laugh of one who loves and yearns, for memories both sweet and fragrant surged through him as his thoughts flashed back and away to where Clarice and Junior beckoned and called him.

Bambino Grimke

The logical way to become acquainted with Bambino Grimke is to be introduced. So . . . My dear Reader, be pleased to meet Mr. B. Grimke, manager and guiding spirit of the Ginger Blues Band.

And . . . if while his face is turned from us, you will read discreetly on for a paragraph or two, you will learn more about the gentleman and be prepared to begin his story.

Bambino is one of those musical mechanisms that are responsible for the controversies among learned white folks about . . . "Who created jazz?" Upon listening to the way one of Bambino's ilk plays it, they are nearly convinced that the little black boys bred, birthed, and reared jazz from the cradle up, but upon thinking it over at leisure, and recalling unwillingly the tantalizing emotions that this sort of music calls forth, they immediately badger themselves into believing that jazz is too much of a coup to concede their dark brethren.

Hence . . . the premise . . . that such exponents of the art as Bambino, have caught the knack of jazzing things up a bit through downright ape-ishness, or when better disposed . . . "An aptness at mimicry."

Beyond a doubt, Bambino himself builds up the argument in so far as it applies to himself. He is somewhat monkey-fied in appearance; not that he isn't good enough looking. . . . Here wait! Take a look for yourself. . . .

Bronzeman Feb. 1931: 18–20, 31–33.

Not a feature askew. His skin smooth as satin, cream-colored, and glistening with health and tonsorial perfection. His hair . . . if ever 'twas kinky, the hair-dresser's magic has stolen the kink. His eyes . . . make the flapper-ish exaggeration: "Simply dazzling orbs!" a mere trite statement of fact that falls short of ample description. His dress . . . is such as best becomes that recently discovered biped . . . the American sheik.

Wait! Move on cautiously, first . . . absorb the picture.

But once let Bambo set himself before the ivories and forthwith he reverts to a Darwinian theory. He twists and squirms and writhes himself into impossible contortions, and plays.

"Yes indeed," as he himself would remark, "Ah plays." He knows music from the bottom to the top, and he makes his knowing music pay. He is very much traveled. The Ginger Blues, the body whose head he is, have skirted every large town in the country.

Bambino holds that your large cities are the money-squeezers. "You can't make them pal." But listen . . . take an outfit like his into your one horse towns and he wagers that inside a week, he can say: "Giddap!" to the town's one horse, if he chose to, and ride out of the town in grand state.

Be that as it may, Bambino's creed is to get money. Another one of his maxims, self-thought, is, Man makes money, solely for the purpose of giving it to a woman. It follows then, for such as he to get money, quickly and unfailingly . . . get the ladies. And in very truth, Bambino is an A-1 ladies man.

Now, Let's on with the story. . . .

It was an exceedingly pleasant morning with a bright sun striving mightily to shine in every nook and corner of the dining room of the Wage Earner's Hotel. It shone full upon a white draped table at which sat the widow Bently and Bambino Grimke. The usually busy widow allowed herself this luxury of loitering here at this unseemly hour of the morning, because she had recently discovered that: "A man does hate to eat alone," consequently, she was taking a bite or two to be sociable. Bambino was there for a consuming purpose, already he had consumed quantities and was steadily at it.

"It's this-a way," he quoted while slowly chewing, as he held aloft upon his fork the securely pinioned half of a still steaming fluffy biscuit.

Widow Bently leaned nearer, waiting upon his words.

"Girls her own age don't know their minds. They're not supposed to." He ended knowingly but generously, as he plopped the waiting tidbit into his mouth.

He chewed ruminantly as might a cow for several minutes, with his dazzling orbs fixed upon the widow, and his mind working neatly and destructively—that is as far as the widow was concerned—as an automatic in the hands of a crack-shooter.

Gentleman bounder of the whole wide world, that he was, he had fallen in love, unthinkable—certainly, foolhardy—surely, but true. What is more to the point, Bambino was convinced that his cause was lost. For to him, falling in love had meant literally not figuratively, to fall; since his adored one rebuffed his advances, and returned his regard with scorn. But he had seen Carmalita, and to see her meant—

It meant moonlight sonatas and roses in bloom, and fireflies flitting along paths of mignonette to pilot one to love—and Carmalita.

Bambino hastily gulped a draught of too-hot coffee, since his cause was lost—well—Here was Carmalita's mother. If his guess was right, the old girl could be made to shove out a dollar or so, and thereby prove herself useful as well as ornamental.

Carmalita's mother was a woman of parts. It was enough, had she been nothing more than the owner of the Wage Earner's Hotel, but no—she was a great deal more than that. She was extremely good looking, she had a mind of her own, and she was the possessor of a most desirable daughter.

This daughter in some respects was to her mother, "a joy forever," as things of beauty should be, but in others, she was bane to the widow's life. It had long been the latter's one intent and purpose that her daughter make a good match. No ordinary, plebeian, burnt-coffee-hued swain would do. None but an artist inside and out—artist of what—that did not matter . . . one of the first water, one with a fat purse. Think then, of what her chagrin had been to learn by chance that Carmalita was madly and staunchly in love with a nobody. To the widow's mind, the very staunchness of her daughter's love revealed how mad the poor dear girl was.

A nobody . . . needless, even to name him at this point, in this short chronicle of Bambino Grimke.

With the faith of desperation, as it were, widow Bently had stretched forth her hand in search of the proverbial straw and had clasped

Bambino Grimke's manicured fingers. In him, she fancied, she had found salvation, and in a spurt of joy reborn, she ordered the "Nobody" from her door and laid down her stern law to her daughter.

It was now, the morning following that last rash act, and she was hopefully listening to the consoling Bambino.

"You have thought, of school, college—a year or two away from home in other surroundings . . ." Ventured he.

The widow sighed gustily. Not for the world would she confess it, but she was one who felt a natural shrinking from expense. Eyeing an empty platter directly in front of Bambino, and hiding her tight-fisted reflections under an apron of solicitude, she inquired sweetly: "Won't you have more cakes?"

Tapping a small bell beside her, she curtailed Bambino's sputter about "Guessing he'd take another," for a lovely head poked through a stingily opened door behind him, and quickly answered the summons.

"Yes Mamma?" queried a girlish voice.

"More cakes, dear, for Mr. Gr . . . . " The lovely head vanished; the door banged shut. Bambino sighed.

The owner of the lovely head, none other than Carmalita, returned quickly, bearing a golden stack of steaming hot-cakes. The widow looked at her daughter in a sprightly fashion, and patted the slender wrist nearest to her, while mentioning in a low dulcet tone . . . "mumsey's got something nice to tell you!" She managed to convey to her daughter that no one but the irresistible Bambino should be thanked for the "something nice."

The young lady responded ungraciously to the inference, by giving an audible sniff and not deigning to look Bambino's way at all.

Hastening back into the kitchen, Carmalita gave a quick glance at the clock, then dashed on into a room beyond to reappear within a second with her apron off and a hat on and a powder-puff plopped to her nose. She traversed the kitchen noiselessly, slipped through the outer door, ran out the back gate, and around the corner where presently she was met by someone, who by the light in her eye and the smile on her lip and the spring in her step, must have been the "Nobody."

A "Nobody" who was exquisitely togged, who was lean and lithe with a thin face . . . but thin, by no means from a lean diet, but from being finely chiseled, and it was lit by a pair of as honest eyes as ever bespoke love to a woman. Now, they were fairly sparkling at the sight of Carmalita tripping towards him. Without a word being said he drew her hand through his arm, when she reached him, and together they sped up the street.

A great yellow butterfly sailed over their heads, and an unseen bird sang them a song, while plainly to their united eyesight, Old King Sol screwed on another jet of light which added a million-trillion beams to his customary shine. And thus we will leave them to turn back to Bambino who has had time to dispose of his third stack of golden-brown hot-cakes.

★ ★ ★

"You know," said he lolling back in his chair, a bit uncomfortably from being overfull. "I have a scheme on foot."

"Oh-oo-oo," cooed the widow, who had not been listening. She had been thinking, how foolish youth is. . . . Her thoughts had been with her daughter whom she supposed was in the kitchen. . . . What a figure the silly chit might cut as Mrs. . . . think of it! Mrs. Grimke.

She was falling back into her reverie when Bambino's voice once again, dripped soothingly into her consciousness.

"You 'bout the one woman who can make my little scheme step out."

He paused here for the purpose of whetting the widow's curiosity, a successful move.

"A baby can stand on his feet," he resumed, "'fore he can do any stepping. That's how my little scheme is, Mrs. Bently, it's on its feet but it ain't stepping."

"Yes . . . but . . . " Giggled the widow delightfully, "I'm done teaching. My baby knows how to step. My baby Carmalita," she giggled teasingly, "Can step most proper. She sure can. . . ." She flung in with a determination to project Carmalita before Bambino.

"Bah!" Exploded Bambino, "Girls . . . your girl, none of 'em can really stand alone. They can't be depended 'pon in a real issue. This here scheme of mine, Mrs. Bently, as I've already said, is on foot, and all it needs now is some mature woman's wit and acumen behind it . . . Ahem." Bambino glared truculently into the widow's eyes, "As for me, Mrs. Bently," he said, coolly polite, I can take my pick of any number of ladies. Ladies with keen insight, keen a-a. . . ." Lost for the right word, at that moment, Bambino again resorted to his meaningful orbs. He allowed them to play carelessly upon her.

"Oh-oo-" breathed the widow strangely thrilled beneath the dazzle of his gaze.

Being for the most part an adroit creature, she closed the embarrassing moment by pouring Bambino another cup of coffee.

"I believe you are beginning to understand me," intoned the wily Mr. Grimke.

"Oh, do go on," beseeched the widow.

"Let's not talk of schemes, but of . . . ." Mr. Grimke broke off, smiled enigmatically and peered into his coffee cup.

"Please go on," again begged the widow.

"With . . . with what?" Questioned the crafty Mr. Grimke.

"Why . . . with your scheme, of course." Pouted the sprightly widow. Thereby swallowing the bait before it had reached water.

"We-el," commenced Bambino in the manner of one loath to begin. "It's this-away. I've kept my eye on you."

"Carmali . . ." ventured the widow, taking a feeble stand for loyalty.

"Please don't interrupt," admonished the schemer, "My regard for that daughter of yours, Mrs. Bently," he went on, "is of the highest, but all the same, I got my eyes on you. Your daughter is but the promise, you . . . allow me to say it, dear Mrs. Bently . . . are the fulfillment. I'm a wide awake fellow. It ain't much that I don't see. Now let's see . . . where was I?" He continued with the air of one who has thoroughly disposed of a troublesome problem.

"How'd you like to expand your business?" His voice dripped with a cloying sweetness, through which a questioning quality that goads one into utter rashness at the same time that it lured one into taking a chance, trickled from his speech. "Start right with this neat little business you got here and expand it into an enterprise. You see, I gets about a heaps. And I know that there's need a-plenty for some good hotels for our people. In some towns there's no place for me and my boys to stop a-tall.

"Of course, when that there happens that town never know what it misses cause we just don't bother about stopping. Us Ginger Blues don't stay nowheres we ain't wanted. And there's a whole lots more outfits on the road what's got that same notion.

"Here's your proposition, Mrs. Bently, all in nut shell. . . . Let's me and you put up a good moderately-priced hotel in every town from coast to coast. You've heard talk about your black belt—well—let's me and you stud it with little hotels for diamonds that'll out-sparkle any other scheme ever put on foot by any of our color."

Adrift on the tide of Bambino's enthusiasm, it is to be admitted the widow was interested. With heads drawn close, they made plans which covered innumerable hotels, beginning at their foundations, they built to the skylights, furnished them, vastly peopled them with guests; then they went so far as to expand a small portion of the imaginary intake on several such trifles as a diamond ring and genuine pearl chokers.

Through it all, Bambino's voice had grown more insinuatingly sweet; until now, when he approached his climax, it all but dripped honey. . . .

"Getting down to actual figures," said he, edging nearer the widow, "Let's see . . . I got by accurate count, penny for penny, five hundred dollars, and what I wants to know," he added dramatically, "Is . . . can you match 'em?"

"Hum-er-er-er," complained the widow. An alert arm slipped around her, squeezing as it came.

"You remember, Mrs. Bently," said Bambino coaxingly. "Our scheme is already on foot, but it's got to step, and it takes maybe a little bit of money for that."

"That is to be thought of," agreed the widow pensively.

Hereupon, Bambino arose and taking a bad aim planted a kiss midway between the widow's eyes and the tip of her nose. It was a satisfactory gesture however, for the widow said instantly when it was over, in a way almost anxiously so eager was she to comply:—

"Alrighty, Mr. Grimke, I'll run down to the bank before noon."

At some time while the weighty plans were being unfolded in the dining room, Carmalita returned. On finding the kitchen as she had left it, she executed a dance of joy. Flitting around and about the room and thence into the one beyond like a bit of thistle-down.

★ ★ ★

The afternoon of the momentous day chanced to be clean-up day at Young's Pool Hall and Barber Shop Deluxe. An unseemly time to be sure, but the young person who then was occupied with mop and bucket had been otherwise engaged all the happy morning hours. Ever and anon, he desists from swinging a mean mop to gaze raptly into space—his thoughts—who desires to encroach on a young man's privacy?

The entrance of customers, curtails the young man's endeavors. A deft shove with his foot and the bucket skids to concealment beneath a combination settee, lounging-cot, and someone's night-bed. A quick swing of the arm and the mop disappears; a hasty ducking into an improvised clothes-press—a length of cretonne swung cater-cornered to protect somebody's somewhat nifty wardrobe, and the erstwhile cleaner is likewise lost to view.

The Ginger Blues enter to a man. They immediately draped themselves around the tables. Chalk their cues and pair to play.

"Hey . . . hows you and the widow these days, 'Fessor?"

"How come, him and that old gal? You're off 'feller,' it's him and sweet little baby-doll, ain't it 'Fessor?"

"Miss Carmalita sure is sweet."

"Wow, oh wow, she certainly is."

"When you all goin'er 'vite us to eat cake? 'Fessor?"

"Pshaw," spat Bambino vehemently. "You all's cold. That poor sweet little gal's plumb gone on a spinding legged, no-count, saucer-eyed, gumpless nobody. She don't even see me, even when I'm close to her as that." To express himself fully, he hunched his shoulders against the wall, and slumped there an instant, the picture of dejection.

This unexpected confession called forth a veritable chorus.

"How's that, 'Fessor?"

"That cannot be."

"I just ain't hearin' right."

"What's up, 'Fessor, you slowing up in your old age?"

"Ah come off," admonished Bambino, "Look—ee here," he demanded springing back to his place.

The strip of cretonne swinging in the further corner stirred as somebody else essayed a peep also.

Nonchalantly, Bambino drew a wallet from his pocket and unclasping it revealed a wad of greenbacks.

"See this doncher? It's down payment on my sagacity, see. . . . Lot more where this here come from. I'm waiting right now, for the next 'stallment. Me and old-lady widow-gal goin'er erect little "Wage Earner's" from this coast . . ." he dropped his cue to hold the wallet in his outstretched hand . . . "To that coast. . . ." He transferred the packet to the other hand and laconically replaced it within his pocket. Whereupon he became loquacious, again.

"Call me slowing up, hey, Brother I opines it calls for sure 'nough fast work to gather in little berries like these." He patted his pocket lovingly.

"Go on, 'Fessor, you're goofy."

"You got burglar notions, them tactics ain't right."

"Oh no," Bambino teased, "my tactics don't do a thing a-tall but build my bank 'count." With marked unconcern, he played a combination in the corner pocket, and looked inconsolable, as all three balls fell.

★ ★ ★

It was five o'clock when some-body eased forth from behind the concealing drapery, kicking out his cramped legs expressively towards the exit. Three hours later he was converted into—what use to name it?—When in the fragrant shadow of a lilac-bush that stood beneath an unlighted window of the Wage Earners hotel, little Carmalita billed and cooed at his side, and clung to his arm and tittered softly and happily until he bade her be quiet. Supplementing his command with a kiss, of course. Then she grew silent and listened attentively while he whispered with great earnestness and at great length.

He was rewarded at the end of his discourse for Carmalita flung her arms around him and hugging him tightly, kissed him and fled. He continued to remain beside the concealing lilac, and presently when a tat-a-tat-tat of approaching footsteps sounded, the nose on his lean face twitched expectantly as he leaned forward alertly.

Soon Bambino came, jauntily stepping and blithesomely whistling until a hand from the dark shot out and grasped his collar.

"Come along, quick and quiet," said a voice that followed the hand.

"None of your monkey business, quit it, I say. Come on."

"C—o—m—e O—n" sharp tuzzling dispersed the words to lengthy dimensions.

The sphere where dwelled the lilac bush was suddenly rent with grunts and blows and tumbling bodies that agitated its very roots. Seconds passed, then the voice. . . .

"Ready to give up that money. . . . What?" More seconds passed.
Biff, biff, biff. . . . "Ouch, Oh will you?"
Biff. . . . Biff. . . . Biff.
"Ready now?"
"Ready for what?" Muttered sullenly.
Biff. . . . Biff. . . . Biff. . . .
"You don't know, do you?"
"What the devil do you want?"
"Are you ready to give up that money. . . ." Intoned the voice like
a Nemesis. . . . "Ready to 'fess up right 'fore me and the widow and
her daughter? Are you?" . . . Biff . . . "Answer me . . . Are you?"
"Yes. . . . da. . . ."
"Look out . . . None of your pretty language either, if it's all forty,
come on let's go from here."

★   ★   ★

Carmalita had done her part well. She had the stage set to a T.
The widow Bently was sitting in her well-lighted parlor, and moreover, she had company. A talkative guest who now seemed determined
to boost her reputation as a talker. She talked but the widow heard
her not.

That lady's thoughts were sadly following after five hundred dollars.
And manifold were the doubts that rose to plague her soul. No kiss,
no squeeze, no man on earth was worth losing those cherished dollars,
somewhat belatedly but nonetheless sincerely. Most decidedly, she
desired her money back.

Thus was her heart yearning when the door to her sanctuary, so
to speak because this room was the one place the widow reserved
for her own among the many in the Wage Earners hotel, was flung
wide, and the intrepid "Nobody" whom she had ordered never to
darken her door again, stood upon the threshold. Stranger still, his
hand was ruthlessly clutching the collar of one—The widow's heart
jumped to her throat. . . . Could it be, no, it could not be Mr.
Grimke. Nor could she tell . . . was she sorry to see him so, or was
she not sorry to see him in this predicament if it meant the return of
her money. To relieve herself of trying to decide, she screamed loudly
and shrilly. And totally devoid of anything else to do, under the circumstances, the talking lady screamed too.

"Mother . . . Mother . . . what is the matter, mother?" cried Carmalita, who came running, with a shade too much dramatics or giggles one tucked in her voice.

"Go on and speak," ordered the "Nobody." . . . This is a propitious moment to present him. He thwacked the musician in the ribs nearest him, and ordered him to speak.

Bambino made an unexpected twist that set him free from the "Nobody's" grasp, while dodging to keep himself free, he faced about, one of his hands struggled with something in his pockets. At last he pulled out the familiar wallet and never stopping, flung it into the widow's lap. Then flashing one or his very best, irresistible, Bambino smiles, he addressed the "Nobody" who still made feints to collar him again.

"Cut the comedy, fellow, I knows when I'm beat."

"To the widow, he said:—

"There's your little nest egg, Madam, without a scratch on its shell." He pointed to the wallet still lying in her lap. "I tried to pull off a stunt, and got the haw-haw-haws instead. Mrs. Bently," he asked, ingratiatingly, "why don't you consent for this young gilly-fish to marry your daughter. . . . He wants to and she wants to. . . . He. . . ."

"Thank you Mr. Grimke," Carmalita chimed in unexpectedly, "But just now, we don't need your importuning." "Tell 'em Bobbie," she chirped gaily as she danced up to the "Nobody's side."

"We married this morning, folks," spoke up the "Nobody" clasping his lady's hand and bowing low. . . . "Please meet Mr. and Mrs. Robert Wilde," he said.

Widow Bently began fanning herself violently. This was exciting, her money back, and her daughter gone; first it had been money gone and daughter . . . but no . . . if the marriage took place in the morning, it surely must have followed that at one time in this momentous day both money and daughter also had been gone. That surely would have been more than one lone widow could have borne. Sheer relief, softened Mrs. Bently's heart. She found herself kissing Carmalita before she knew it and pumping Bobbie's arm with an evident intent to welcome him, her new son, into the family.

Bambino: Star Boarder

ANOTHER FASCINATING EXPERIENCE OF THE DAPPER
MAESTRO, WHO DISPLAYS A REMARKABLE GENIUS FOR
GETTING IN AND OUT OF TROUBLE

Carried off though it had been with flare and flourish, Bambino heaved
a sigh of relief when he said farewell to the Widow Bentley and to her
newly acquired combination household protector and son-in-law and
to the charming Carmalita.

It is indisputable, that when once a jewel has glinted and sparkled
within one's hand, it is difficult to watch it slither through the fingers
into another's palm. Bambino felt a like sentiment towards the little
project which he nearly put on foot with the widow.

In a way, the feeling had been only a bud, but when he, as the
head of the Ginger Blues, alighted first, the others following upon the
station platform in Altondale, it blossomed into flower.

An I-ain't-got-no-home feeling descended and enveloped the Ginger
Blues to a man when their attempt to hail a squawking taxi was ruthlessly nipped with: "White fares, only!"

"Sold," ejaculated Bambino in a voice which despair made almost
majestic. "Sold again! ah tell you boys when yo' hand gets called
when you're playing these womenfolk, you got'er run hard before
you catches up with yo' luck, ever."

Bronzeman Feb. 1931: 18–20, 31–33.

"Tell it 'Fessor," sighed the trombonist in a husky whisper, "tell it."

"Fellows, this ain't so worse." Soothed Chunky, one of the banjo boys. "Look-ee here, ah was raised on this dope, and worse," he sighed humorously, "but ah just natcherly eats it up. You alls rest easy. Let me rekonoiter." He all but cooed in his throaty southern voice. "Cause when you gets in these dumps, you got'er seek yo' own, yessuh, seek yo' own."

With these words, he eased his prized banjo cautiously down beside Slim's polished boots and departed. Slim played the tenor banjo, and he and Chunky were inseparable.

"Me . . . Me . . . I don't stand for no such," blustered Collins, the drummer, stalking angrily up and down the platform. Turning sharply on one of his angry marches, he bumped heavily into Chunky, who was just returning with a dusky companion. A stranger, with white eyes shining from an inky countenance that surveyed all they beheld with dog-like friendliness.

"Pardon and excuses, suh, pardon and excuses," he beseeched, quite disregarding the fact that he was not the one to offer excuse or to plead pardon. When he had been assured of utter forgiveness from all the Ginger Blues, singly and in unison, he generously offered to find shelter for all and sundry.

"Knock me down to yuh buddies, Cap'n," he begged in a loud aside to Chunky. The service was then performed speedily and thoroughly by the ingenious Chunky.

"Ah declare, ah do declare, yo . . . suh . . . yo is the head of this here musical organization," spoke the new-comer, Dusky, as the boys had instantly dubbed him. He suddenly doubled over like a jack knife, gave a loud guffaw, slapped his thighs and goggled his eyes at Bambino, the flawless. "Well suh, ah do be pleased to meet yuh. Yo is show-e-nuff royal'ty, and yo is goin'er have the best on the market. Just yo come wif me, suh, yo is fust."

It is to be supposed, the head was reluctant to leave the body; Bambino already deep in a hurried whispered confab with the boys was "Bucking the situation," as he said to "A real come down."

"Ah'm a-leaving yo," he admonished them solemnly, "in the flesh, but my spirit's a'staying with you."

The Jazzers actuated by an eagerness to get settled somehow and somewhere and an ever ready willingness to please the 'Fessor did their level best to cheer their crestfallen head.

"Everything is jake, 'Fessor. Go 'long," they urged him, and presently Bambino allowed himself to be towed away by the obliging Dusky.

"Ah'm carryin' yuh to the Dabneys. Yessuh to the Dabneys, and they is dicty, dicty folks . . . unhuh what is!"

"Is that so? Hey, what!" cried Bambino arousing himself from the gloom of parting, and awakening to sniff the scent of sompin' doin'.

Dusky waxed dumb at the transformation.

"You sure," questioned Bambino, "that they are dicty-dicks?"

Dusky whistled, and looked down at the luggage that he was obligingly helping Bambino to carry.

"'Cause," boasted Bambino. "Ah'm used to class, and ah don't mean mebbe. Tell us somethin' 'bout the folks in these here parts," he urged, "the Dabneys, fer instance."

"Nope, Mr. 'Fessor-man . . . seein' is believin'; ah keeps muy mouf shut; minds muy business, and eats muy squares three times a day and evahday. Hyah we is!" he sang out cheerily, and stopped before a neat little cream and white cottage. A cottage that was plainly articulate that someone lived in it and liked the living.

★   ★   ★

The happy owners of the cottage had been married seven years. Sometimes, seven works two ways, good and bad. Good housewives are aware that sheets, pillow slips, napkins, and cloths must be replenished every seven years. And so should love, for if the lesser materials fray with use, the finer fabric ought surely to develop "runs." At least, Lucy Dabney's love was wearing thin around the edges, and for no reason at all, except from wear. Tobias, her husband, was a good man . . . but so . . . the cutting tooth is good for the baby, but ouch! It hurts!

In seven years they had done well, their snug little home attested to that. Even though Lucy had bedecked it within with too many pretentions, too many over-trimmed cushions, too much too-frail, and too glossy furniture, too many over-dressed shades over too many colored lights: Tobias saw to it that their few square feet of town frontage yielded exquisite verdure . . . honeysuckle twined the porch railing and climbed the slender columns; roses nodded beneath the windows, and a patch of smooth green sward lured one to their door. Behind the cottage another garden grew, a hardier, more practical one, where lettuce and cabbage and string-beans gave up their fruit and seed beside sturdier flowers, marigolds and zinnias.

Always, there was a bowl of cut-flowers in Lucy's house. During their years together, Tobias had never failed to gather her a bouquet morning and evening. They cluttered things up, she secretly considered . . . but after all Dan Cupid knew his arrows, so the dart that had struck a corresponding spark in the breast of Lucy and Tobias was still sticking on the job. Hence, morning and night when the flowers were presented, Lucy kissed her husband's rough cheek, called him "Old Dear," and if in particularly good spirits, tweeked his nose or pulled his ear by way of emphasis.

Yet and still there was a humdrumness to married life, and she was beginning to see it. She craved for a fling. Things were happening all around her, and she was shut off from everything. She was sick and tired of breakfast, dinner, and supper, the Evening Herald, and the monthly bills . . . Oh gosh, what a life! was growing to be her everyday slogan . . . when . . . Wait! Hush! The doorbell rang! And Bambino Grimke, Bambino, the head of the Ginger Blues, Bambino the ladies' man, invaded her domain.

★   ★   ★

The pretentious Dabney interior caught Bambino's eye simultaneously with Lucy's babyish well-cared-for prettiness.

"Hey! What! A find . . . attaboy," he said to himself.

Playing one of his major strokes, he let his long-lashed lids waver and fall beneath the smiling Lucy's very nose, then tilting his head ever so slightly, lifted his lids fully and swept Tobias with his meaningful orbs. In case you fail to get him, he looked not on the vassal, but upon the master of the house.

Poor Tobias was taken off his feet, though to be exact he was not really upon them, for he was sitting, rather uncomfortably upon one of Lucy's "infernal foolishnesses,"—the secret regard in which he held his wife's new-fangled furniture.

A loss of equilibrium, however, was really experienced by the good Tobias at this unexpected sight of such a figure of a man, Bambino at his best! Soft pearl-gray Fedora prest to his bosom; a slight crook in his elegantly tailored back as he stood bowing before them; his black plush hair glossing and sheening beneath one of Lucy's orange colored lights; his "dazzling orbs" holding Tobias' gaze like magnets; his wide mouth smiling.

Lucy stood; her hand upon the knob of the door which she had flung wide; her eyes fixed, entranced at this apparition of a perfect man.

Here Dusky, who had been completely eclipsed by Bambino's stellar properties, stepped forth.

"Eek," squealed Lucy in unfeigned amazement.

"Mr. and Mrs. Dabney, hyah is a gent'man what's just come to town. What wants a room . . . Ah don't zackly know him, but ah vouches fo' him just the same. He's got a band what's got more boys in it, and they all is a room hankerin', and a standin' stock-still fo' me to he'p 'em. Ah don't 'tends to be perdum'in, but I done gi'n muy word, and muy word's all ah got, ah'd put him up hyah fo' a couple weeks. Well'um good night evahbody." Dusky slid out of the door, contented with Bambino's disposal.

The Dabney household was agap. Emotions therein, dovetailed for a little ways then zigzagged in opposite directions. She thought: The perfect darling, of course he might stay. He thought: Indeed not! My fine fellow, this home was built for two.

Bambino was thinking: go slow, Bo, slow. Watch yo' step. 'Cause now, any little move yo' make, might be a bad move. And boy, howdy. Ah sho' wants to put up here. Convinced of the persuasive powers of his tongue, he resorted to speech.

"Allow me," he motioned the hand containing the Fedora, gracefully toward Lucy, but with a grander sweep, included Tobias, "Mr. and Mrs.— Mr. and Mrs.— Ah—"

"Dabney," supplied the nearly dumb-stricken Tobias.

"Thanks, thanks—Mr. Dabney—You heard this here case stated, but ah feels certain, that yo' ain't heard it stated e-nough! I ain't got no place to stay and nowhere to go." He flung his hands out and down, dramatically letting them drop, like dead weights at his side, allowing his new hat to fall to the floor unnoticed, in a motion of finality.

"Oh," cried the tender-hearted Lucy. "No place to stay and no place to go." Echoing Bambino like a polly and with the words it was evident that the gentleman had found a confederate. To batter down Tobias' resistance was a matter of seconds, for Lucy was armed with three weapons, any one of which usually caused a surrender, namely, a plea, a pout, or a kiss. When all three of them were brought to play upon him at once, as Lucy intended doing now, capitulation was swift and certain.

"Let the gentleman stay, Toby. It would be cruel to say 'no,'" she said, slipping over to Tobias' side. "That's a dear," she added, laying a playful thumb and forefinger against the lobe of his ear, and the thing was done.

★　★　★

Altondale was a pokey enough place in everyway, but when it came to the social swirl it was a flop. In a week's time Bambino had not signed up a single engagement. There had been neither dance nor celebration that needed to solicit the aid of the Ginger Blues. Bambino admitted that his decision to stop over in Altondale had been a dumb-bell scheme. It was simply nothing doing for his Jazzy-Jazzers.

The saxophones, the clarinets, and the banjo boys had been housed together on Duncan street with Big easy-going Kate. Kate of the slipshod habits, and the careless ways. The drummer and the bassoon artist were stowed in the rear of Jake's, The Tailor, the coronets were camping over Stintson's Chili and Chitterling Parlor. And, pardon the repetition, Bambino, pianist, was enjoying the fussy coziness of the Dabney's guest room.

Widely separated were the Ginger Blues, but with one accord, Big Kate's place became their mecca. There it was, they congregated for their daily practice, for their gentlemanly gossip, and for their recreation.

Big Kate, herself, played a mean game of cards. Making the boys a cup of coffee—and supplying the makings—having them send out for a mess of fish, and frying it to a turn, and serving it with good-natured enjoyment, was but a few of the little services she performed for them, and it goes without saying that her place was a shelt'ring nook in the time o' storm.

Considering everything, Bambino was forced to pay divided attentions. He had so much on his mind. Essaying a rough estimate of his emotions at this time, one would say that his inclinations abided at Big Kate's and his interests dwelled with the Dabneys. There was nothing to be had from Kate's but much, yes, much, to be gained in philandering—carefully, you understand—at the Dabneys.

Reduced to neat terms, the state of affairs resulted in the Ginger Blues being minus their head most of the time. Headlessly, they played cards, danced and dined as it were, with Kate, while Bambino spent long hours playing his inimitable jazz on Lucy's tinkling toned piano. Dimming Lucy's timorous rendition of the "Maiden's Prayer" to nothingness with his ponderous syncopation.

Tobias came home day after day to find Lucy enthralled beside the piano, and Bambino manipulating the ivories like one possessed.

It never occurred to the head of the house of Dabney that a subtle system of love making was going on right at his finger-tips. The obtuse soul of him never suspected that the popular air, "If I Could Be With You," doctored and ministered by Bambino's clever touch, was more potent than a moonlit bower, say on the twenty-fifth of June at three o'clock in the morning.

Added to his other qualities, Bambino was a present-day exponent of the term, speed. His creed was fast-work. Be not amazed then, at this bald statement of facts. The thirtieth instant exactly two weeks to the day of their first meeting, Lucy and Bambino planned to fly the coop, fling discretion to the four winds and cast their lots together.

At two o'clock of that afternoon, Lucy dolled up like the Princess Zita, finished penning the missive which she had painstakingly prepared for Tobias. One of those, you know, as-old-as-the-world-Dear-Boy-things: I don't love you anymore, but can't we still be friends? I hate to hurt you, but you will understand. I have found my heart's ideal, and honey ain't love grand? Don't look for me, I'm gone forever, with my own true love—To be sure, not Lucy's own words, but the import was the same.

A moment spent to slip into her street coat—a new one recently purchased by good old Toby. A pause to lock the front door and to hide the key in the time-honored place under the door-mat—

And—"Baby, we'll pick each other up at the station. There ain't no gumption in being careless, Sugar. No use in rousin' the neighbors. Keep down 'spicions, keep 'em down."

Bambino's last words, his last bit of advice rang in her ears—Oh, now wasn't he cautious and cute? Wasn't he sharp and wise? Wasn't he adorable? The darling!

So danced her thoughts to the tripping of her pretty feet, until in less time than it takes to tell, she had found a seat in the crowded waiting room. For awhile, her breath came in little gusts of excitement. Her bright eyes beamed brighter, and her little foot tapped a restive tattoo upon the floor.

A tattoo, that before it was done reverberated in exasperated protest throughout an empty room. Protest because Lucy Dabney waited there. Half past two . . . half after three . . . four o'clock . . . five! And Bambino did not come!

How could he? The heart . . . how often it has led poor mortals astray. That Bambino had a preference for the all-inclusive warmth of Big Kate's hospitality has been afore-mentioned, but that he had a liking, a leaning, a penchant, no—a passion for the hoary game of pinochle, has not been stated. Now then, combine these two heart-felt preferences, and say for instance, he rushes to Big Kate's all a-gog and full of business, and one idea in his mind—to tell the boys where to meet him down the road. What further need to hang 'round a hick hole like Altondale? Then, presto! To be there, and find it so warm and so comfortable! A blazing fire in Big Kate's air-tight heater. A half of her spacious, sparsely furnished room cluttered with the Ginger Blues and their instruments, almost to a man. And each man teasing and tormenting his respective "weakness" to a fare-thee-well. Trembly runs on the banjoes, muted wails from the clarinets, muffled screams from the coronets, husky bellows from the trombones and grunts from the bassoon, and above and below and around and about the moaning of the saxophone making a not unpleasant accompani-ment for a musical fellow like himself, to lounge by. But don't stop here, for occupying the place of vantage, nearest the heater, closest to the sunny windows, just about in the center of the floor, stood a long low table, and before it spread good-natured Kate, and opposite sat a nondescript person with whom she was playing . . . Hey! What! Boy, Howdy! between them a pinochle board, before them the cards!

"Ah-chew, ah-chew," cried Bambino, rubbing his hands together in pleasurable anticipation. Lean and dapper, he hovered over the players like a moth attracted to a light. His every mission forgotten: his one and only aim to play old Kate, a hot one. The sheer intensity of his longing soon drove the nondescript from the table, and Bambino—a smile wreathing his lips, his eyes shining—his nervous fingers already caressing the cards—slid into the place . . . Two o'clock . . . three o'clock . . . four . . . five . . . !

Long since the gay little Lucy had lost her aplomb. Even the perky velvet bows upon her bonnet looked crumpled and done-for. Her slender shoulders hunched forward; her brown little hands lay tightly clasped in her lap, and tears, great big ones that just wouldn't dry up, rolled down her cheeks and left salt upon her lips.

Nasty, mean old Mr. Grimke to stick her up, like this! . . . And her! The idea, to her—Lucy Dabney. Used to having her own way! Her every whim gratified. She grit her sharp little teeth, and dug with her sharp pointed nails into the cloth of her skirt.

Well, he'd see, he couldn't make a fool of her, she'd go right straight home. Good old Toby would stand by her, and after this, she was going to stand by Toby.

Lucy's feet had carried her swiftly to the station, but they skimmed the distance back, that is, until they reached the corner nearest home. Then it was that her feet became leaden things: her heart pounded dully—suppose, suppose Toby had found that note . . . "Oh, she couldn't face that."

Pretty though she was, Lucy looked exactly like the "Hungry cat come back." Hoping against hope, she lifted the mat. If only the key were there . . . It wasn't . . . Toby was at home.

She sped through the front of the house, into the kitchen. . . . On the table where Toby always came first to put down his fragrant offering of love—freshly cut flowers—Lucy had elected to leave that farewell note. She had written it upon pink note paper . . . Where . . . where . . . where was it? She fearfully snatched up the flowers and beneath them, a bit blotched and stained, written side down, scarcely discernible against the rose-colored oil-cloth, lay the note. Apparently, some vagrant breeze had tossed it about and turned the cruel scrawl so that it could do no earthly harm. How glad she was! Her hand shot out and crushed the horrid pink paper into a tight little wad, and her hot little mouth brushed the cool flowers, as she darted away to find her Toby.

The Ginger Blues left town at midnight on the fast through train. Next morning a special delivery wrote finis to Bambino's sojourn in Altondale:

"Dear Mr. and Mrs. Dabney:

Allow me to tender sincerest regret at taking French leave. Important business forced my hurried departure. Enclosed find money-order to cover two weeks' lodging.

"Most Cordially Yours,
"B. Grimke."

Lucy leaned on Toby's shoulder to scan the note, and one arm found its way around his neck.

"Here," said the discerning Toby. "Buy yourself something nice," and he handed her the blue slip.

"A pretty nice sort of chap," he went on, "pretty nice chap," and he tore the letter into little bits. "Yes, sir, a pretty nice chap, that Mr. Grimke, but Honey, let's never keep any more boarders."

Rich Man, Poor Man

Drusilla Evans was a rich man's daughter. Old big black double-jointed Daniel Evans was her father. So big was he, that he towered above every other man in the community; so black, that his genial wrinkled old countenance shone strikingly where-ever he went; and so shrewd and industrious was he that the Evans ranch and the Bar-Crescent-E brand was as widely known as other longer standing ones like the Diamond D and the X–Z outfits.

Drusilla's mother was just such a woman as most sure-footed men choose for a partner. A tall, slender woman was she, with a delicate, fragile air—a woman with soft warm eyes and a gentle voice and a smiling mouth above the roundest, stubbornest chin.

Drusilla herself was just such a daughter as one would expect to spring from such a well-matched team as old Daniel and his wife. She was sparklingly pretty, a jolly twinkling star of a girl. And because she was so pretty and perhaps because she was so rich, the suitors she had in tow were not to be numbered. However, gossip said it would be a long time before Drusilla married, for who, pray, would be able to match old Daniel's dollars, and wouldn't Drusilla be a fool to marry a poor man?

One of the main impressions of Drusilla's childhood coincided with this line of gossip. Day in and day out, her father's friends had gathered

Half-Century Magazine May 1920: 6, 14.

in her home of evenings to partake of old Daniel's hospitality. They played cards at times; but the main business of these little gatherings had been to talk—and how they had talked. Sometimes politics, sometimes religion; at times a long drawn-out tale of Indian-War days, but the one sincere, palpably sincere argument was the Race Question discussed again and again and over and over.

In red headlines some paper would herald some atrocity done a Negro—always some unknown, far-off Negro; but the little band of black men gathered in the Evans parlor were wont to discuss it pro and con in subdued and sorrowful voices.

From listening to these talks, Drusilla had learned to know and honor Douglass, Washington, Cuney and Langston. She knew and admired the race benefactors and having heard the race haters like Vardaman, Tillman and Dixon, Jr., ridiculed with true American humor, she was able to laugh her jolly, twinkling laughter at their piteously self-belittling antics.

Often the men would bring their wives and then the women joined with the men in a friendly combat with words. Race men, versus race women, was the topic of the day whenever this occurred, and one of these arguments had stuck and sprouted like a seed in fertile soil in Drusilla's mind.

"Now men, you know," one of the women would declare, "our menfolk are slack about letting their wives work—" That would start the bout.

"Work—Work"—little peppery Mr. Stinson would shout, "What can we do—how's a black man to support a wife and children on the mere pittance he gets a day!"

"Get a job that pays more than a pittance." Some crisp tongued woman would return.

"Indeed, indeed—wouldn't we, if we could. A black woman can always get a good (?) job in somebody's kitchen—but a black man can't get a good (?) job cleaning the streets; if some white man happens to want it."

Now Drusilla as a very little, twinkly star of a girl decided that no matter what came or what went—she would not work for any man alive.

"When I marry," she would say, "my man is going to take care of me." Then she would quote a remembered fragment from some of the old arguments. "It's a sorry man who can't take care of his own family."

Then came a day when Drusilla's sparkling prettiness forgot to twinkle and glowed and shown instead. Drusilla's mother discovered it first. It had been she who first likened Drusilla to a twinkling star. Long ago, when Drusilla was a wee mite, Mrs. Evans had held her close in her arms while looking into her sparkling eyes and chanted the old nursery rhyme:

"Twinkle, twinkle, little star, how I wonder what you are?" And the little Drusilla had answered: "Why, muvver, I'm your little daughter." So now, that she no longer twinkled, Mrs. Evans was the first to notice.

Drusilla came in one evening after she and a party of young folk had been on a hike to the mountains. John Condon had been with them—John Condon, young and poor as a church mouse, possessing a lovableness utterly compelling, working at the menial task, of chauffeuring, and newly arrived from the East in the train of his wealthy Eastern employers.

"Oh Daughter," Mrs. Evans had exclaimed, "My little girl."

Then Drusilla had walked straight into her mother's arms and hidden her starry glowing face on her mother's bosom, and both had cried a little and gazed into each other's face, wet-eyed and trustingly.

Said Mrs. Evans, "Daughter, John is a poor man, a poor black man, daughter; have you thought of that."

"Yes, yes," cried Drusilla, "but John can make his way."

"*So* he can, Daughter, if you are willing to help." But little Drusilla, shocked through and through, sprang up at this, crying: "Why mother, I wouldn't work for any man alive. John shall make his way alone."

"Daughter," returned Mrs. Evans, "you do not know how your father got the money to buy our first cow. I'll tell you. I, your mother, did days work, washed and scoured from house to house. That cow, a heifer, cost us thirty-five dollars, and it took me two solid months to earn enough to get her."

"Oh Mother," exclaimed Drusilla, pityingly. Then brightly, "but times have changed. So I'm not going to wash and scour for John Condon, cows or no cows."

Mrs. Evans smiled understandably, and little Drusilla snuggled down beside her, and they sat down together with their arms entwined, silently, knowing they had reached the bitter-sweet moment that comes to every mother and every daughter who reaches the parting of their ways.

Said old Daniel Evans to young John Condon a day or two later:

"I want you to know son, that I've liked you from the first moment I set eyes on you. Though I hadn't figured on you taking my little girl away from me, but—" old Daniel crinkled his black genial face into a whimsical smile and continued: "You know that everything I possess goes to my little girl, too, don't you?" Old Daniel asked the blunt question unexpectedly, and young John fidgeted under the surprise of it; but his eyes so boyish and straightforward, met the older man's unflinchingly, and he answered, "Yes Sir."

"All right, then," resumed old Daniel. "I'm going to tell you something most people do not know. I don't intend to choke the manhood out of any man with my money." He paused, and a full moment elapsed before he spoke again. "I love my little girl, son—so well that you can rest assured that if you never make good, she and her little ones, if there be any, aren't ever going to suffer—no, never, so long as old Dan Evans is in full possession of his strength and mind. But I'd die mighty happy, son, if I had some way of knowing that the man she'd tied to was a man—that the family she was a-building was being built on rock foundation. When I'm gone every cent goes to my children; but figuring on their chances compared to what I had, my children ought to leave their children a fortune treble the value of mine. Sounds like a Chinese puzzle, boy; but what have you to say?"

Old Dan laughed heartily, and grasped the youth's shoulder, swung him about easily and looked into his face. "Is it a go, my girl, but not a red cent goes with her, not one red cent until you have proved your metal. I'll fit up a little house right nigh my own—."

"Oh, no you don't," interrupted John. "I'm in love with your daughter, but not with your West. When we are married, back East for us."

"What? Well, it's all right, Son, but it pricks my hope bubble. I'd set my heart on keeping my little girl close."

Of course Drusilla's friends were aghast when they heard of her engagement. Their own dear little Drucy going to marry a poor nobody. The idea. The overly-wise young fellows about town on hearing it winked their eyes, cocked their heads to one side, exhaled pungent cigarette smoke through their burnt-out nostrils, and gave vent to much conjecture; namely, "How the deuce had that Eastern fish managed to hook in all that money?"

Nevertheless, John and Drusilla were married and went away to make a home of their own. John with very high hopes, indeed, for was not he taking with him as a bride, the prettiest, sweetest girl on earth? world? In little cozy moments when they were alone, Drusilla would say, "John, dear, dear I'd die for you." And John would say gaily, joyously, "Right, o'right girl, but just keep on living, won't you?"

All this was very well and good, and yet better, John found a cute little nest of a house and eventually another job as a chauffeur in a private family. They were very happy. Drusilla cooked spicy, tasty little dishes, and kept them piping hot for supper, which was a variable affair owing to John's employment. She kept their tiny rooms shining like mirrors and her own pretty self as trim and neat as a rose-bud. But the butcher, the grocer, the fuel—the bills climbed up amazingly, and at the end of a month when they were all paid, what was left of John's wages looked like a small boy's Christmas gift from a maiden aunt.

John worked like a galley-slave. He added the care of several offices to his other tasks. He grew lean as a foxhound. In his spare moments he was far too tired to play around with Drusilla. He would even forget to tell her how pretty she looked, or how good the supper tasted. This of course aroused a vague uneasiness within Drusilla. Yet, needless to say; the remarks that she had heard on every side concerning John's poverty, and the solicitude which well-meaning friends bestowed upon her before her marriage all had their effect. Indeed, she considered John's effort to make ends meet, an acknowledgement of the sacrifice she had made to become his wife.

Then something happened. One day, as John was about to take a dangerous curve with his usual careful precision, another chauffeur who knew next to nothing about carefulness, and had no preciseness whatever, took it from the opposite direction with a devil-may-care recklessness. There was a smash-up. Everyone of the occupants of John's car were more or less shaken and John was painfully cut by flying glass from his broken wind-shield. They sent for Drusilla from the hospital whence John had been carried.

It was a very frightened and contrite Drusilla who was ushered into her husband's presence. Her first impulse had been to send an S.O.S. call to her doting parents; but the first glimpse of dear old

John's bandaged face which revealed better than anything else could have done, the square line of his determined chin, with its distracting cleft peeping out beneath the folds of gauze, dispelled that notion entirely.

Perhaps this accident would not have changed things materially for in a few days John came home from the hospital, still swathed in bandages and rather sore; but fully decided to go to work within the next forty-eight hours had not Influenza quite accommodatingly lent itself to the situation. Ignoring the time honored rule of the game— not to strike when a man's down—it took a tenacious hold upon John, all bandaged and sore as he was, and gave him a race for his life. During the first few days of his illness, John, who couldn't stand pain any better than a day-old kitten, had to endure so much that his mind rambled and he muttered all sorts of queer odds and ends and bits of nonsense—such as a delirious person can.

Drusilla's eyes would mist with tears as she listened; yet her twinkling laughter would ripple out huskily, then she would flash a look at the clock and glance at the medicine schedule beside her. Lord, she would rather cut off her right arm than to miss that medicine right on the dot. One of the things she kept thinking about was the way John muttered about bread. It puzzled her. "Bread, bread, bread," he would say, then he would begin to count, seemingly endless loaves of bread, bread, bread.

When John's fever spent itself, he began to mend rapidly, and the remainder of the time he passed in bed was like a holiday. It was luxurious, to be sure, to rest among cool pillows and fall asleep, to awake with nothing on hand to do, other than locating Drusilla, who, knowing how to amuse a fellow, kept her sparkling self just within range of his waking vision. When he was himself again, Drusilla asked why he had raved so about bread. John smiled at that, and reached for his wife's hand, then he answered:

"Girl Dear, I'm not a chauffeur. I've as much love for driving a car as you have for running a washing machine. I'm a baker; got the first taste of it working around a French bakery, when I was a kid, then somehow my folks scraped up enough to send me to a school and I specialized in baking. The one thing I've wanted is to own a bakery-shop. I bummed around a great deal after I left school, trying to find an opening; but my trade seemed to be the garden of roses for Germans and Bohemians and nobody's even give me a chance to keep the ovens hot. To come down to brass tacks, I had to live so I capitalized on buzz-cars, and Oh, girl, you know I'm the nifty kid at the steering-wheel.

Drusilla often ran out to purchase a loaf of bread, or a pie from the little bakery around the corner, owned by a florid-faced German and his round-tub of a wife. The round-tub of a wife was a friendly soul, and always chattered with Drusilla; yet John's good angel must have prompted her to speak thus a day or two later:

"Mein Gott, the trades fallen off dreadfully. Mein Gott to think we are Americans, but our looks are the German, so no onces comes to buy."

Said Drusilla quick as a flash, "Turn over your business to me." The smooth brown braids of the German woman and Drusilla's curly tresses mingled as their heads bowed to make speedy calculations over the counter.

"Two hundred and fifty dollars, my dear," exclaimed the proprietress; "two hundred and fifty dollars down and one hundred every six months and the shop, also the little delivery car is yours, with blessing of Mein Gott."

Drusilla forgot her parcel, left it lying upon the counter and ran into her own spick and span little house. She went straight into her room, never stopping until she ransacked her belongings, disclosing a veritable garden of gay little dresses; some of these she sorted out and made into a neat pile, saying, "Lovely dresses, you are quite the thing for a rich man's daughter, but you are outlandish for a poor man's wife, so I'm going to sell you to the second-hand man, and tonight I'm going to have $250." Then she laughed gaily, thinking how lucky she was to be in an Eastern city wherein a second-hand clothing shop could be found. She was exceedingly busy all the afternoon, and John having yet to remain indoors, wondered why she did not come to entertain him as she had been doing.

Late that evening Drusilla burst into his presence. Excitement made her sparkling prettiness a dazzling thing to see. She brushed aside John's compliments and rushed on to what she had to say.

"John, dear, haven't I always told you, I'd die for you?"

"You bet," responded he. Drusilla laughed her twinkling laugh, and said, "Well, I've changed my mind. Instead, I'm going to work for you."

John sat up at that, and said harshly. "Yes, I guess not. No woman will ever remember working for me. I'm a man who wants only a man's chance—a man's chance, do you hear, and I'll do the man's part, I'll—"

"John, John," laughed Drusilla, "Will you listen to me?"

Then, as John leaned back among the pillows, Drusilla told him all about her business venture. He could only gasp and stare.

Said she, "It's you, and I for the night work, until we get on our feet. Of days, you can peddle our wares in that little antediluvian Ford and I'll sell them over the counter."

"Oh, girl," said John, "that means you will have to work. . . ."

"Yes, boy, I've always said I wouldn't work for any man alive, but I've found the one I'm willing to work with."

Then altogether irrelevant to the business in hand, John repeated ever so softly: "Twinkle, Twinkle little star. . . ." as he put his arms around Drusilla and drew her close.

Pot Luck: A Story True to Life

Life is a capricious woman who delights to twist away the thread with which man weaves the tapestry of his existence. She dresses love like a merry little elf and sends him to meet a dusky nurse-maid in a flower garden or she rolls love in the mud and sends him a sordid little imp to intrigue a queen in her court. She flavors her broth with wondrous herbs and condiments and skims off the top, which is tasteless, giving it to those who receive first serving, while those who chance on pot-luck are given the strength of her porridge. She juggles men together, mixes them, shuffles them as a dealer his cards and no one wonders who plays her game if the loser draws a full house and the winner holds a rotten, rotten hand.

Life was capricious to say the least when she tangled the thread in the fabric of Mrs. John Borden's career by snapping the cords which kept Mr. Borden suspended on this earth and tumbling him into eternity, thereby forcing his widow, a hitherto comfortably cared for wife, to take in washing to eke out a scanty livelihood for herself and three-year-old daughter.

Mrs. John Borden with a resignation quite unbelievable in one so fed-up on a diet of petted and cared-for wife-dom submitted to life's whims and became a sweating and grim-faced wash-woman.

Life smiled complacently as she viewed Mrs. Borden sweating over her tubs, decided nonchalantly to keep her there, and passed on.

Competitor Aug.–Sept. 1920: 105–8.

Widow Borden, the supposedly meek, spat at her passing and determined that Life, Life the capricious lady, herself, should be made to push the finest of plush upholstered perambulator in which Anne, Mrs. Borden's own daughter, should ride.

An unwise determination to be sure—a veritable flying into the face of destiny—a silly jumping from hot skillet into fire, but nevertheless, a determination that calls for the fortitude of a God and the patience of a saint. Just think of it, resolving to make Life, the capricious woman, push someone in a perambulator. As yet no man has ever conceived such a thing and no woman save only she, whose womanhood is set with the priceless gem of maternity.

This determination deeply rooted in her motherly bosom, squared Mrs. Borden's shoulders and furnished stamina for her ceaseless toil. At night when her back twinged with pain and her arms swung like dead weights from their sockets the flaming glory of it, like the colors from a golden sunset, flared before her tired eyes causing her to forget the numbing weariness of her aching body and lulling her to sleep. Then of days as she would glance over her steaming tubs and behold little Anne at play at a distance just far enough to be undefiled by soapy suds and dirty linens, the glory of her determination would scintillate and shine like many diamonds and the sound of soiled clothing being rubbed against the rough washboard was as a mighty paean sung in its honor.

Life smiled derisively as she passed.

Little Anne thrived and grew. Grew fast like a fast-growing flower. School demanded her presence, and Widow Borden deprived of her constant pleasure—which was to pause unnumbered times with her arms half hidden in soapy suds supporting the weight of her bending body, while she gazed adoringly upon a dusky child at play—fell to planning small surprises against Anne's homecoming—the dough for sugar cookies was made over night while Anne slept, cut out and baked in the intervals when clothes steamed or irons heated or a gay hair-bow was surreptitiously purchased to be pinned beside a pillow or hidden beneath a plate.

Following swiftly the time arrived, when Anne was no longer short-skirted and easily pleased with a sugar cake fashioned like the badly done caricature of a man. She was grown tall and slim and her skirts swished against her slender ankles. Forthwith Widow Borden advertised for more "Fine Linens" to be "Hygienically Done by Hand." And sent the young Miss off to an expensive, exclusive, genteel, finishing school for young ladies.

There, Anne continued her piano lessons. To be sure she had taken music years and years before she could sit and touch the pedals with her toes. Yet even the best of expert teachers failed to teach her any sort of technique. Her greatest endeavors drew from the ivory keys a simple melody rendered always in too-slow a beat.

She studied languages, too, but her French was a woeful pot pourri of unrelated terms, her Spanish was a lob lolly as hard to get away with as a dish of that people's chilli con carne; her Latin, no food combination. Italy's spaghetti or an Irish stew could equal it for a mixture of wasted effort, time, and money. She took up sewing, but they who taught her that domestic art surveyed her crooked hems and puckered tucks with eyes registering horror. For some unknown reason higher mathematics are always taught even in a finishing school for young ladies. Anne's was no exception, but her teachers soon came to know that the well-known and easily done symbol for naught was devised to be used in connection with Anne Borden's work. She had no taste for literature. All the old estimable poems from the time-honored poets, which are usually thrown into curriculum in young ladies' finishing schools went a-begging with Anne.

Mind you, don't start in blaming Anne. For really, she was a peach of a girl, appealing and charming as it is good for a girl to be. She dressed very very fetchingly. Widow Borden with the help of her tubs and washboard saw to that. Her manners were the pink of perfection, and she was entirely kind and lovable.

What more could you ask? In the face of the fact that her father was just a plodding, good natured colored man, lacking enough fore-thought to provide for the future welfare of his family, who knew nothing whatever about Longfellow and no less than that about Plato and cared never a fig about either. Her mother, poor soul, used to enjoy listening to Anne strumming, which is to say, she did not know music; and barring her great capacity for unstinted devotion, she was dis-qualified for everything else in the world, save washing and ironing.

So if any of you expect Life, Life the capricious woman, to pitch her decorum to the winds and do a handspring for the sake of converting the child of a clod-hopping hodcarrier whose mate is a washwoman, into a finished musician or a distinguished linguist, you simply don't know Life. It's far more befitting her caprice to make the sons and daughters of musicians and poets the rag-pickers and scullery maids of tomorrow. If you notice, she takes generations in which to produce and only moments in which to destroy.

But withal, Anne was a real little lady. Didn't somebody say, "that artists and linguists—and cooks—wasn't included—are born?" Leastways, it's a fact. But a lady—bah, a lady—any female who chooses can be that. Take for instance, a little bit of natural inclination, a fair amount of right association, a smattering of education; and a knack at imitation, and you have it.

Life complacently passed on. However out-doing her own capriciousness and quite as Widow Borden willed, condescended to lightly clasp the handle of a fine-upholstered perambulator, in which a dusky little lady luxuriously reclined, and shove it along. Eighteen years, Life did just. Who can say, what Life, the capricious woman will do.

Anne Borden at eighteen was a lovely thing to behold, as round and plump and as merry and carefree as youth when it is cherished and nourished can possibly be. Also, Anne had a gift, you might say half a gift, the gift of song. She could sing liltingly like a bird, warbling as he sits on a dew drenched vine to watch the sun rise like a golden ball tossed high into the blue bowl of heaven—and as blithely as a boy whistling as he starts off on a coveted half-holiday, headed for his favorite swimming hole. Only, this voice of hers lilting and blithe though it was had not one bit of range, and honest, given a voice like hers and possessing no range the Pattis*, white or black, would turn over in their graves.

And again, as a real insight into just the kind of girl Anne was; her class staged the well-known playlet: "Mothers and Babes." In the last act in the role of a young mother bending over a crib, crooning a lullaby, she brought down the house. For her voice had just the right quality of sweetness and the exact quantity of softness to hush babies to sleep and make hardened adults remember their own mother's arms and recall the stilled lullabys of long ago. She brought down the

---

*Adeline Patti (1843–1919) was a Spanish-born Italian soprano. She had a voice remarkable for its range, timbre, and flexibility.

house, I tell you, and the stage floor was literally covered with sweet-young-girl-graduate-boquets when her act was finished. Mrs. John Borden sitting back out of the way and somewhat hidden by row on row of more pompous and prosperous parents allowed tears—of joy—to flow unheeded down her cheeks and fall heedlessly upon the real lace jabot dear little Anne had hastily and lovingly pinned about her scrawny neck just before the performance.

★   ★   ★

The post-haste methods with which joy turns into sorrow and laughter merges into tears would be strange and ridiculous besides being sad; if one did not know that Life is a capricious woman. Hence it was only in keeping with Life's whims that poor self-sacrificing Widow Borden died one short week after accompanying little Anne home from boarding school. All of the meagre sum over and above board which had been culled during all the years of hard work was squandered to enable Mrs. Borden's presence upon the memorable occasion; when Anne brought down the house.

It could not have been spent better. It gave Widow Borden the joy of a life-time—it illumined with a dazzling glory the dimming flames of her ambition. It caused the years on years of toil and sacrifice to roll from her tired shoulders like the great waves out at sea. In short she tasted of the sweet honey-dew melon of fulfillment and Life, the capricious woman, who flaunted so many tantalizing gifts has none to offer more entrancing than that.

Life passed on quite unmindful of the fact that she had unclasped her hands and let go a fine upholstered perambulator that immediately overturned a dusky fairy-like creature in the open highway. Poor Anne Borden. The question, "What can you do?" was flung at her so often until she smarted with the pain of it as if each word was a cat-o-nine-tails lashed about her body. She was completely befuddled and oh, so helpless.

Then a good old family doctor, a kindly intentioned man; who often intended far kinder things than he ever performed, took her in charge. His intentions toward Anne was kindness itself, but even as he carried her home, he was considering the expense she would be to him. And he was such a poor man; as all doctors know that a sick man grown well makes a hard paymaster. Money was a thing to be thought of, besides his widowed daughter and four lusty grandchildren were depended upon him. How was he to carry another burden. Quite plainly the thing to do was to get Anne Borden settled as speedily as possible—off his hands anyhow, any way. And at that wouldn't he do a Christian act?

Moodily, he tabulated in his mind different possibilities to get Anne Borden speedily off his hands. The shops nearby were closed to her because of her color. Theatre-goers would scoff at buying tickets from such a dusky maiden. Central, the mecca for girls with pleasing voice and goodly patience, would ring with alarm should so dark an operator strap the gear about her head put forth her hand to a plug, and call sweetly, "number." He enumerated all the divers things set aside for the dainty maidens whom Life has teetered downward and decided they were taboo to Anne Borden on account of a too-brown complexion. And on the other hand all the things accommodatingly tossed to one side for the benefit of dusky maidens down on their luck were likewise out of the question. To wit, no one would be willing to pay Anne Borden to concoct chafing dish delicacies and delectable fudges, not this day and time, when sugar is twenty-eight cents the pound and the very best of us are using oleo-margarine and camouflaging it for butter, no indeed, it requires an old head at the business to stir the pots these days. Laundry work, well I say, the idea. She was not fitted to teach and she could not sew.

Yet there still remains many many things for an untrained person to do. You are right. But remember, Anne Borden was not untrained. She had been trained actually trained throughout eighteen years to ride in a fine upholstered perambulator. Life had capriciously pushed it. Even Life can carry a joke too far.

A week or two passed in which the good old doctor worked as hard as a sleuth on a mystery case, and finally with the unconscious aid of his grandchildren he was able to place Ann alongside the very pattern Life probably cut out for her use.

The grandchildren had taken to Anne at once. Since her advent among them, they had babbled of no one else. And Anne, poor bereaved creature secured what solace she was able to get hold of, by occupying the somewhat stormy position of being the center of their attraction.

One day as the old doctor perplexedly stroked his beard and watched Anne with the children all clustered about her, he had an inspiration which revealed itself a couple of days later; when he came in and said to Anne in a manner he considered benign:—

"Get ready, my dear, I've found you a place."

Then with Anne's eyes grown suddenly wide and startled full upon him he was unable to go on in his benign fashion, so he dropped his benignity like peas burst from their shell, and flared out meaningly.

"Come, come, I've found you a place—er—er a job, you know. Nursing, private family, one child, good pay, good room, a real home you might say, start in at once. Get ready, quickly as you can. We've a long way to go, across town, 1212 Sonnet's Drive, that's the address. Come, come—"

Anne set to, quickly as she was bidden. And the trunks and bags and boxes, which had so shortly arrived with her from an exclusive genteel finishing school for young ladies, were piled unto the doctor's rattley old car along with herself and carried across town to 1212 Sonnet's Drive. And so it was that pretty little dusky Anne Borden entered upon the arduous duties of nurse-maid in the home of the Lewis-Osbornes.

Fie fie, a nurse-maid. Widow Borden's dusky little lady. The very Anne whom life had allowed to ride in a fine upholstered perambulator, now forced to push a rather sumptuous perambulator herself, containing a husky kicking, red-faced, too-fat, bawling youngster.

Life, Life, you are derisive just as much as you are capricious. For a long time, Anne suffered sheer martyrdom. Truly was she an alien in a foreign land. She, who in all her days, saving for the fleeting moments on streets and in shops, whence she had glimpsed the haughty visages of another race; had beheld none but the pleasing countenances of her own people. It was worse than bondage, for bondage teaches first of all, to expect any and all indignities; but how was a girl like Anne to know, that because she toiled as nurse-maid she had not even the caste of a bondsman nor the consideration that is given to the family's dog. It had to be learned and her lessons were hard.

Her grief for her mother instead of abating grew more acute with the days and she yearned piteously for the sound of the silent voice and a pressure from those resting hands.

But the inherent will-power which had propped up Widow Borden beside uncountable washtubs, now enabled Anne to carry on. It masked her dark-hued face in inscrutableness. It laid low the clinging longing for the old life of ease and—yes—splendor. It aided her to learn the art of simple every day washing and baking and sewing. And of course it didn't take much of a wrench to unloose her little store in knowledge of music and languages and the preparation of a chafing-dish feast. Yet the sobs which she stifled of nights against her pillow and the ache in her heart which grew and grew until it lessened under its own weight, seemed a needles, heartless price to pay for a comfortable ride in a fine upholstered perambulator. But Life is Life, and youth is youth.

Anne kept tenacious hold unto Life's skirts even after her tumble. And more to be commended she held tightly to her ladyhood, that attainment so easily acquired and as easily lost. Something in a way so startling that it attracted the attention of Mrs. Lewis-Osborne, Anne's mistress.

That august lady was often wont to declare over her luncheon, at tea, and even while dining out; whenever the servant-problem was discussed:

"Oh, my servants—la—la," then with a gush of very pleasing laughter—"but I have one jewel—my nurse-maid—with me four years this June; as straight as a string and even more a lady; why her poise is wonderful and she carries her head high, like a queen. My Dicky-boy's manners are due to her and I intend to hold her by all means for the sake of Elizabeth." Then with the manner of one handing out a rare tid-bit, in lowered tones. "It's odd, too, she's colored." And always that information was followed by a grand chorus, "Oh, you don't say, colored."

Then came a summer, when Anne went to the coast with the Lewis-Osbornes, to a little town, which she thought was the prettiest spot in all the world; where mountains and valley and ocean suffused their beauty in a matchless rivalry; where the purple of mountains misted and shaded through a thousand hues into the green of valley, while the valley's green caught the gold of sun and the silver of moon's and merged tremblingly into the green of ocean. And Life so wondrously kind when she chooses, followed Anne over the mountains down through the valley, on by the sea.

A high rock wall surrounded the premises of the Lewis-Osbornes. A high rock wall that shut in an old-fashioned garden, a sundial and many rustic seats and a musical fountain—and here it was that Anne spent the mornings with her charges. She always sang for the children, and here singing was easy, the thing to be done amid flowers and a tinkling fountain. Whenever their dusky nurse-maid sang the children left their play to draw close, listening with the wonder and appreciation of childhood.

All unknowing, Anne had another listener. Big Jim Moore, the neighborhood gardener; a genius in his line. A wonderful sight to see, great bronze giant that he was, handling flowers with the exquisite finesse of a master. Any artist, who knew his business enough to depict feeling, soul, or art, or whatever you call it, and expert enough. To catch that great black fellow with his brawny arms bared as his great hands played lovingly over a rosebush, while more or less little children tugged at his garments as he was to be seen any summer morning would make a canvass fit to be placed side by side with any of the great Shepherd and Lamb paintings and its significance would be by far the greater.

One morning, so sunny a morning until the sky had a golden sheen, Anne sang and the little ones stopped their play to listen—on the other side of the wall Jim Moore stopped his work to listen. And Life draped in rosy garments danced around and about giving ear to the song she sang:

"I feel the sap to the bough returning,
I knew the skylarks' transport fine;
I feel the fountains' wayward yearning,
I love and the world is mine."

Jim Moore listened until he caught the refrain, then roguishly chimed in with a deep-throated whistle. And the singing and the whistling combined faultlessly and sweetly and continued on until the song was done.

With one accord Anne and the children stood up.

"Let's climb the wall and see," cried the elder.

"Oh, do; oh, do;" piped the younger.

Without a word, Anne swung across the garden, the children in hot pursuit. A moment and the wall was scaled. A moment and Anne Borden looked down deep, deep into the gentle eyes of big Jim Moore.

"It's you." They exclaimed simultaneously, as though this their first meeting was but the renewal of an age-long friendship.

Ah, Life, what a woman you are, with all your capriciousness and derisiveness and your jokes which you sometimes take too far, yet do you ever pause to bow in obeisance to youth and love such as these clasping hands to follow after you.

Two Old Women A-Shopping Go!
A Story of Man, Marriage and Poverty

Without a doubt, Nell had Horace on her mind. There was no forgetting the way he had pleaded with her, the night before. She had fallen to sleep thinking of him, not as on other nights when imagery made vivid by love, brought his dear presence near in her last wakeful moments to drift pleasantly through her dreams. No, not that way, but an unhappy picture of him, nervous and moody, penetrated her sleep and leaped to aliveness with her first wakefulness.

She remembered every word he had said, unfair, cruel words; now they formed crookedly and apart like bits of a jig-saw puzzle as she dressed. His arguments repeated themselves:

"Each day, we are growing older—"

Nell leaned nearer the mirror, and scanned her piquant face. Could it be that she really was aging and losing her charm, as surely as yesterday's flowers that drooped beside her in their squat, brown jar. A tiny line brought Nell's brows, silky, high-arched brows like the sweep of bird wings, together. She brushed her hair with brisk strokes, while thinking dejectedly:

"You will be old and gray."

Suddenly panic seized her; she would not look for gray strands; no, not yet. She was not old, and she would not allow Horace to hurry her, frighten her into marrying him.

Crisis May 1933: 109–10

She put on her hat, a little round crocheted affair that she had made herself. She put on her coat and drew on her gloves, picked up her bag, and went out, an altogether lovely colored girl.

Nell thought how many mornings had she gone out, thus. Five years and every morning except Sundays, she had taken this same way: three steps down the cobble-stoned walk to the green latticed gate; half a block to the corner, turn North; four blocks to the car-line; a wait five or more minutes for the car; an hour's ride to work.

Last night, Horace had said, pleadingly. . . .

"You'll be worn out, all fagged-to-death and, I—I—don't want the girl I marry worked to death before I get her."

Nell tried to brush her troublesome thoughts aside and quickened her steps, then as quickly found herself agreeing with Horace. She was tired, so tired. Unconsciously, the line that drew her lovely brows together, deepened.

She heard voices, and looking up, she saw two old women come trundling towards her.

One was a very black and very stout old lady with near-white-folk's hair straggling from beneath a brown bonnet. She was buttoned into a red knitted sweater. She wore a heavy worsted skirt, and over that, a white, starched apron that tied around her waist. She carried a black shopping-bag in her hand.

Thought Nell: two old ladies out to do their shopping. Making a lark of it, too, she decided as their high cackling old voices came to her. Said one:

"No suh, they'll never come through what we done come through."

The other old woman tuned in quaveringly:

"Lord, chile, they couldn't begin to do 't."

"Not wantin' 'im 'cause he ain't rich," chimed the first.

"Ain't none of us that, neither," vouchsafed the other.

"The ideas and the whimsies of these 'ere young 'uns do beat me." They broke into high cackling laughter. The black old woman changed the basket to her other arm. The old white woman shortened the strings of her bag.

Then they were abreast of Nell. They smiled broadly upon her. The old mulatto nodded her head until the brown feather atop her brown bonnet danced like a live thing. The black old woman called out: "Howdy!"

"None of 'em will ever stand what we done stood," floated to Nell, like the refrain of a song, as she waited for the car.

Somehow the passing of those two old women changed Nell's day. For the first time, she noticed that the morning was very bright, the sky was blue and tiny knobs of green were putting out on a tree near by.

"They were so cheery, the dears!" she said of the two old women, and sought to dismiss them. She wanted to think of her own perplexities, but the old ladies insisted upon rising up before her. . . . Their cackling words: "None of 'em will ever stand what we done stood," caused Nell to toss her head defiantly. How could they know, those two. . . . Old issues that they were! Why, she herself had had her share of trouble, and she was but one of a legion of "Young'uns" as they termed them.

Had she not toiled every day except Sundays for five years, denying herself everything save sheer necessities for a chance to enjoy at some future time the heritage of every human creature, love and home and children? Undoubtedly, she had saved a little, her dowry, she called it, but its amount was written in her brain and on her heart. Tolling off their joint income, dollar by dollar, penny by penny, she and Horace together, was a part of their Sunday's routine.

Sundays Nell often said were Horace-days. Horace had Sundays off also, and they spent their one free day together. For the most part they spent the day, planning, making schemes to make their dreams come true. While she had merely worked, Horace had slaved; he had scraped together a sum that matched her own savings and there was a little place up-state where he wished to make their home.

He wanted to marry at once, now that the little place was paid for, but then, Nell countered, when during the long years since they had known they belonged to each other, had he not wanted to do so?

As though some of the glow from the steady flame of his adoration reached out to her, Nell felt her cheeks grow hot.

Suddenly, she knew that it was hard on Horace, harder than upon herself. Black men really had tougher sledding than black women, she thought, tenderly. She loved him so, she communed in her heart. That's why she wanted things; demanded them, those things that later, would insure their peace and contentment in their nest of a home. That's why . . . She checked herself, smiling whimsically at finding herself beginning to use all the arguments that she was wont to use upon Horace over and over to convince him that they must work on and wait a little longer.

Then for no reason at all, two old figures lumbered through her consciousness, glimmeringly like moving shadows on a wall.

One very black and stout old lady, one very stout and white old lady said: "No suh, they'll never come through what we done come through."

"Lord, chile, they couldn't begin to do 't."

Nell tossed back her head and laughed . . . The darling funny old dears!

Aroused from her day-dreams, her slender brown fingers played for a time on the keys of her typewriter, but thoughts of Horace would not down. As the moments sped, her thoughts became laden with foreboding: she decided to call him. It was against the rules, but just this once.

—Employees must not use telephone during working-hours, except emergencies.—

A placard advised her as she dialed. It was an emergency, she concluded grimly. Never before had such warning intuition driven her. Never before had a desire to call to Horace through space tormented her as it did now; never before had longing, intense as pain, made her want to stretch out her arms and encircle him, close to her heart . . .

"Horace Canning has quit the company," an ironic voice informed her over the wire.

"Horace—quit—his—job?" Nell gasped the words foolishly and was restored to sanity only by the sound of the faint click striking into her ear.

She alighted from the car four blocks from home. She had not found Horace, though she had verified the information received by telephone. Horace had given up his job, though, that no longer mattered; she has lost hers too. She had given it up to look for Horace.

She could not avoid seeing the knot of people gathered on the corner. A cursory glance revealed it to be several boys in their teens and younger mingling with the usual motley street-crowd that is attracted willy-nilly to anything that happens. Intent with her own concern she was hastening on when some horrid cataclysm rushed out to

meet her, paralyzing her until sight and sound and feeling swirled
and clashed into one agonizing tempest of emotion that sent her running,
screaming headlong into the crowd. Horace was in the midst of it, a
disheveled funny-looking Horace, but her Horace!

Magically, they made way for her to pass . . . Save for a few taunts—
a prolonged "Boo," "Sic 'em, Sic 'em," "Atta Girl," "Geese"—nothing
was done to hinder her. Presently she was beside Horace, placing
trembling hands upon his shoulder. At her touch, he turned, looked
at her a moment, unknowingly, and announced thickly:—

"I need-sh my girl, hic, but she-sh won't-sh have me!"

Nell's grasp on his shoulder tightened; she shook him furiously . . .
"Horace, oh Horace, how could you? How could you?"

The crowd dwindled away. As for that, Nell had forgotten that
there ever was a crowd. She looked for a taxi. Horace lurched
heavily against her, and asked in ludicrous bewilderment:

"Is-sh you, hic, Nellie by-sh any chanc-sh?"

"Tut, tut . . ." said someone close beside her, with a voice whose
high old cackle dropped through Nell's dismay like a ray of sunlight
into a dark crevice.

"He be your'n honey, your man? queried the voice. Nell knew it
belonged to the old black woman of the morning.

"Take 'im, chile don't you dast to leave 'im, when he needs yo',"
chimed in another quavering old voice.

"Just you take 'im home. A cup of right hot coffee'll fix 'im or a
speck of tomatoes 'will be better."

Without more ado, they were walking together. The trundling gait
of the two old women matching nicely with Horace's unsteady steps.

"'Tis a trouble men folks be," offered one.

"But a sweet trouble 'tis," proffered the other.

"Trouble ain't never harmed nary one of us. What's more, us wimens
can make men folks what us choose to."

"'Deed so! Us 'tis what makes 'em or breaks 'ems."

Then they performed a tempered replica of their high cackling
laughter of the morning. Soon afterwards, they left her, turning off
down the street.

The next day, while Nell sat waiting proudly high-headed looking
straight a-head, she was not certain that these two old ladies had really
joined her. Yet without effort, she could vision the black old woman

in her queer black coat and the old white woman in her brown bonnet and red-knitted sweater. Oddly enough, their high cackling old voices still rang in her ears:

"Trouble ain't never harmed nary one of us," made a tune like a Spiritual . . .

"The idees and the whimsies of these 'ere young 'uns do beat me," was an epitome of the wisdom of old age.

"No suh, they'll never come through what we done come through."

"Lord, chile, they couldn't begin to do 't," was like a skit of Negro comedy and Nell tossed back her head and laughed.

The intangibleness of those two old women enthralled her. Life, too, was like that, Nell mused, made up of intangible veils that became real only as you lifted them one by one, always, to find others and yet others, on and on. Love was one of the veils, so gossamer and fine, so fragile and easily broken. Love was one of life's veils that could never be brushed aside to grasp another. If you dared, once having it, to let it go, it was lost forever. You had to take it when you came to it, but once you caught and held it, it became for all time, a magic carpet.

Horace was coming towards her; tickets were in his hand. The porter was calling their train. Above all the ensuing bustle of departure, she caught the sound of a high, old cackle:

"'Deed so! . . . 'tis us what makes 'em or breaks 'em."

All Aboard!

At last, Horace and she were settled in their seats, on their way to the little place up-state, still short thousands of dollars of what they intended having. But she was glad, oh so glad.

"Happy?" asked Horace suddenly, his arm going around her.

"Happy!" breathed Nell with a great content.

The Mechanical Toy

Jonathan Connors and Haven Addams were friends . . . That is, they were, until the day they fought over a golden butterfly. Such friends, that their friendship attracted the attention of Benjamin Silas Billinger . . . To him, a noted professor, near-sighted and kindly to a fault, an old dreaming sentimentalist, it mattered not, that Jonathan Connors was a black lad and Haven Addams a white one. He adored friendship wherever it was found . . . "Damon and Pythias as sure as I'm alive," he said to himself, whenever he met the two boys on the street, or upon looking up from his work, caught sight of them trudging past his window.

He began to dream of ways to encourage their attachment. "Friendship," he mused. "There is not enough of it in the world . . . friendship must grow." . . . Upon musing further, he was convinced that friendship was not a lasting fabric if woven on the looms of play, without work, or an association that withheld intimacy . . . "In short," said old Billinger, "playing together is nothing more or less than bubbles on the sea of friendship . . . They play always as boys will . . . tut . . . tut . . . tut." He clicked his tongue against his teeth in mild disapproval. "They must work together . . . Then we shall see. . . . We shall see whether the tendrils of their affection has taken root." He squinted his near-sighted eyes thoughtfully, "Yes, they must work together," he decided with finality.

Looking Glass 9 Dec. 1925: 7, 11; 16 Dec. 1925: 7, 11.

Being one of the foremost scientists of his day, he had no difficulty in finding work, pleasant work he fancied, for them to do. He employed Jonathan and Haven to catch butterflies—specimens—he called them, in the field and outlying thickets, down in the old creek-bed and on the hill-sides that guarded the little town, to the west. He agreed to pay them for each insect. If the specimen was large and uninjured in any way, he paid accordingly; while for any that chanced to be mutilated, they received rebuke.

All one summer Jonathan and Haven worked side by side. With the coming of autumn, they gathered a veritable harvest of butterflies, butterflies of every hue and size, and the old professor paid them royally. And had much to do, opening the back windows of his laboratory to release the fluttering captives. He would stand, a benign old gentleman framed in an open window, watching the butterflies which an instant before he had liberally paid for, uncertainly flutter like autumn leaves in a wind to earth, then assured of their freedom, soar upwards, splashes of gay color, living flowers a-sail beneath a twilight sky . . . Old Billinger watching them until they were lost in the fading light would say . . . "Ah, friendship, if only it would be as buoyant, as soaring, as beautiful as that."

To root, friendship needs more than the kindly—if fantastic—assistance of an old gentleman, or does it need less; since no one has yet explored the recess in the heart where friendship grows. For the friendship of Jonathan and Haven came to an end, despite the fact that they toiled together joyously for many, many weeks. What boy is there who would not have enjoyed the headlong leaps from rock to rock in the old creek-bed; the wild scramble up the rough slopes, the race down, the strolls through the wooded places, the long rests under a tree or in some sheltered nook; the lunches eaten together and shared alike; the male's enjoyment of the hunt, even though the game sought were butterflies; and the human love of gain . . . ? Though it was the latter that severed Jonathan's and Haven's friendship.

Jonathan saved his share of their earnings. In his mind was a vision of an industrial school where some day, he would study and learn his chosen work . . . Every penny counted . . . Every penny was needed if ever he attained the desire of his heart; for his widowed mother was poor and he was black.

Haven, having much and knowing that he would have more, squandered his. Finally, he bought a bicycle from a second-hand-dealer; who agreed to take his pay in dribbles as the boy earned it. The entire arrangement being an outcome of one of those strange alliances which a growing, headstrong boy is liable to fall into . . . For the asking, he could have had the pick of any bicycle; but the battered, disreputable object of his own selection was his dearest possession. The former owner, an evil, ill-favored fellow, was pressing him for the final payments now, several days over-due. Here again, Haven could have easily gotten the money from his father, but guided by the unexplainable caprice of youth, he did not choose to do so. Yet, he was greatly troubled over his indebtedness that clear autumn day when friendship ended between himself and Jonathan.

He was out-of-sorts, burdened with his troubles, which he stubbornly nursed in secret. And on the other hand, Jonathan was very, very happy, for his little savings were growing, and if all went well, who could say, what better way of earning money would blossom from his present task . . . On an impulse . . . He told Haven all about his desire . . . How much he had . . . How much he thought he needed . . . What he hoped to do . . . Oh yes, what was it he couldn't do, if . . . Everything, all things did the black lad tell the white one that day. And the white one listened surlily, though unnoticed by his companion; who trusted him greatly.

Then silence fell, while the boys worked . . . Jonathan made swift with happiness was on the trail without pause . . . catching one after another beautiful, shimmering insect. Haven worked slowly, broodingly, with his eyes on other things than his work . . . He caught only a few butterflies and bungled them . . . a broken wing . . . a crushed body . . . was his reward, though he worked himself into a fury. And all the while, he thought about his debt and saw before him the evil eyes of his creditor.

They had separated widely during the chase, but each knew an appointed place where they would meet. Jonathan was already there, waiting, when Haven reached it. And it angered him to see that Jonathan's spoil was great. Added to this, one of his butterflies, a gorgeous golden creature was a beauty . . . Even to their untrained eyes, the butterfly was a specimen, indeed. Haven demanded the insect from Jonathan. And Jonathan surprised and wounded at Haven's belligerent manner, refused . . . .

They quarreled . . . They came to blows . . . These two gawky, adolescent boys, fighting solemnly . . . alone . . . Their battle unwitnessed save by a timid rabbit, that paused in consternation and leaped in terror at the antics of human beings, into a fear-propelled lope which carried him far, far from their vicinity . . . By a flock of crows that cawed noisily high above them and circled and re-circled over them in an effort to make-out what was going on . . . By a score or more butterflies, escaping from confinement, bewildered, to flutter here and there, aimlessly an instant before sailing away . . . Valiantly, they fought and hard . . . Haven the quicker and Jonathan the stronger . . . The blows the former plied in quick succession were offset by the weight and sureness of his opponent's fisticuffs.

But quick of wit even in the thick of battle Haven caught a fleeting glimpse of Jonathan's net . . . Saw that it was empty save for one or two bottom and one of these was the beauty over which they fought . . . In an eye's twinkling he broke from Jonathan. Caught up Jonathan's bag and ran with it, down the winding road . . . swiftly he sped and was swallowed in the distance, before slow-moving Jonathan realized what had happened . . . Overwhelmed with a sudden pain greater than his physical hurt, he started in pursuit. Vowing vengeance in stifled sobs. Determined above all things to recover his stolen treasure . . . On and on he ran but he did not overtake Haven . . .

In truth, before he had covered half the distance, Haven had composed himself, removed as best he could, all traces of the recent fray from his wiry little person . . . and presented himself at old Billinger's laboratory.

As the boys had suspected, the golden butterfly was a magnificent specimen of an almost unknown species . . . At sight of it, old Billinger asked no questions . . . even though it was an unwonted happening for the boys to appear before him singly . . . He was enthusiastic and openly delighted over the golden butterfly. In an abstract manner, he gave Haven a lavish sum . . . and dismissed him . . . And at once, fell to work defining the captive insect . . .

A dreamer he was and the kindest of men, yet first and foremost he was a scientist . . . An ant, a bee, a grasshopper was important enough for him to give many years of his life to study and observation to learn their habits . . . His very soul feasted upon research . . . Now, here before him was a butterfly out of the ordinary . . . Indeed, he had work to do . . .

Then it was that Jonathan burst into the room, disrupting its shadowy quiet like a sudden explosion, disturbing the old gentleman into a startled surprise; which rapidly changed into vexation as he beheld Jonathan's disheveled appearance, and tried vainly to follow his incoherent speech. Then some words he said, clung and served to upset the old gentleman profoundly . . . Jonathan was loudly voicing claim to the rare insect . . . Not wholly released from his recent abstraction, old Billinger recalled that he had already paid someone—supposedly both boys—with wrath more terrible because from one so wildly gentle . . . he rebuked the lad before him, accusing him of lying and cheating . . . And his scathing words were like oil poured into a blaze . . . Jonathan never remembered a single word of his own angry reply . . . Yet it is certain, that the hot-headed youth and the kind old gentleman let ill words fall between them that night.

Old Billinger very much flustered at the end of the occurrence muttered something about the "Cussedness of Negroes," as he returned to his contemplation of the golden butterfly.

Jonathan Connors, susceptible as sculptor's clay and sensitive to a fault suffered because of the happening as one suffers with a painful illness . . . He was never again as carefree nor did he soon forget or forgive Haven Addams' part in his misery . . . For a long, long time, he brooded over it and always vowed to "get even" . . . But like that current which rushes on and on regardless of setbacks and heedless of promptings, caught him up and away from Haven Addams and old Billinger and the incident became submerged in the backwaters of his consciousness, rippling forward only in subconscious moments; when he dreamed of golden butterflies and mighty battles and of friends that never betrayed a trust.

To a little town as like hundreds of other little towns as peas in a pod; except for its far-famed university and its unique mechanical toy-shop, life settled its swirling eddies into a quiet pool for Jonathan Connors . . . And strange as fate itself, life drew Haven Addams into the selfsame pool, while the currents rushed into the channel that led out into the sea for one of the two who had once been friends . . .

Jonathan had not realized his dream . . . Yet his dream, for which in his youth, he had hoarded pennies, had woven itself into his life, revealing itself at every turn and peering out from its hiding place to direct his every act . . . And so instead of being a great mechanical genius, as he had dreamed, Jonathan Connors was the owner of a little mechanical toy-shop . . . Once in a while, some one of the toys that made his shop unique was fashioned by his hands.

Haven Addams was an eminent authority in Science . . . Old Benjamin Silas Billinger who had hired Jonathan and Haven to collect butterflies, had afterwards taken Haven Addams into his laboratory and in a manner had shed his cloak of glory upon the shoulders of his pupil . . . Haven now held a professorship in science in a university whose alumni boasted many master-minds of the present day . . . What he had to say concerning this or that appeared as if by magic in every periodical . . . He was quoted by lecturers . . . His books were the text-books used in unnumbered colleges and schools . . .

He was extraordinarily small of stature and his shock of fine hair was snow-white . . . In many ways, as sometimes, studious men are, he was extremely effeminate . . . A little man of quick and unreasoning impulses, changing moods and varying tempers, given to strange antipathies, burdened with peculiarities which served to antagonize his associates . . . In spite of his wonderful mind, his brilliance and his genius, he was the most unpopular man in the university. His brilliance forced a toleration from his colleagues . . . His uncommon appearance caused him to be sought after by persons unacquainted with his eccentricity . . . But his pupils who saw him as he was, hated him . . .

Half in jest and half in grim earnest a class made up of prankish young men conspired together to play a joke on old (White-head) Addams . . . After a session of good-natured plotting, they resorted to Jonathan's shop of magical toys . . . bent upon purchasing—to use their own parlance—"Some sort of jim-crack that would give the old codger a fright."

They were aware of Haven Addams' habit of going every evening an hour before sundown, for a long walk, which invariably led the same way, along a rather lonely road that wended through a small Negro settlement and ended on the outskirts of the town; where a large low-branching tree stood solidly as if for the sole purpose of preventing the road going further. Here, he would rest probably an hour or more, beguiling the moments with a book or by scribbling learned thoughts upon a pad; which he had brought in his pocket. Always, he brushed the ground around and about him, very, very carefully and peered cautiously here there, and everywhere. Some wit had declared that: "Addams (Old White-head) had been on such intimate terms with bugs that he was afraid of them."

Such were the hints upon which the young fellows hinged their joke . . . Sheer accident or perhaps fate made it correct. For of all Haven Addams' antipathies his aversion to crawling, creeping insects was the greatest. It amounted to such uncontrollable horror that it produced internal disturbances great enough to bring on fainting. And the insect he detested above all others was a spider . . . Long since, he had had the conviction that a spider—a loathsome spider—would somehow cause his death. Like most men, Haven Addams did not want to die. So for that reason, he brushed carefully whatever space he occupied and peered cautiously around and about him.

It was another autumn day, when the little bell—a mechanical device over the door of Jonathan's shop—tinkled merrily and Jonathan's wife, a buxom, pleasant woman, called to her husband: "Come, come quickly . . . The shop is over-full."

Mechanical toys are not best-sellers so Jonathan eked out his income by doing repair work. And his little work-shop was under a tree in his back yard. At times when he was busy, his wife minded the toy shop.

Jonathan came. The young men from the university had come. The university that set on a hill far on the other side of town and further than that in Jonathan's thoughts . . . He scarcely, if ever heard it mentioned and at no time before, had any one from there ventured into his shop. That these came from the university was revealed to him by their conversation . . . They were very young and laughed a great deal and talked overmuch; because youth loves to flaunt itself and is never secretive. They told Jonathan for what purpose they had come . . . "To give an old skin-flint professor a fright." And they wanted it should be the one genuine fright of his life . . . It was their custom to speak of Addams as "old White-head" and they did so now.

Falling into their mood—since few are the men, who entirely shed their prankishness or who never condescend to play a joke; and fewer yet are those who are able to withstand the hilarity of youth—Jonathan put himself to a good deal of bother to oblige them . . . He displayed all his toys . . . Then of a sudden remembered one that was tucked away in a box, waiting for a more opportune season, and went and brought it forth . . . A thing he had designed himself and it could not have been done better.

With the pride of creation lighting his heavy features, Jonathan placed it upon the counter . . . Life-like as life itself an insect leaped, then writhed a moment contracting a leg, extending another . . . then upon several legs which moved together, it began to crawl . . . Creeping, crawling, a huge spider made its way towards the young men . . .

And the young men shouted and bellowed with satisfied glee . . .

"The thing . . . the thing," they cried in unison.

Glowing with pleasure because they were so pleased with his handi-work, Jonathan instructed them how to attach a slender wire fixture to the spider's back . . . Showed them how it would swing life-like, with wriggling legs, when suspended in midair, like a spider swinging from its web.

The young men departed . . . with even more laughter and chaffing and more talking than when they had come . . . Taking advantage of every short-cut, they arrived in quick time to "Old White-head" Addams' resting place. It was a moment's work to climb the tree and swing the mechanical toy fashioned by Jonathan's hands among the branches. Tomorrow, they agreed, they would return to witness "Old White-head's" discomfiture.

But another mind than theirs had planned the denouement.

Haven Addams had been delayed and did not take his stroll at the accustomed time, but loathe to forget it, determined on going never-theless and reached his resting place, a full hour later than usual. . . . He brushed the ground very, very carefully and sat down. . . . It was growing dusk. . . . He peered very, very cautiously about . . . around him . . . behind him . . . before him . . . then upwards . . . his eyes riveted in an upward stare . . . one—two—three—heart-beats in rapid suc-cession . . . one, slow . . . two, slow, slow . . . the third, silence . . .

A breeze stirred the branches of the tree. And the mechanical toy rattled, making a thin metallic sound among the leaves.

Love for Hire

Old Mrs. Goebbles' family noticed with increasing alarm how she doted on the one person who seemed able to relieve her suffering. All in all, it was an appalling situation. Old Mrs. Goebbles, worth her weight in gold, and turning to her help as a sunflower turns to the sun, for sustenance! Hired help, mind you, a colored maid! And supposing Mother Goebbles should in a rash moment, well—just suppose— hasn't many a rash deed been done with a pen and a scrap of paper? Mrs. Goebbles' children were beside themselves with worrying.

Mrs. Andy J. Cooms and Mrs. Heinrich Heine, daughters of the old lady, came and went continuously. Beneath their mother's roof, they spent their time peering into this drawer and that, looking into cupboards, moving the furniture and opening chests. They went about mumbling to one another about silver spoons and china cups.

"Wonder what's become?" one of them would say.

"You don't suppose she gave it to—" the other would gasp incredulously.

"And those napkin rings, the ivy patterned ones?"

"Haven't you found them? But she couldn't have the least use for them." The manner in which Mrs. Cooms said "she" was enough to have scorched the maid.

"What do they talk about?"

Pittsburgh Courier 21 Aug. 1943: 13.

"What, indeed! We shouldn't have allowed this to drift."

The Goebbles' sons, Maurice and Steve, Bernard and Otto, came as often as the girls.

"Just dropped by," they muttered explanatory to each other.

"She's pretty low . . . d'you think?" They always talked in broken phrases, exclaiming, conjecturing.

"Suppose she's written anything?"

"If it's down on paper, our goose is cooked."

"You know . . . meaning, that is, understand don't you, if she's written anything lately."

★ ★ ★

Mrs. Andy Cooms' sharp nose was given to quivering. It quivered now as she said:

"Mother pulled through another night."

Maurice Goebbles, who had not gotten on and looked it, lifted his brows. He was straddle a chair, with his chin on the back of it. With his brows still lifted, he stared impudently at his sister. He always knew just the words to upset her and make her nose quiver more:

"That maid stayed all night, too."

"Mercy on us!" Mrs. Cooms collapsed into a chair.

"Just the maid?" Mrs. Heinrich Heine's voice was always high with offended notes, as if she was always being insulted. "You all knew I couldn't stay another minute away from Heinrich and the children. You could have stayed Steve!"

"O yeah!" Steve was immediately on the defensive. He was not one to have obligations thrust upon him, but it happened that he was not in a mood to quarrel with his sister, so after another repetition of "Oh yeah?" he subsided.

Bernard Goebbles, who had fallen heir to his mother's corpulence, along with her knack of securing things for herself, spoke up:

"I've brought along a nurse. I should've from the first. If I hadn't been in Milwaukee when it started, I'd have sent that maid packing."

"There's no telling what she hasn't done," Mrs. Cooms offered from her chair.

"I can't find those napkin rings, high or low."

"You can stand losing napkin rings," Otto Goebbles spoke darkly, "if mother stopped there."

"How could we've been so thoughtless," moaned Mrs. Heine.

"How were we to know that she was letting that maid twist her around her finger?" parried Steve.

"And her impudence. She's that close-lipped, she drives me mad. You'd think she wasn't the maid, but the Queen of Sheba."

"Just you wait, I'll put an end to her." Bernard waddled back and forth across the floor. "Nobody's maid is going to get between me and mine. I'll send her packing."

"If!" Steve raised his brows and turned his gaze ceilingward.

"Suppose Mother has fixed it so we can't?" Steve's suggestive "if" had brought cold sweat to Maurice's brow. "It's possible, you know." He was shrieking.

"Stop it!" snorted Bernard, waddling faster and faster across the floor. "There's the courts."

★   ★   ★

Unexpectedly, in the midst of great expectation, old Mrs. Goebbles died. The brothers and sisters were crushed. No longer could they endure being in their mother's house; like goats they scattered. Only the newly-hired nurse and the colored maid kept vigil in the silent place.

Nurse Murray was touched by the maid's devotion. Such fealty could spring only from a true and loving heart. While the nurse pondered these things, the maid sat on a couch and wept. Finally, the nurse's sympathy grew so acute she also began weeping.

"Lamb o' God, woman, what you crying fo'?"

Scarcely able to believe her ears, Nurse Murray lowered her handkerchief and lifted her head to meet the red-from-crying eyes of the dusky maid's.

"I asked yo' what yo' crying fo'? You can get yo'self something else as good or better, but me, I ain't never goin' to find another one like this."

Startled into inquisitiveness, Nurse Murray gasped, "What?"

"I ain't goin' to ever find another job like this one. I got five dollars a day here."

. . . G'Long, Old White Man's Gal . . .

"What youalls reckon. . . . what youalls reckon, now?" old Nancy Little, shriveled and black as an aged prune, had just entered Newman's drug store. Newman, himself, lolled against one of his counters and super-intended the black "Sheik" of a fellow in clean white coat and apron who waited to serve Newman's customers. Couples were grouped around two of the little tables. A dark-eyed yellow Miss with her "company," a big shining black lout were perched on high stools at the soda fountain.

Old Nancy looked over her audience gloatingly. She was so little and thin that one wondered what had consumed her. Having attracted the attention of her audience, she walked over to the waiting sheik and mumblingly requested a fifty-cent box of stuff. This done she again inquired in her crackled old voice, "What youalls reckon?"

The audience, there was always one to be had at Newman's, obligingly shook its head and discreetly assimilated keen interest. They knew old Nancy.

"Well, I tells youall," Old Nancy spoke tantalizingly slow. "Some ol' white man's done willed that thar Mercy Kent ah fortune." Envy. It was so patent in her manner that one decided it was envy and envy alone that had eaten her up.

Silence ensued, a murky, smudgy silence in which evil thoughts could breed.

Messenger Apr. 1928: 81–82.

After a while, Newman, himself, condescended from his state of surveying boss to the extent of pooh-poohing old Nancy's statement. She wheeled on him like a startled cat, saying with vehement conviction, "I was right thar when the news come. She's got a legacy I tells youall. Some ol' white man's named her in his will 'n' everythin', and beque'thed Mercy Kent a good sized fortune."

"Uhuh, now what'd I tell yuh?" exclaimed the yellow Miss at the soda fountain.

"Pshaw," laughed her escort sneeringly. "Don't you 'spect I allus knowed it?"

"A leegacy?" inquired one from among the group at a table. "Say, sister, couldn't yuh be mistaken?"

"Humph! Don't youalls start that, young feller; whatever ol' Nancy talks 'bout she's either heerd it, see'd it, or smelt it. Ain't I done told youalls I was thar when the news come?" Here old Nancy dropped her belligerance and spoke confidingly. "Those fool Kents were so brazen they just lets me hear all on it. Some ol' man or nuther named Endlidge—Mr. Endlidge, Mis-ter Endlidge youalls understand done paid youalls high filutin' Miss Mercee Kent for a lots she's done, I reckon. Now youalls can take it or leave it. I done told what I knows. And if it's a lie, youall hear me, the mail what the postman brought and the envelope what was tore open and the paper what was took out the envelope and read right fore these here eyes and the words what these here ears of mine heerd, they's all done lied too."

Old Nancy took up her small packet from off the counter and dropped her fifty cent piece down with a clatter. She hobbled towards the door, then turned and came back. She was like a little black spider in the midst of them, weaving a web with which to catch flies. And the flies, see them, flies will always be caught. "Listen here, them Kents never let us know when this here started now it ain't for us to be runnin' after them when the things ended. I reckons youall know no white man's ain't ever left no black gal somethin' for nuthin'."

At old Nancy's departure the remaining coterie drew closer together.

"Whats I allus told yuh," were the words most rampant. At last, so they surmised, they had the clew to Mercy Kent's high-hat manners.

"Oh no, she don't go with nobody, Oh no, Oh no." All but chanted a slim youth who had been one of the many who felt it was worth Mercy's while to pay attention to himself.

"Deed, ain't this rich? But I allus suspected some such," drawled another.

"Oh brother, little pussy-cat done jumped out the bag."

"Its some reason for being so high and mighty, I'll say."

"It's your high sailing kite what gits tangled up in the telegraph wires."

"That's cold, feller, nuthing but bombs explode."

"Go way, Bud, this here is one of Lindy's planes that's gone and punctured her wings."

"Say, I heerd th' crash."

"Didja?"

Old Nancy hobbled along with unwonted speed. Soon, she reached Brothels, the green grocers'. Pete Brothel the proprietor was a fat, pig-eyed, greasy, salacious gentleman of color. He hailed Nancy's gossip with loud-mouthed laughter that made his fat shoulders billow and shake. "Well yes," he ejaculated, "Well yes."

"So the bile's busted right in th' ol' hen. . . . well yes." He leaned far over a fruit stall to wag a pudgy finger in old Nancy's face, then he winked an eye meaningly and slipped a slobbery tongue around his lips by way of preparing for further discourse. A necessary but an inopportune and transient customer came in, whereupon old Nancy having other places to go darted out, grimacing with unctuous satisfaction as she went for she knew that greasy Pete would do his bit towards spreading the gossip after his own foul fashion.

The Kents were not popular among their neighbors, for Welsh street demanded free and easy manners of all its habitues. It welcomed display; it encouraged ostentation, it lauded opulence; but it fully and decidedly resented and denounced what it called, "Airs."

Long since, the Welsh streeters had attached "Airs" to the name of Kents. The Kents lived in the white and green cottage at the end of the street. White and green mind you, when all the other nondescript houses on Welsh were drab greys and ugly duns. There were many grievances piled onto the account that was stacked against them such as screened doors and windows and of all unheard of airs a screened-in back porch. Neat flower beds in their front yard, and not a singly scraggly chicken to peck a livelihood at their back door, and when all the neighborhood youngsters had wallowed at will in the dusty street the Kent young one in stiffly starched gingham and ribbon bows in her hair had spent her time among the flower beds, playing "a'leery" with her rubber ball or mimicking grown-ups with her dolls and china tea-set. Or "airs" untold, Sarah Kent, mother, the unpardonably guilty one with her "yaller" face and straight hair had taken the small though albeit stout and stumpy Mercy by the hand and gone off walking, strutting scandalously down the length of Welsh street, looking neither to the right or to the left but dividing her attention between her small daughter who clung to one hand and to the gay red parasol which she held carefully over herself with the other. The neighbors said it was because she feared black; they joshed each other about it, and declared that they could mark the seasons by watching Sarah Kent for all summer long, the red parasol, and when the shrill winds blew, Sarah left off the parasol and adopted veils to shield her complexion. When grown older, Mercy went off to school, and upon her return the Welsh street youths had never quite dared to approach her. True, they delighted to group them-selves on the corner and look her over. The more intrepid ones made remarks at ear-shot distances, but something in Mercy's manner piqued them. They couldn't say that she did not notice them, because she did. She looked at them impersonally from wide-set eyes with a cool tolerant stare that ruffled them amazedly, nor could they explain just how she made them feel except by shrug of shoulder and dis-gruntled "humph."

Old John Kent, father, had been employed up town for a good many years—"'snooping' 'round Buckram white-folks," Welsh street said. How-be-it, he earned enough to foot the bills for all the "airs" his folks put on. He had grown old in the performance of simple service; he had aided any fellow-man who needed his assistance. To him, it had seemed neither strange or unfitting to reach out a helping hand to Pat Endlidge when Endlidge, a white man, had slumped beneath successive loads of hard-luck. He had considered Endlidge's fervent promises to pay back, double fold just so much chaff threshed out from his field of fertile service. Moreover, as for being paid, Old Kent imagined that his white and green cottage, his flower-beds, and his women-folk were recompense enough for anything he had ever done or might ever do. To partake of one of Sarah's dinners after a hard day's work; to sit back, deep in his old arm-chair, listening to Mercy's tinkling touch upon the piano keys. He had long thought that he wished for nothing else.

Then like a long-in-coming boomerang, a letter bringing the information that Patrick Endlidge after twenty-five years had kept his promise. It was something to thank God for and to be proud of. It proved many things which had smouldered down in the red glow of kindliness in old Kent's heart:—that now and then, white folks did remember the hand that fed. . . . that bread cast on the water does come back. . . . that the righteous—not that he set himself up as being so righteous, but he tried to be—was never forsaken and his seed would never beg.

"God a' mighty, God a' mighty. . . . now Mercy need not beg!" Like a revelation it came to him, that all along he had wanted money, money, money, that all along he had been worrying over what he was going to leave behind for Mercy. He thought with warming chuckles of delight how Patrick Endlidge had put one over on him, repaid him one thousand-fold. A gift to himself would have been alright, but no, Endlidge, the crook, had reached further than that. He had given to Mercy, his child, his little old gal, his Mercy.

There was rejoicing within the little white and green cottage, the sort of joy that bubbles over the rim and splashes down the sides, and makes little puddles about the bottom of the bucket and eventually forms into little rivulets to run here and there and everywhere.

The Kents thought gleefully that it had been propitious that old Nancy the neighborhood gossip had been there to share their news. They wondered in innocent merriment what folks would say. . . .

Sarah who had secretly bemoaned that her daughter Mercy at twenty-eight was yet unmarried, immediately re-lit her hopes. Money— how sweet the thought—would conceal her daughter's shortcomings like smoke does flame. Who could care now, that Miss Mercy Kent was a roly-poly, that her features were blunt, and her complexion swart or that her none too luxuriant hair was stubby and kinky, and that Mercy for all her usual good-nature was too stubborn or too lazy—Sarah could not decide which—to resort to cosmetics or to submit to the hair-dresser's art of pressing her crinkly locks into rigid straightness.

From the instant, that she knew of her "luck" Mercy had been in a dream, a veritable daze of pleasure that enwrapped her. To think of having more money than she had ever imagined. To think she could go places, some place, maybe, that would be more friendlier towards her than Welsh street. Yes, they would all go, go somewhere and start all over. No. That could not be; it would break her parents' hearts to pull up and leave this spot of their choice. It was funny, she thought, how black people became rooted to the soil like stumps, and besides, her father and mother were old, so old they did not sense their neighbors' hostility or perhaps they had grown hardened to it. Leastway, they did not mind the ostracism which Welsh street levelled upon them. Although—her sudden good fortune was softening her heart—perhaps, she herself was too critical of Welsh street. She would stay, that's what she would, among these people whom she had always known. Stay among them and spend her wealth with them and on them and for them. They were her people, she too was a stump rooted in this soil.

Unnoticed by either Sarah or John, she slipped out of the house. She wanted to walk, an urge beset her to wander among the old familiar surroundings of Welsh street with its ramshackle houses, and its wallowing youngsters, and its idling youths, and its loitering grown-ups. She went briskly in the rolling gait that was hers. Her heavy breasts jostling with each step, her hips rippling beneath the folds of her skirt, her trim ankles and small feet catching the eye almost forcibly. Though she was unaware of it, her head sat at a haughty angle, and bobbed slightly as she walked as the head of a spirited horse does.

She was thinking about the money that would be hers, when some unkempt youngsters suddenly sprang up before her and scudded away. She laughed at their sudden flight, never once, suspecting that she was the cause of it, and instantly decided that it would be nice to use some of her legacy to build a play-ground for the youngsters on Welsh street. Supposing, so ran her thoughts, she would take in that vacant lot out by Simmons, and fix it up, swings, and slides, and. . . .

Of a sudden, she was aware of Newman's, and as usual, it swarmed with black folk. A victrola screeched "blues." Mercy could see into the store, and across to the soda-fountain as she approached. Two couples sat before the counter smirking at her disdainfully. As she drew in front of the entrance, a slim black youth in spotless attire sauntered out, rudely crossing before her, and without lifting his cap, he met her eyefully, and spat.

Above the waves of laughter that rushed at her, loud flung words struck her, sinking like lead in deep water, down, down, into her heart. . . . "G'long ol' white man's gal."

Instinctively, Mercy's chin gifted, and her head bobbed a trifle faster, the rippling of her hips beneath her skirts became a bit more marked just for the interval of her passage before Newman's. Then, as she reached the corner, she staggered like a wounded beast, fighting to stand on her feet, fought desperately, before plunging head-long down the street for the haven of a white and green cottage.

Phoebe and Peter up North

Phoebe and Peter had come with the first avalanche of eager wide-eyed Negroes to answer the call of the North.

Oh, isn't there something about people; who play the game fair; who take what comes and wrestle with it to victory or defeat that makes you long to grasp their hands and cry, "My brethren!" Phoebe and Peter played the game that way and this is just one little move they made on the checker board called life.

They landed in a big Northern city in September and before the first snow fell, Peter had launched full-fledged into the ways of the city. He dressed the part, acted the part, and very nearly overdid the part. But Phoebe still remembered the old home down South. She dressed the part of good, staid, a-way-down-South-colored matron. She acted the part and also almost overdid the part.

Peter used to say, "Honey can't you fix your hair like the ladies do up here?"

And Phoebe used to answer: "I'm not going to stretch and pull *and grease and burn out my hair, hear me, Pete?*"

To which Peter used to respond patiently, "I can't say how they do it, Honey, but it looks mighty nice, their heads do."

Phoebe cried ever and ever so often, as often as Peter asked her about her hair. Tears you know cannot be hidden. It is real funny how they

Half-Century Magazine Feb. 1919: 4, 10.

sag the cheeks, darken and inflate the nose, and make eyes weak and watery. Her tears weighted her down, consequently Phoebe didn't stay even as pretty as she was.

She did not look pretty to Peter when tired and hungry he came home from the foundry. Between the conflicting forces of fatigue, hunger and ugliness, Peter was a cross man. To think of seeing pretty women, thick as daisies in a field at every turn, until you get home, and there to find an ugly one. Why this would make a discordant note in heaven!

Peter began to delay his coming. He tried standing on the street corners or loitering in the parks, marking off the prettiest woman from among the merely pretty ones. That attracted him as an alluring game and you know it grows upon one like a taste for olives. So it made Peter a disciple. At times he skipped dinners and suppers and came home in the "wee small hours" of the morning, just in time for an early breakfast.

Phoebe quarreled and Peter quarreled, so they both quarreled. They quarreled and quarreled until Peter told Phoebe this:

"You can take a girl out of the country, but you can't take the country out of the girl, that's why you and I can't get on. You are chuck full of country. You won't dress and you won't look pretty. You are— you're—you'r—." He searched his vocabulary for something fitting to say, then burst out with, "You are a thorn in my side, that's what you are." He slammed the door behind him to drown out Phoebe's sobs.

This happened in the morning and the noon hour found Peter still angry, so he spent his time down town with the boys and ate a solitary sandwich over a lunch counter. But during the afternoon, when nothing could be heard but the sizzle and buzz of machinery—which is silence to the foundry worker—his thoughts stole back to Phoebe. He remembered how pretty she had looked to him in another setting, in old Jenkin's cotton field where they had met, under the vivid blue of a Southern sky.

In memory, he saw again the fields of cotton, beautiful as newly fallen snow enhanced by glowing warmth and living green, and Phoebe's laughing face above it; her nimble fingers picking cotton faster than all the other hands; her skirts played with by the wind and showing her slender ankles; her strong young body poised erect despite its heavy load. He recalled how his blood boiled the first time he saw her in the field. It was then and there that he had vowed to take her from it and give her all the pretty things women yearn for. Over and over he had repeated to himself, "I'll love her forever and forever," and now he had called her, his own dear little Phoebe, a "thorn in his side."

The hours dragged until quitting time. On his homeward way, he bought her candy at the first confectioner's, and fruit clustered prettily in a basket from a vender on the street. He paused once to look at some beautiful, ermine in a window and felt in his pocket, sadly wishing it were pay-day. He hastened on, never stopping until he turned in at his own gate.

He pushed on the door; it was locked. This was something strange, he thought, as he fumbled in his pocket for his key. Finally, the door was opened and he was inside—but no Phoebe was there.

He placed the little packages carefully upon the table and looked about him, as he recalled, how back at home, Phoebe used to jump out at him with her face wreathed in smiles from behind doors and other hidden corners, but a moment's expectant wait told him that hoping for such now was useless.

He went into the next room and there found, spread on the table where his supper was invitingly laid, a note. It read:

"Dear Peter:—I won't stay with you to be a thorn in your side. Good bye, Phoebe."

Peter dropped down disconsolately in a chair and buried his face in his hands. He smiled wanly as he went over the words of the note. How like Phoebe they were, his own, dear, high-spirited Phoebe, who wouldn't eat bread that she thought was given without welcome.

One, two, three days swept by, then a week, two weeks and still Phoebe did not return. Peter wandered the streets most of his spare time, only now, he was there for a purpose. Grimly he strode about, watching, watching, scanning every passing face with the hurt look of a collie in his straining eyes.

Then one evening when it would have been dusk, had not the city lights kept springing up one by one and in clusters, here and there and everywhere, in brilliant illumination, Peter glimpsed a woman—

blooming, well-poised woman with very slender ankles. Her crowning glory was a head of hair. She was gone in the crowd, however, before the truth flashed over him that it was Phoebe—Phoebe—his own Phoebe.

Phoebe cried and cried after Peter left her; but his words were too stinging not to bring forth action. He had called her "countrified." She vowed that he should see. She gathered up some papers and searched their want ads for something that she might do. Like most gentle folk, Phoebe was a little wasp in action. Presently, she arose from her task and began to rummage in her wardrobe. She chose her most becoming dress, then remembering painfully about her hair, she sat down before her mirror, determined to do it up. She placed her hat carefully upon her head. When it was done, she caught up one of the papers and hurriedly slipped away a portion of it, putting it securely into her handbag and hurried out.

All the working force at the Bell-worth Hotel paused for a moment, as their manager strode pass them, followed by a slender and some-what doughtily clad, little Colored woman, and disappeared with her behind the doors of Bell-worth's spacious pantries.

"Can't be the candy artist's helper?" was the question conveyed by each raised eyebrow.

Contrary it was so. Besides the art of picking cotton, Phoebe's tapering and nimble fingers could ply a needle deftly, but their real aptitude lay in molding, molding any plastic thing into any shape or form her fancy willed. She had made mud-dolls and mud-furniture, when a child; while her playmates had struggled with the intricacies of plain mud-pies. And once down South she had filled a white girl's place for a week, making sugar roses and frosting cakes. This was her meagre store of knowledge. No object looms up so large that it cannot be overcome if we are determined to overcome it.

Monsieur Jacques Adonis watched the only one who had called in answer to his advertisement, for five minutes as she busied herself converting a shapeless lump of candy-syrup into a silver butterfly, before he spoke:

"You'll do: your pay starts at once; help me make these tulips for tonight."

Phoebe, an exulting Phoebe, stole into their apartment at five o'clock, one whole hour before Peter would come. She saw with dismay that he had not been in to dinner and then rebellion, born of independence, sprang to the surface. Though tired from her new employment, she flew about preparing something to eat for the man of her choice. While supper was cooking, she gathered a few belongings into a small valise, wrote the note and placed it where it could be found; and once more set out, this time to find a lodging place. In this she was successful, entirely so, because she found a room next door to Mayme.

Mayme Wilson was city through and through. Her coiffure showed it, her figure revealed it, her gait proclaimed it; and her speech was the essence of a city's slang. She was the most expert of all the hair-dressers at Jaynes and Hendricks Parlors.

Phoebe and Mayme became friends or as friendly as two so widely differing beings could be. It was the motive which causes a great big dog to stand motionless while he is being inspected by a very, very small one, that made Mayme kind to lonely little Phoebe. And Phoebe worshipped Mayme because she was all the things from head to foot that Peter had found wanting in her. She meant, oh, how she meant to learn of this glorious creature.

Mayme had a way of throwing the weight of her body back upon one foot, then thrusting out the other in a manner to show off its pretty curved instep, and of placing her slim bands upon her slender hips, while dropping sweet crumbs of wisdom from her painted lips for the enlightenment of Phoebe.

"No, kiddie, don't straighten your hair. It's already ready got the very wave that most of these old Janes around here would die for. Now, kitten, take it from me, be the wise Virgin, always do your hair low—that's your style. Listen, honey-bug, a man's loony, you've got to bluff him. You can't be easy. Don't wear your heart on your sleeve, hide it, keep him guessing, get me, Hon?"

Thus it was that two weeks of nightly lecturings from Mayme and two months of pleasant lucrative employment found Phoebe a changed Phoebe. Her hair was worn in a way that Mayme could no longer scoff at. It would surely delight Peter. Her clothes had style and they were worn with a graciousness that was inborn.

In the meantime Peter had spent two dreary months. He no longer walked the streets but spent his evenings at home, in loneliness and bitterness. The thoughts: "Where could Phoebe be? What is Phoebe doing?" haunted him like bitter memories; pursued him like phantoms in the night and crushed him like terrible weights. It came dreadfully to him that wherever she was, whatever she was doing he had driven her to it.

He imagined all sorts of dire things befalling his poor "countri-fied" (he still called her that), gentle, timid Phoebe. It took the taste for food from his mouth; and sleep away from his eyes; but he worked harder at the foundry and was promoted to a better position.

Phobe's mirrors revealed the improvement in herself, but her heart yearned to have Peter see it also and tell her of it in his own pictures-que way. She wanted him despite Mayme's "super-wise" advice.

"Don't you hunt him up. Don't you do it, let him find you. Take it from me don't be E-Z. That's a girl."

Such conversations were beginning to end lamely thus: "But Oh, Oh, Oh, he'll never, never find me." Then a hasty shutting of a door and poor Phoebe would evolve out of her tearful state to find herself alone, no Mayme in sight.

It was one evening when she came in at five. It was one whole hour before Peter's quitting time, that she entered her lonely room, filled with genuine disgust. And how she did want Peter! She wanted to cook his supper, to prepare his favorite dishes. She thought of the little nut cakes he liked so much; she smiled in memory of the vast numbers he could demolish. Then like a flash, came the conclusion that she was going home to make him some in reality.

Mayme from the next room called: "That you, honey? Come in here."

Phoebe answered, as she hurriedly stuffed some things into a bag: "Can't dear, I'm going home."

"*Home!*" A door flew inwards and a disgusted Mayme in a bright red kimona, stood framed therein saying stridently: "*You Boob!*"

Phoebe was already out of hearing. Peter's lagging footsteps threat-ened to fail him altogether as he entered the hallway. His eyes flitted along the passage and he saw that his own door was a-jar. Could it—could it possibly be Phoebe; but who else could it be?

He ventured to enter and sure enough Phoebe—his Phoebe, a radiant Phoebe was there. There was a rapturous moment of laughter and tears and kisses all intermingled. Then Peter with masculinity asserting itself asked:

"Where have you been?"

Phoebe told everything she knew. Suddenly assimilating a well-known pose, with one foot back supporting the weight of her body, and with one foot front thrust out to show its prettily arching curve, with arms akimbo, with her hands on her slender hips; she quoted glibly stolen words from Mayme:

"And believe me, I'm the only lady of Color on my job; the only one in my line. Why, Pete, I'm helper to the best candy artist in this old town—get me?"

But Peter being just a mere man could not see, he couldn't grasp the importance of Phoebe's employment. All he could sense was that his homing mate was about to fly, his drab, little housewife was spreading her wings. His male instinct cried out, "Beware," and a cold wave made a pathway of his spine; until some occult intuition, his guardian angel maybe, caused him to say these words:

"Listen, little girl, you can't work down there. We've enough money now to start on that little home you wanted, out in the suburbs."

Then not too sure of himself, he added:

"You used to want it, sweetheart, don't you yet?"

"Oh! Peter, dear Peter!" Then remembering Mayme's advice, not to carry her heart upon her sleeve, she stopped midway, poised herself with that lady's favorite pose—flung up her rounded chin and said:

"I'll be the only lady on my job. I'll have the homerule in my hands. Why, I'll be helper to the best old scout on earth, Mr. Peter Nettleby."

And with a hidden heart or not, Phoebe found herself cuddled closely in Peter's arms, his lips upon hers.

Phoebe Goes to a Lecture

Tell you, Kitten, you come with me next Friday," said Mayme to little Phoebe, as they sat together in the latter's cozy sitting-room.

"Get this straight, Hon, you're staying too close. It's the ticket, maybe, to always stay to-home and run your household ship-shape—but take it from me, kid, it's killing. I would not do it. Why, Hon, a gold man couldn't take all my joy out of life. Now, listen to me, doll-up your prettiest Friday and come in to town. I'll be at Donald's sharp at two for ices you know, then we will beat it to the Wise Acres' Women's Club-rooms. There's going to be a lecture and I'm the appointed queen, Kid, who has to attend to boost up trade for Jaynes and Hendricks Beauty Parlors. All I have to do is slip 'em over some especially printed cards—some swell they are too—we figure on getting some mighty paying trade. All you got to do is once get your intellectual doll-babies headed for beauty, Kid, and they make a home-run every time.

"Say is it a go?" she wound up a bit breathlessly to gaze scrutinizingly at Phoebe.

Phoebe sat listlessly beside the open window, the sewing in her lap forgotten.

Half-Century Magazine June 1919: 6.
Preface to the original: "In the February issue of the magazine Phoebe and Peter left their home in the sunny South and came North to take advantage of the many opportunities for members of the race in big northern towns. Most of our readers wanted to know more about them and their life in the North, and here they are with us again."

"Why yes, I suppose so," she agreed as she turned to face her friend somewhat languidly. "Peter was saying this morning, that he thought I should go out more, but Oh, dear," she sighed, "this place is so large Mayme and I do not know the people and most of them I meet are so distant and unfriendly. I'd rather stay at home. You see I love my flowers and my book, and haven't you noticed, I am collecting copies of famous paintings, it's such fun to get them and read up on the lives of their painters."

Mayme's assent to this was a dismal "grunt," then she added: "I think you've a twinge of homesickness, honey-bug, but you'll outgrow it. Magnolia blossoms and sunny weather are pow'ful fine I'll admit, but I'll take the North and snippy-snappy city-life for mine—see? Gee-ee, I'm overstaying my time," as she spoke, she was up, and rapidly gathering her belongings, prepared to go. She darted towards Phoebe impulsively, pecked a kiss upon her cheek and patted her shoulder affectionately "You are down in the dumps, Kitten, but meet me Friday. That's a girl." And so saying she hurried away.

"I declare," murmured Phoebe, "Mayme is a real tonic—what would I do in this lonesome place without her?" Then wonderingly, she thought: "Dear old Peter, what would he do if he really knew how dreadfully homesick I am. It's a shame, too," she thought contritely, "everything here is so different, so uplifting, it's inspiring just to be here, and down home," she pressed her lips tightly; as she thought pityingly of the friends—"down home."

"I am a goose," she said the words aloud uttering them vehemently— wholly absorbed with her thoughts.

Tut-tut, I don't think so," returned Peter. He stood in the doorway regarding her roguishly.

Phoebe, startled, sprang from her seat, then laughing ran to him flinging her arms about his neck.

"How on earth did you get in without me hearing you?"

"Easy enough while you were busy calling yourself names," retorted Peter. "How long have you known you were a goose and how does it feel?" he teased.

"That's my secret," rejoined Phoebe. "Guess who's been here."

"The Mayor's wife," responded Peter in mock surprise.

"Guess again."

"Nix," laughed Peter, "I met Mayme on the corner—gave me a raking over about you, said I ought to see that you got a little diversion—

bet me a dollar to a doughnut I'd find you crying right where she had left you—that's why I slipped in—the old girl owes me a dollar—I'll make her pony up too," he declared, relishing the outcome of their goodnatured wager.

"But see here, little girl, aren't you happy?" His gay manner changed instantly to one of honest concern; as he drew Phoebe into his arms and turned her face to his, that he might search her eyes.

"Why, of course, I am, Peter—but—," Phoebe's mouth trembled perceptibly. "I am a goose, Peter, just as I said awhile ago because there are times that I can't help thinking about our old home. I seem to smell the flowers and I see old Aunt Susan and Uncle Alex and all the youngsters. Why, I even miss the cotton-fields and I seem to ache for the warmth and friendship that we left behind us. I long for the smiles and the "howdies" that everyone used to give me as I passed along the street—and here—oh, Peter, everything is so strange and so unfriendly."

Peter's arms tightened about her, for he too had felt; but kept hidden, the mighty tugging of his heartstrings for the old home and the old environment so full of good-humored friendliness; which all the limitations and restrictions put upon his race could not smother. It was there, say what you would, the open hand and the open heart of friendship, a blessed thing, grown luxuriant among his oppressed people, back there in the sunny Southland.

"You can forget it all in time, sweetheart, only," he added soberly, "we don't want to forget, do we little girl? We are going to hold on to our pleasant memories as we would to sacred things, but there are unpleasant memories too—hateful ones, Phoebe, and they are the ones that are going to make us hold on here and keep us here. No! We must never forget, neither the good or the bad, for together, they are the chains that bind us to the path we are started on. We've got to live and make a way for others—the little ones—our little ones maybe, and down there, girl, we can't even have the chance."

Phoebe's arms were flung upward now to encircle Peter's neck; as solemnly they stood oppressed by the weight of color; but dauntless, determined to surmount it.

★   ★   ★

Friday came. It was a clear day, warm and sunny. The scent at budding things and the fragrance of newly upturned earth was everywhere, for in the city, little plots of ground were already spaded up for planting—thanks to the high cost of living.

Phoebe inhaled the balmy air joyously as she went along Broad Street. It was almost two, and she knew Mayme was even then waiting for her at Donald's. "Dear, kind Mayme, is always as punctual as the old clock, in the city hall back home," thought Phoebe happily.

"Oh, you doll," sang Mayme gaily as Phoebe entered Donald's exquisitely appointed ice-cream parlor. Donald, himself the brown and dapper little proprietor ushered her to Mayme's table.

"I second the motion," put in Gordon Moss rising from a seat beside Mayme to greet Phoebe cordially, while Roscoe Donald's eyes implied that he thought the same.

"Oh, Gordon," exclaimed Phoebe delightedly. "Mayme, didn't say you would be here too."

"Why, his real name is Goatee Buttinsky," drawled Mayme. "Can any one tell just when a goat decides to butt? Oh, no," she answered her own query drolly. "You never know until he has landed the butt."

"If that's the way you feel," replied Gordon dolefully, "I'll leave." He began to rise but was restrained by a deft move on the part of Mayme.

"Oh, no you don't, not on your life. You talk to that waiter!" she ordered threateningly.

Gordon laughed and settled himself comfortably in his chair, pleased as he always was, to be commanded by the sparkling, audacious Mayme.

Half an hour later Phoebe and Mayme were on their way to the Wise-Acre Women's Club. The lecture-hall was spacious and Phoebe found herself in a maze of women—big ones, chubby, fat, and slender ones, women manicured and tailored, business-like and militant, be-spectacled and lofty-browned; but in all that throng of women, Phoebe herself, was the only woman there belonging to the time-honored school of home-loving wives.

Now and then, she caught glimpses of Mayme in her place near the entrance standing there so alert, so busy, distributing the little cards, one after another to the ever gathering horde of women.

Presently an exceedingly aggressive looking spinster mounted the platform, and instantly, the buzzing of many subdued voices ceased, as if by magic, there was quiet.

The lady before them was Doctor Patty Pugh, the foremost and most accurate authority on birth-control known.

Ah, and she could talk. Her sonorous voice made itself heard, and felt in every corner of the vast room; and besides she was such an ardent devotee to the science she was eulogizing.

Phoebe felt that it was indeed a heinous crime to be a mother. Also, she thought by the determined quirk that sat upon more than one mouth, that few indeed would be guilty of the grave offense among those present.

She wished she had not come. Was this the sort of lectures women attended? How different to her old home training wherein, maternity had been upheld as woman's crowning glory, and little ones as the Lord's anointed.

She was glad when she was outside. Glad indeed, when Mayme threaded her way painstakingly to her side and cleverly maneuvered a way out of the crowd and into a quiet side-street, where they could talk alone leisurely.

Mayme watched her amusedly; finally asking, "How'd you like the speel, Kitten?"

"Gracious, it was horrid," blurted Phoebe earnestly.

"D'ye think so? Oh, well it's good food for thought. You've got to go some to refute all that old lady-quack's arguments, now don't you? Own up."

"Yes," faltered Phoebe.

"Alright then," exclaimed Mayme. "Honey-child, that's why I urged you to come, not that I thought you'd enjoy that especially, but get out, see with your eyes and hear with your ears, and give your brains an airing. That's what city life is for, to put the "*pep*" in living. You don't need to think other people's thoughts. Think up your own; but you can't think looking inside yourself. You've got to look out. Do you get me? Then you won't have time for such nonsense as loneliness."

"What a dear, dear friend you are," cried Phoebe.

They had stopped at their place of parting while a jitney drove up to the curb.

"Bye-bye," chirped Mayme gaily and her sparkling eyes beamed lovingly upon Phoebe an instant before the door of the car swung shut.

"Good bye," sang Phoebe, and then, quite contentedly snuggled back among the cushions to gaze out upon the broad smooth road; which led to home and Peter.

Part II

Poems

Hands

Gnarled and knotty,
Iron-wrought hands,
Fashioned for the spade and plow,
Padded hard in calloused flesh
To rescind the spring of steel,
Hands . . . his, yours . . . mine,
Old black working-man's hands!
They wielded an ax felling trees
In new country
They have tilled the soil of an alien land.
They have builded a house in an unfriendly habitat.
   Slender and lovely,
   Musical hands,
   Dusky in hue, fluttering over ivory keys
   Like a raven's wings;
   Do raven wings make music,
   Beating their way through inescapable air
   Mounting higher?
Hands, brown as snuff,
Wash-tub hands,
Curled like claws from clutching and squeezing

Beatrice M. Murphy, ed., *Ebony Rhythm: An Anthology of Contemporary Negro Verse* (New York: Exposition P, 1948) 50.

Heavy wet garments.
Water-soaked, sudsy, rheumy, old hands—
    Only when they are folded thus
    In the quiescent pose of death
    Are they stilled.

Impressions from a Family Album

Grand-Pap

Grand-Pap was very old,
When this was struck. So old!
But he could recollect . . .
The way 'twas told
That Annie was the p'utt'est gal
On ol' Marse Tom's plantation,
And Annie was his mammy.
   'Could recollect . . .
How he was allus kept
To wait 'pon ol' Marse Tom
To shoo off flies, while ol' Marse slept
And when ol' Marse woke
Go fetch his pipe and bring his book
And mix the mint-julep . . .
   'Could recollect . . .
The w'uppin's, Marster gin him
'Lowing fo' to teach him how to show
The proper 'spec's where 'spec's were due . . .
Lawsy! Ol' Marster sure insisted

Crisis Feb. 1930: 56.

197

Wid a great big strop
That he say:—"Thank-ee, Yessuh . . .
Yessuh, Thank-ee", in de proper way.
    'Could recollect . . .
The w'uppin's sure enuff
And all the times he said:—
"Thank-ee," and cussed ol' Marster . . .
Underneath his breaf.

★   ★   ★

Old Praying Sue

My man is black . . .
God . . . You alone, know why.
Shed but one briny tear
For all the drops of sweat
That fall from off his brow
Merciful God . . . mark one little smile
That wreaths his trembling lips
See but the mite of faith and courage
In his eyes . . .
That I might learn with blest humility
Even though, my man is black
It is not he, but Christ
They crucify.

★   ★   ★

Melissa—Little Black Girl

DOLLY, my dear . . .
A kind lady gave you to me
I'm grateful too . . . 'um, yes.
    'Cause you're pretty and sweet
    And you're dressed up neat.
But I don't love you . . . I positively don't . . .
    'Cause the man that made you
    Gave you long flaxen hair.

And God made me . . . But look at my hair.
The man that made you, didn't put any feel
Inside your cold little breast.
He left the feel out
From your head to your heels,
But he gave you blue eyes, instead.
Now suppose you were me . . .
Oh . . . my doll-baby Rose . . .
And you knew how it felt
To be lonely and black
And I . . . just sat on a chair
And gave you . . . a cold stare . . .
Wouldn't you . . . give my head
A hard whack . . . Just like that!

Oh . . . oh . . . My dolly . . .
   My doll-baby Rose . . .

*   *   *

Jim—A Weary Traveler

I been a weary traveler
But I ain't goin'er be no more . . .
I'm 'bout to take my chance at lovin'
'Cause my heart tells me to.
I been a weary traveler
But I ain't goin'er be no more.
When a man's dry, he wants licker
When he's weary, he takes his rest.
When he finds a sweet woman . . . .
To please her . . . he tries his best.

*   *   *

Little Samson—Philosopher

Some white folks are anglers
   They throws the bait . . .

Some white folks are fishes
   They swallows bait.
Us, black folks?
   Go 'long, don't bother me.
     We is bait.

Portraiture

Black men are the tall trees that remain
Standing in a forest after a fire.
   Flames strip their branches,
   Flames sear their limbs,
   Flames scorch their trunks,
   Yet stand these trees
   For their roots are thrust deep
   In the heart of the earth.
Black men are the tall trees that remain
Standing in a forest after a fire.

Crisis June 1931: 199.

Idle Wonder

My cat is so sleek and contented;
   She is a real house-cat
She has not seen any other cat
Since she came to live with me.

   I wonder does she think,
   I wonder does she dream
   I wonder does she ever imagine
   Herself out, among cats
   I wonder is she like poor Agnes

Agnes lives with the white folks
And they think she is contented
And actually delighted with being
   Their house-maid.

Opportunity May 1938: 150; *Reason for Singing* (Prairie City, Ill.: Decker P, 1948).

The Shining Parlor

It was a drab street
   A white man's street . . .
   Jammed with automobiles
   Streetcars and trucks;
Bee-hived with fruit venders' stalls,
   Real estate concerns, meat shops,
   Dental clinics and soft drink stands.

It was a drab street
A white man's street . . .
But it held the shining parlor—
A boot-black booth,
   Commandeered by a black man,
   Who spent much time smiling out
Upon the hub-hub of the thoroughfare.

Ever . . . serenely smiling . . .
With a brush and a soiled rag in his hands.
Often . . . white patrons wait for
Their boots to be "shined"
   Wondering the while
   At the wonder—
Of the black man's smile.

Crisis Sept. 1929: 302.

Black Faces

I love black faces:
   They are full of smouldering fire,
      And Negro eyes . . . white . . . with white desire,
      And Negro lips so soft and thick,
         Like rich velvet within fine jewelry cases.
I love black faces.

Opportunity Oct. 1929: 320; *Ebony Rhythm* 51.

America Negra

I am Indian;
I am grown old
Huddled beside sand dunes
Cradled in the lap of a plateau.
Cacti my shade,
Sky and land,
Land and sky,
The sky is clear as a mirror,
But the land is a painted desert;
Many the pictures I see there.
I am weary of seeing them. . . . . . .
Mirages of misery.

I am Irish and Scotch and Welsh,
Islands of rock,
Islands alone in the ocean,
Waves of the ocean bombarding;
Inflowing tides wash my shores,
Tides ebbing wash my shores clean,
Wash, wash mighty waters.
Is not England and France,

Ebony Rhythm 48–49.

Germany and Spain,
Singapore and Shanghai in my veins?

Yes. . . . . . .
I am Africa.
Africa stealing forth to meet
A lover in the everglades,
Chief Heartache,
Parleying with famine and sorrow
With never a war whoop.
Africa,
Singing the Irish caoine
Bewailing in accents of Scotland;
Mute are the harps;
Why are they voiceless?
Silent the bagpipes—
There was no victory.

I am Africa,
Africa the maiden;
My breasts are sweet apples;
My limbs are the flowering
Limbs of the fruit tree.
My body is fertile oasis
Alone in the barren desert,
Ever green in the sands of the desert.

In my veins the blood of all nations,
In my hands the jewels of all nations,
In my being the wisdoms and the passions of all nations.

I am Africa
Rooted in America,
Africa the maiden,
Africa the conquered and the conqueror;
Beat, beat my heart
To the sound of the tom-toms;
Throb, throb my heart

To the roll of the drums.
Transplanted from Africa,
Nurtured in America,
Son of many races,
Fathered by many,
I am become
Man universal.

Baptism

They were so amusing,
The black folk all dressed in white
Deacons, sisters and a preacherman
    And the candidates,
      Every one in spotless white.

They stood together on the river's brink
And I watched from the side of the hill.
The preacherman strode into the water
And the brothers and sisters and all
The little dark children sang:

    "Wade in the water chillun,
    Wade in the water chillun,
    God goin'er trouble de water."

Then I guess . . .
The "Spirit" fell on me
Suddenly I forgot that the people were black folk
And that their religion was funny and mysterious.
All memory left me, all time and all space

The Chicago Defender 8 June 1940. Awarded First Prize at the 1940 Robert Browning
Poetry Contest, University of Redlands, Redlands, California.

I was down by the river
Mingling my whiteness with my brothers black

I think I was lifted up.

The heavens opened or else the sky was bluer.
The sun was warm and ran hot in my veins
The fragrance of flowers, mingled with
The river's smell of left over rains,
Hung sweet in the air.
The heart of me softened,
Tears wet my face.
I guess I got "Happy"
And the brothers and sisters and
All the little dark children sang:

"Wade in the water . . . wade . . .
God's goin'er trouble de water."

I heard "Amen" shouts,
And the preacherman saying
"I now baptize you,
In the name of the Father, and of the Son
And of the Holy Ghost,"
And the river water flowed over me.
Then they raised me, and I walked straight up
Out of the water
I felt clean as the newborn day.
I felt free as the wind blowing in
From the sea.

I am a new creature
    Rejoicing to tell
    How I went to the river
    And got baptized.

Words, Words, Words

Words, words, words
Have power of saints
And of devils.
With words weave a song
Or break a heart, or
Rule a Nation.
Words, words, words—
Have power of saints,
And of devils.

Previously unpublished.

This, Then, Is Courage

This–then is courage–
To be earth—bound at mountain's pit—
And, yet have faith that lifts the inner-man
And sets him there-upon the mountain's summit.

Previously unpublished.

The Colorist

God is an Indian; He loves gay colors.
Red, yellow, orange are in the sky at sunset
And at the sunrise, too.
God is Irish. He loves green color best,
For all the trees and grasses in green garments
Oft-times dress.
God is Saxon, stern and cold,
For snow is white and ice is cold,
The downy clouds are white, and a white moon peeks
When lovers pledge their troth.
Cotton is white and snowy lambkin's fleece.
God is African. . . . . . .
For night is robed in black;
The twinkling stars are black men's eyes.
The black clouds tempests tell,
While little seeds of flowers birthed
Are tans and browns and black.

Crisis Sept. 1925: 224; *Ebony Rhythm* 50–51.

Humility

They charge me with humility;
I who walk with an Humble One.
They taunt me, because to their eyes
I am poor;
I, who am daily fed!
They say:
I am lowly and poor and weak—
All of these things, they say,
Not knowing that my humility
Is the shadow cast,
The mighty shadow of an Humble One
In whose Hand my hand is clasped!

Opportunity Sept. 1933: 271; *Ebony Rhythm* 51.

The Pool

The pool was very cool and quiet
I thought to plumb its depth,
But all I did—was see a mirrored sky,
And pendant there—myself!

Previously unpublished.

Steps to Transcendence

(Step 1)

When I was young,
God was to me,
A huge bright bird
Perched in a tree;
Audacious child I used to be
I dared toss stones into the tree.

(Step 2)

As I older grew,
God became a Spirit-being
With dazzling wings effacing light,
A mighty force that from me flew
Ever skyward was his flight
Casting shadows across my view.

(Step 3)

Now I am old and
God is . . .

Reason for Singing.

When husband spreads a napkin white
Upon his thigh, and ladles food
Into our child's deep plate,
A father kind and good,
Benevolent and wise.

A Tale and a Moral

Once three wise men journeyed far
By following a distant star, which
Led them straight to a prize surpassing
Anything that one could ask for.

And since that day and long before
Wise men come and wise men go.

Until three wise men of our day
Glimpsed a shining distant star,
And sought to reach it without going far
By taking devious crooked trails
They thought to reach it without fail,
Instead, they lost themselves . . .
And lost the star.

And since that day and long before
Wise men come and wise men go.

L'en-voi . . . there are no short-cuts to a star.

Reason for Singing.

The Treasure-Trove of Andy Kane

Old Andy Kane, a rugged fellow
Tugged with a boulder,
Until he turned it over.
For underneath the mighty stone,
He thought to find a treasure sown.
With his aged limbs creaking
From unaccustomed toil, he strove
With the rock until it was moved.
Then he crouched down where the rock had been
His searching fingers raising a storm,
Expecting to find golden doubloons,
All he turned up was a fat earth-worm.

Reason for Singing.

Mystery

He wished to die,
A listless, soured old man
He longed for death, and hated life
Like clinging moss,
He lived.

She wished to live
A pretty, gladsome maid
She treasured life and grew as
Flowers do, and like them
Died.

Reason for Singing.

This Knowledge Springs

I am glad this knowledge springs
Within me, that you live, you live.
The people here and all around me
Are so sure that you are dead.
But I have culled the sweet significance
Of these words our Saviour said:
"I am the Resurrection and the Life"
And I am certain that you live.

Previously unpublished.

Freedom Is A-Borning Still

"That this Nation under God shall have a new birth
Of freedom. . . ."
  Freedom is the Nation's destiny,
  To this, we are dedicated!
Slow. . . . are the birth pangs of a Nation's travail
Freedom is a-borning still.
  Lesser nations scorn us,
  That opulent with nature's bounty,
  And fat with sloth and greed
  We sleep in the face of wrong,
  And stand before barred doors
  Made fast by our own hands,
  Like mendicants in fear
  Of losing alms;
  The while our kindred
  Torment little children,
  And stifle the cries of: "Lord, Our Lord";
  That rise from sable throats.
  Slow. . . . are the birth pangs of a Nation's travail,
  Freedom is a-borning still.

Previously unpublished.

221

And that government of the people,
By the people,
For the people,
Shall not perish from the earth!

Awareness

The sacrifice was made for men
But not until awareness splendid
Caused me to heed the benefice
Did His Spirit loving, tender,
Rise from the tomb to dwell in me.

Patriot I, of humble mein, who saw
With pride, great silver airplanes
Ride the sky, who marked with grief
Most reasonable, a million youth
Go forth to war. Yet not until
They marshalled my sons, did my
Heart strive with the combat.

'Twas then I sought the Councilor,
'Twas then I went to Him and cried,
'Twas then I learned the ageless truth:
That my Lord, the Savior, died that we
Through ravages of war and scourge
Through death and trial and times like these
Could watch in peace, the ceaseless turmoil

Reason for Singing.

Could hope in faith, while all is chaos
Could ask in prayer, in trust believing
That valiant sons of every nation
Be buckled well and shielded ever,
And though, they fall in heat of battle,
Shall not die, because God lives.

Peace Talk

Today, down at the theatre they talked about peace.
Maybe, you know that when folksy folk fall to arguing
Their voices rise and rise into crescendos of
"I know's,'" and "I remember's" and "I've seen's"
Or else settle into sustained expressions of "Ifs" or
"Musts"
It was, oh, so enlightening the ways and means by which
Peace was relegated to a politic platform of behaviorism
by these good theatrical folk. Big Jim Barber got up
and said:
    Peace is an essence, fellows. In the name of God
    Don't try putting a bit and halter in its mouth,
    And a saddle on its back. You and nobody else
    Can straddle peace and go riding. Peace is like
    The air we breathe, untrammeled and inexplainable.
    It just is, when it is, and we have to attain it.

Reason for Singing.

Peace Item

Her pastor often told his congregation,
"Sister Alkins was Job clothed in femininity."
She made no lamentation when her four sons
Marched off to war. And no complaint when
Their crops failed, because her John had lost
The knack of putting his shoulders to the task
Without the aid of his sons' strong arms.
John Alkins died at the year's end.
   Sister Alkins bowed her head in acquiescence,
   And went about her daily chores humming a melody
   A hymn-tune which dear John had loved,
   The same one she had used for lullabies,
   Completely unaware that peace,
   Like death, goes ever undisturbed.

Reason for Singing.

The Land Where Silk Came From

A silken land was China
Where men and little children
Wore silken coats and slippers,
And ladies wove with silky floss
Upon transparent cloth.
An ancient land was China
Where courtesies and manners
Were suave and soft as silk,
And days were filled with silences
And time was folded silk.
Alas war came to China
To tear her silk in shreds,
But found that deftly thru the years
The Chinese had wrought iron wills
While spinning silken threads.

Previously unpublished.

Peace Is a Little Bird

Peace is a little bird that
Must have her freedom . . .
If she nests, protect her,
If she rests, refresh her,
If she sleeps, "shoo, shoo" her away
Peace must have her freedom.

Previously unpublished.

Whence Cometh Strength

Because . . .
We have scaled high mountains
And restrained our stride descending,
We now walk with sure tread along
Intricate ways called streets.

Because . . .
We have seen the rugged bulk
Of a mountain thwart the sun's rays
From sun-up until noontide, when the
Sun rode supreme in high heaven
Flooding its golden glow on all things beneath,
Turning the bulwarks of earth into
Altars of amethyst, we know that
Light scatters darkness.

Because . . .
We have known the beauty of mountains,
The rounded protuberances, bosoms of earth,
Long distant ranges blue as the sky,

Reason for Singing.

Imperturbable mountains clothed in thin mists,
Triumphant mountains head in the clouds
Calmly we lift up our eyes to these hills
And find peace.

Travel-Log

Yesterday in Hamburgh
Today in New Bedsford.

★   ★   ★

I left behind, a likely lass
In Hamburgh's mart,
As true as truth,
I spied today, on Bedsford's street
Her counterpart.
I stood amazed and watched her pass,
And saw her kiss a handsome lad
Upon New Bedsford's square.

★   ★   ★

As like as two peas in a pod,
That's how the lass in Hamburgh's mart
Greeted me but yesterday.

Reason for Singing.

Veils That Blow

Between us there are veils that blow
Hindering our eyes that see but darkly,
Still, we are brothers this, I know
For it is mirrored heart-framed starkly.

Previously unpublished.

From a Trolley Window

Panoramic scenes flashed on and off,
Plate glass windows reflected the fleeting
Pagentries. Pavements, dusty and hot,
Clacked accompaniment to innumerable feet,
As humanity pushed and shoved in ruthless
Progress, swarming, at cross purposes one
With another. Then a boy and girl appeared,
Spot-light in the midst of the throng.
   Their young bodies touching shoulder to shoulder,
   Arms locked, hands clasped, eyes intent upon
   Each other, straying but enough to mark their path,
   A miracle occurred, we board the trolley
   Heard their gay young laughter, high and clear
   Above the roar of traffic.

Reason for Singing.

233

Proposal

What am I that I should tell you what to do
Or who are you to tell me how or why or when?
You cannot guide me nor I lead you, hence
Let us marry and be at variance ever.

Reason for Singing.

What Choice?

Love brought me his treasure
He gave it me to choose
Would I have a passion flower
    Or a tender rose?
Would I have a falcon swift
    Or a white dove flying?
Would I have a torrent come
    Or translucent pool?
Would I have tumultuousness
    Or quiet after quest?
Love brought me his treasure
    Alas, I could not choose.

Opportunity Dec. 1933: 380.

Lasting Impression

Before we met . . .
My hope was dim as a distant star,
While you were here,
My hope turned golden as the sun.
Now you are gone,
I find my hope is golden still;
Gold endures, so does the sun!

Previously unpublished.

She Was Not Wise

Call her the moth that gleefully died
For a moment's gay swirl with a flame.
Or say of her, she is that woman un-wise,
Who plucked down her house with her hands.
Yet . . . poor foolish woman, she once
Spread a fine cloth . . . and the flame was
A sun to the moth!

Previously unpublished.

Inspiration

I vowed with courage high,
When circumstances brightened to travel far
From busy street and crowding houses, and
Tracks, where street-cars rattled by each quarter-hour.
Removed to sylvan spot, I would weave sonnets
to beauty, or paint a picture worthy of Angelo.
Then, into my ken, a child appeared—
A youngster five or six at most.
One, who loved him well had dressed the child in scarlet.
His head was high, flung upward, like a colt's,
From startled flight, arrested,
His eyes were wide with wonder,
He was beholding beauty everywhere!
Contrition like a whip-lash stung; led by a child,
I knew: Eyes have I; but eyes that do not see!

Previously unpublished.

Black Baby

The baby I hold in my arms is a black baby.
   Today I set him in the sun and
   Sunbeams danced on his head.
The baby I hold in my arms is a black baby.
   I toil, and I cannot always cuddle him.
   I place him on the ground at my feet.
   He presses the warm earth with his hands,
   He lifts the sand and laughs to see
   It flow through his chubby fingers.
   I watch to discern which are his hands,
   Which is the sand. . . .
Lo . . . the rich loam is black like his hands.

The baby I hold in my arms is a black baby.
   Today the coal-man brought me coal.
   Sixteen dollars a ton is the price I pay for coal.—
   Costly fuel . . . though they say:—
   Men must sweat and toil to dig it from the ground.
   Costly fuel . . . 'Tis said:—
If it is buried deep enough and lies hidden long enough

Opportunity Feb. 1929: 53.

'Twill be no longer coal but diamonds. . . .
My black baby looks at me.
His eyes are like coals,
They shine like diamonds.

Adventure

Sung for Mary

Come climb the hills with me . . . these three!
The hills of faith and hope and charity
And at their summit unsought treasure find
A joyful soul, a lasting peace of mind
Then in the realm of each great velvet hill
Find manifold signs of God's great will
And too, behold, at end of human strife
The serpent death become the bird of life.

Reason for Singing.

A Year Is Not Long

Sung for Mary

A year's not long;
The tree adds but an inch
The century, a year
Yet, candle moths live out their span
And hearts beat continuously.

A year's not long
But twice the sun
The equinox descries
Yet a child's conceived and born
The flower blooms and dies.

Reason for Singing.

Parenthood

(*Infancy*)
He cries
And time was and is
And will be evermore.
Being mother, I am
One with God;
Holding immensity
A babe in my arms.

(*Child*)
Small moist hands
Clutching mine.
Eyes filled with wonder
Looking up, brightened
With faith, shining with
Trust; seeing the universe
In me, his mother.

(*Youth*)
Aimless, I stand
With hands poised

Reason for Singing.

Knowing, I have made
Motherhood's sacrifice.
What more can I do for this
Stalwart one? Bone of my bone,
Flesh of my flesh. He who I once
Carried, now walks alone.

Life Is a See-Saw

Life is a seesaw
Sorrow strides one end of the board
And joy is poised upon the other.
   Sorrow rides low
   Joy rides high

   Joy cannot lift up sorrow
   Sorrow cannot bring joy down.

I have ridden with sorrow, low so low
I have seen him of my heart bereft
Seen him weeping for a well-beloved one
Who had grown cold and quiescent in death

   Joy cannot lift up sorrow
   Sorrow cannot bring joy down.

I have ridden with joy, high so high,
I have seen a babe new-born, and
Heard his new-born cry, beheld his tiny
Hand scarce more than petal of a rose,

Crisis Mar. 1929: 85; *Reason for Singing*.

Flutter with infant quest, and fall to rest
In peace beyond all worldliness at my own breast
   Sorrow rides low.
   Joy rides high.

The Good Tomorrow

Only now this moment this hour
Pan and sorrow hold sway,
Afterwards, the good tomorrow
Swallows the bitter hyssop today.
Not throes of travail, but birth is remembered.
Not scars of battle, but victories won,
Not the long fast, but the purpose is reverenced
Not the dream, but the deed is emblazoned.
Sorrow leaves only the marks of its passing
Joy is ensconced in time everlasting.

Reason for Singing.

I Am Glad for Tears

I am glad for tears
Like freshets that sweep
Debris from streets,
They wet my cheeks,
Cleansing my heart of
Burning fears,
   Embers of sorrow and
     Ashes of joy.

Reason for Singing.

Boarding Home for Children

Maybelle in the autumn of her years
Keeps a boarding home for children
In a cozy place which nears the city's edge.
Larkspurs, hollyhocks and children
Seem to spring alive in Maybelle's path.
She is a silent woman, knowing more
Of childish jingles than she does of life.
To set her talking mention the sign upon
The house that's down the street:
    "For Rent, No Children Wanted."
    "I can't understand those folk
    Who won't let children light.

    "No it's no trouble 'tending them
    They're mostly all alike.

    "Love is what they want the most
    Give it to them and they'll turn
    To you like plants toward the sun,
    "Unlike grown folk, little children
    Are never hard to please,

Reason for Singing.

249

They never bother about the reason,
They only understand the deed.

"The way they look at you
With their pure souls in their eyes,
I just can't see how grown-ups
Can deceive them or despise.
"I like any child,
I like to see his eyes
Fill with happy wonder,
When he's given a surprise.

"I like to keep them 'round me
They keep me mindful of the time
When mine were home.
"It's fun to tell them stories
Tales of bears and cats and dogs,
Tales of other girls and boys,
Tales of chairs and stoves which talk,
Tales of friendly rats and frogs,
Tales of mountains that can walk!

"Say it's nonsense, call it chit-chat
But such fare keeps children fat.

"And here's the secret out for a
Boarding home for children anywhere.
Keep them clean and fat and jolly,
Give them all they want to eat,
Teach them goodness by doing your
Share of good.

"It beats most anything, how a child
Can imitate. The little tykes
Can mock the way you think!

"I've never seen the infant yet
Who wouldn't clap his chubby hands

When you clap yours before him singing:
   "Baker's man
   Patty cake, patty cake
   Fast as you can!"

"And there's not a child alive
Who does not like a rocking-chair
And a tuneful lullabye.
   "Rockabye, rockabye mother is near
   Rockabye, rockabye nothing to fear."

What about their going?
How long do they stay?

"That's our risk
At times, it makes me groan;
When you care for babies, not your own,
They are bound to come and go!
But Tommy here, has lived with us since
He was one month old, and Jane's been here
Since she was just three weeks, and Michael
Came when he was turned a year."

How Glad I Am

How glad I am to see another Spring
The cares which long years bring
Can drape no age upon me,
If each successive Spring
Makes my heart sing!

Previously unpublished.

November

Like a door gently closed,
To open, at the touch of a finger
Is November;
Leaves, russet and brown and gold
Have done with falling; they carpet
The earth with color,
The harvest is gathered, housed.
Open door at the touch of a finger!
Come in, Winter, come in!

Previously unpublished.

Lamps

First the burning brand,
Then the candle's flame,
The smoky lamps of Greece,
And Rome's lamps of knowledge.
Thence . . . step by step to the myriad lamps
Of a lamp-lit civilization.

Man's progress is measured in light
Lamps of his lighting turn night to day,
And dare obscure the stars.

Reason for Singing.

Dry Bones

Dry bones . . .
Bleaching in the sun,
Make a spot of whiteness
On the sandy dune,
Bones of some dead animal,
White like the whiteness of the moon.

I heard it said,
The moon is a planet, dead.

Reason for Singing.

Barter

She was foolish it was said
She bought flowers instead of bread.

But they who each day feasted well
Sat at meat while beauty fled;

While she who dined upon a crust
Held much of beauty's store in trust.

Reason for Singing.

Tribute

High, high your purpose,
Gnarled old tree.
Staunch in your beauty stand,
Timbered to Earth Mother's breast,
Pith and fibre, leaf and bark
Breathing loveliness!

Reason for Singing.

Routine

Night after day
Spring after winter
Infancy, childhood
Maturity, age;
All things written
Stilted, precise
On red, dotted lines
In the ledger of life;
Work a little,
Play a little
Joy leavens sorrow,
Each day a cycle
That wheels in tomorrow.

Reason for Singing.

Decision

When I consider the
Intricacies of one short day,
The saffron of sunrise
The gold of noon
The slumberous amber of
Early evening
The tint of countless blades of grass
Of trees and shrubs no two alike
The warmth of sun
The cool of shade
The wind . . .
I know man's gamboling is naught
His wars, his deeds of valor, his cries,
His laughter, all . . . is a garment wrought
Of shabby fabric, thin cloth
That soon will tear
That souls released may winging go
To God for reckoning

Reason for Singing.

The Dust of the Streets

Out of the dust of the earth men are made.
Even now our feet tread on
The minute particles of forms
of unborn men,
Here in the streets.
And men will come
To tread upon our breasts
When they are stilled,
After aeons of time have sifted us
Into the dust of the streets.

Crisis July 1929: 232.

Respective Flight

Birds flying high into a sky of blue
   Is beauty of a common hue
   Beauty is for beauty's sake
   It merits small ado.

Birds flying low beneath a leaden sky
   Is dauntlessness anew;
   Fearlessness is sturdy fare
   That nothing need subdue.

Reason for Singing.

Modes

Night's affair is embroidered in stars
    Edged with the laces of trees
    She is robed in opaque velvets
    Lest her charms be revealed.

Day's apparel is threaded with gold
    Striped with slender trees
    She wears chiffon and nets
    Her limbs are never concealed.

Reason for Singing.

Definition

Night is a velvet cloak
Wrapped 'round a gay Lothario
Day is a flash-light
In the hand of a prude.

Opportunity Nov. 1927: 340; *Reason for Singing.*

Prima Donna Musing

The applause was wild and loud,
Beneath the shaken rafters;
I bowed and bowed.
The critics say:
"Mine is the voice which soars once
In a hundred years."
Acclaim belongs to lesser things
Such as: "A servant's worth his hire."
For all the while,
I sang tonight, I saw
My mother's eyes.

Reason for Singing.

She Is Not Proud

She coldly listens,
While they say:
"You're marvelous!"
"Your voice is grand!"
"My dear, you will go far!"
   She is not proud,
   But, oh, so bored
   Of pomp and circumstance.

Reason for Singing.

On Hearing Four White Men Singing Spirituals

Well sir, a white quartette trying Spirituals!
They should not, their voices are unsuitable.
Imagine, "Steal Away To Jesus" or "Roll Jordan Roll."
Sung through a nose.
Spirituals require deep resonant voices,
Pulsing with heartache and laden with sorrow.
Voices of people who are full-up with trouble,
And potent with woe.

Only, listen to these white men sing!
Guess it must be true; other folk
Sing sorrow songs now.

    ("He calls me by the thunder,
    The tempest rolls within my soul,
    I ain't got long to stay here.")
Indeed, it's a good concert and a full house,
Negro Spirituals being sung and
White men singing them. Oh my Lord.
("Steal away, Steal away, Steal away Home.")

Reason for Singing.

Audition

Only when the heart accompanies the voice
   Goes the song right;
Pray that my heart cuts no capers tonight
   For the master I sing.

Reason for Singing.

Folksong

I'm so glad my Lord's got wings,
I'm so glad He's a being what flies

He flaps his wings and nations rise,
He spreads his wings and peace abides,

He circles here and there and wide,
He swoops down low and he goes up high.

He brings joy to such as I, and
'Neath his wings great peace abides,

I'm so glad my Lord's got wings,
I'm so glad He's a being what flies

Reason for Singing.

Theme with Variations

(The Theme) *Played on a flute*
  A sorceress gave it to me,
  A crystal goblet rare and fine,
  And bade me drink.

  I drank the draught.
  The goblet drained—
  And lo! a strange sweet madness came.

  Now I am drunk,
  Intoxicated with a gladness . . .
  Rejoicing wildly in a madness . . .
  Drained from a crystal goblet fine—
  A copious draught of Love is mine. . . .

(Var. I) *On a Cello*
  Your passion is as strong sunshine,
  Your tenderness as healing rain.
  You smile upon me, and I see
  A radiance like flaring sunset;
  You speak . . . . and heavenly music is
  The utterance I hear.

Negro Voices: An Anthology of Contemporary Verse (New York: Henry Harrison, 1938) 36–39.

And violins answer
My love for you has brought to me
A strength, a glad new life . . .
My love for you has brought to me
No pain, no sacrifice. . . .
Loving you has made me glad,
Has made me joyous, free—
And every wrong and every woe
Is now immersed forevermore
In love's refining caldron.

(Var. II) *And Drums Reverberate*
On a black, black night we journeyed . . .
Stumbling blindly, sought our way. . . .
Ours the road that wound over mountains;
While, in the valley far below us,
War, a mighty war, was waged.
Ever to us came the clamour
Of the fearful din they made:
The strident calls of angry men—
The wailing cries of men sore-wounded—
The hapless pleas of dying men.

But. . . .
This the chant that marked our footfalls—
This the burthen of its lay:
"Fear not, fear not, Love is thine . . .
Love is brave and never weary.
Love has sight of soaring eagle . . .
It matters not, if you be blind.
Love is nourished in God's bosom.
Rejoice, rejoice that its glowing beauty
Nestles in the hearts of humans
Making them as beings divine."

(Var. III) *And Trumpets shrill*
The heights, the heights,
The heights we've climbed!

No further dare we go . . .
See, far below, how red they glow:
Night lights from distant windows . . .
Then Love drew close, enwreathed us both—
"Dear hearts, climb higher, higher.
The stars are yours; those silver stars,
With all their fulgent fire."
We kissed, embraced, shed tender tears.
Repentant of a moment's fears. . . .
We looked no more on the red, red glow
Of the night-lights from distant windows. . . .

Violins and cello . . . sing
Hope, like a jeweled pendant swung
Before us, when our love begun.
Hope, like a jeweled pendant shone
Upon our breasts, when love was won.

(Var. IV) *Drums, trumpets, cello, violins, and flute*
Love's consummation is regeneration . . .
   All glory surpassing;
Love is Life's veneration . . .
   'Tis the seedling, the bud, and
The flower full-blown.

Part III

Essays

Unfinished Masterpieces

There are days which stand out clearly like limpid pools beside the dusty road; when your thoughts, crystal clear as water, are pinioned in loveliness like star-points. Solitary days, which come often, if you are given to browsing in fields of past adventure; or rarely, if you are seldom retrospective; and not at all, if you are too greatly concerned with rushing onward to a nebulous future. Days whereupon your experiences glimmer before you waveringly like motion-pictures and the people you have known stroll through the lanes of memory, arrayed in vari-colored splendour or in amusing disarray. Days like these are to be revered, for they have their humors and their whimsicalities. Hurry your thoughts and the gathering imageries take flight. Perplexity but makes the lens of introspection blur. And of annoyance beware, for it is an evil vapour that disseminates and drowns the visions in the sea of grim realities. Such days must be cultivated. Scenes for their reception must be set. Cushions perhaps, and warmth of fire. Above all, the warmth of sweet content. Ease and comfort, comfort and ease and moods of receptivity. Then hither, come hither the places and the people we have known, the associations that withstand time's effacements. Backward ho, through the mazes of the past.

Stop! "Why howdy, Dora Johns." Darling playmate of my child-years. With wooly hair a length too short for even pigtails. Mud-spatters

Crisis Mar. 1927: 14, 24–25.

upon your funny black face. Mud-spatters all over your dress and your little black hands mud-spattered too.

Why? What? Come on and see. And lo! I am a child again.

Hand in hand, unmindful of her muddy ones, we skip around the old ramshackle house, back to the furthest corner of an unkempt yard, impervious to the tin cans, the ash-heap, the litter, the clutter that impedes our way, our eyes upon, our thoughts bent upon one small clean-swept corner, where there is mud. More mud and water in a battered tin can. And row after row of mud. No, not mud—not merely mud, but things made out of mud. Row on row, drying in the sun.

Carefully, I sit down, doubling up, to be as small as possible, for only this corner where mud things are drying is clean and corners are seldom, if ever, quite large enough. Besides, I must not touch the things made out of mud. If the dried ones fall, they break. If the moist ones are molested, be it with ever so gentle a finger, they lose their shape. Moreover, I must not disturb Dora.

Her little hands are busied with the mud. Little moulder's fingers are deftly plying their skill. Her child's face is alight. What has splashed her grave child's face with such a light? I wondered. I wonder now. The glitter of brittle talent, a gleam of sterling genius or the glow from artistic fires burning within the soul of a little black child?

Little Dora shaping figures out of mud. Vases and urns, dolls and toys, flying birds and trotting horses, frisking dogs and playing kittens, marvelous things out of mud. Crying aloud as though dealt a blow if one of the dried mud-figures is broken. Working in mud for endless hours, while the neighbor children play. Their hilarious merriment dropping like bombs into the quiet of our clean-swept corner. Deadly missiles seeking to find a mark. The insistent halloes of futile mirth forever bubbling on the other side of a high-board fence. The dividing fence and upon one side the clean-swept corner and the row on row of mud things drying in the sun. And Dora seeming not to heed the seething bubbles upon the other side, shaping, shaping marvelous things out of mud.

Yet, Oh Dora, now that the day is ours, will you not say, "When did the bombs of futile mirth strike their target? When did the tin-cans and the rags and the old ash-heap crowd you out from your clean-swept corner? What rude hand caused the dried mud shapes to fall and break? Who set a ruthless foot in the midst of your damp mud things?" Or were you too plastic, as plastic as your mud? You dare not tell. Only this you can whisper into the mists of our today. You are one of the Master's unfinished shapes which He will some day gather to mould anew into the finished masterpiece.

A lump of mud. Now, there is a sobriquet for you—you funny, funny man. Mr. William Williams. I saw you but once. We chanced to meet in the home of a mutual friend. I thought you so very funny then. Uncouth and very boorish, but ever, when these pageants of the past, these dumb shows of inarticulate folks arise before me upon retrospective days, you appear garbed in the tatters of pathos.

"I am fifty-one years old," you kept repeating. How pitiful those fifty-one years are. You wear a child's simplicity, the sort that is so sad to see upon a man. Fifty-one and penniless. Fifty-one and possessed of naught else but the clothing you wore. Fifty-one and no place on earth you might call home. You confessed to being a vagabond though "bum" was the term you used and you were very proud of your one accomplishment, an ability to avoid all labour.

"I've given no man a full day's honest work in all my fifty-one years," you boasted. "I gambles. I ain't no cotton-pickin' nigger." Your one and only boast after holding life, the fathomless fountain of eternal possibilities, in your possession for fifty-one priceless years.

Nevertheless you have lived and so intensely. You held us against our will. Clustered around you, listening to you talk. Relating clippings as it were from the scrap-book of your life.

Tales of the road, of the only places you knew. Roads leading away from plantations where the cotton waited to be picked by number-less "cotton-pickin' niggers." Roads leading to pool halls and gambling dens. Roads beginning and roads ending in "riding the roads," carrying backward and forward, here and yon through the weird goblin land of the South's black belt.

With a hardened casualness you told stories that revolted and at the same time cheered us with an all sufficing glow of thankfulness that life had spared us the sordidness of yours. Offhandily, you gave us humourous skits that tempered our laughter with wishes that we might know at least a bit of such a droll existence as had been yours. With magical words, you painted pictures so sharply they cut scars upon our hearts. You drew others so filled with rollicking delight their gladsomeness was contagious. With the non-chalance of a player shuffling cards you flipped your characters before us, drawn directly from the cesspool of your contacts and spellbound we listened.

Someone remarked how wonderful you talked and you replied, "Once, I sorter wanted to write books. Once, I uster read a heaps. See times when I was broke and nobody would stake me for a game. I'd lay around and read. I've read the Bible through and through and every Police Gazette I could lay my hands on. Yes, suh, I've read a'heap. And I've wished a lot'er times I'd sense enough to write a book."

Lump of mud. Containing the you, the splendid artist in you, the soul of you, the unfinished you in the ungainly lump of you, awaiting the gathering-up to be moulded anew into the finished masterpiece.

What a day! Here is my friend at whose fire-side I have lingered beholding Mr. William Williams, great lump of mud. To be sure, she also is an unfinished production. Though it is apparent that the Master had all but done when she slipped from his hands and dropped to earth to lie groping like the rest of us thereon.

Let us sit here together, friend, and enjoy this day.

I shall try to discover what recent gift you have given to the poor the while you are quietly stitching upon the garments, linens and scarlet, with which to clothe your household. Sit here and smile with the welcoming light in your eyes, knowing that your door is open to such as William Williams and Dora Johns, the Dora who is become as the mud beneath one's feet. Kind mistress of the widely opened door where white and black, rich and poor, of whatever caste or creed may enter and find comfort and ease and food and drink.

Let me sit awhile beside you upon this day, hearkening again to your simple philosophy. A philosophy stirred with the spoon of kindliness and seasoned with the essence of love. Very simple indeed and yet sufficient to sustain you in every trial and of such resilience it rebounds in the presence of tribulations unto itself and findeth peace.

What is it you say to back-biters and gossips, all those who wrongfully accuse you? "Everything will come out in the wash."

And when a haughty one is being superior? "Birds fly high but they come down to get water."

And when something or someone has failed you in duty or in word? "Every tub has to stand on its own bottom."

And your simple panacea for intolerance? "Man is 'apt' to fall as sparks to go upwards."

What boon would I not forswear to sit beside you in reality, my friend, who boasts no art save the art of friendliness?

Friendliness encased in a crust of black mud, awaiting also the Master's final touch, when all outer semblance and material hindrances shall fade into nothingness and His gifts, be they the one talent or the five, shall be poured into His scales.

So thinking, retrospection sudden done with, retracing with leaps and bounds the journey through the fields of memory, I arrive at the stile of the present. Whereon there is a sign as vividly lined as the present is drawn from the past and the future from the present. Quite plainly it reads:

"We one and all are God's unfinished shapes, ungainly shapes, ungainly lumps of mud, waiting—waiting to be moulded anew into the finished masterpiece."

Arizona and New Mexico — The Land of Esperanza

It is singular, that most persons think of Arizona and New Mexico in unity. The fact is, that Arizona was a part of New Mexico until 1863 when it was divided by Congress into a separate territory. Since, each, not so many years ago attained the status of Statehood, they have striven diligently, albeit amiably to establish a distinct and separate individualism.

Yet for this once, we shall consider them as one.

Together they cover an area of 235,654 square miles, a boundless region of vast treasures.

Their mineral resources are limitless. Manganese, iron, coal, oil, zinc, copper, gold, silver, onyx and marble, meerschaum and turquoise, emeralds, sapphires, garnets and opals lie buried in level plains and rugged mountains.

Great stretches of timbered lands are protected in forest reserves, and one forest in Holebroke, Arizona, is so old, it is petrified, its trees but solid rock. The lower mountain ranges and hills are covered with stunted growth of pine, juniper, piñon, cedar, and oak. The rolling prairies are arrayed in the wonder vegetation of the Southwest—the cactus, the sagebrush, the mesquite, and the yucca.

Its surface is traversed by rivers. The greatest of these being the Rio Grande, the old reliable, of whom legend says: obligingly changed

Messenger Sept. 1926: 275–76.

its course to suit the whim of "el Gringo"; cleaving the State of New Mexico from tip to toe as it wends its way to the Gulf. This and the Pecos and the Gila rivers along with their tributaries water extraordinarily fertile valleys; in which wonder apples, figs, apricots, grapes, wheat, corn, cotton, and alfalfa are produced. While the Colorado River in Arizona is that small and turbid stream which has wrought through centuries the mighty marvel of the Grand Canyon.

The animals and the insects of these States, like its arid vegetation, are unique. Here is the home of the Gila-monster, the vinegerone, the rattlesnake, the centipede, the tarantula and the niña de terra. The coyote and the prairie dog keep watch upon its plains, the fox and deer, the wolf and bear, sheep and mountain lions, and countless feathered "game," bestow upon their natal states the title: "The hunting ground of the United States."

Another natural resource is the climate. Rarely does the sun hide its face from these two states. Endless breezes lilt and sing as effective as an electric fan in summer and as bracing as a tonic.

Natural resources are the gifts of generous Nature, and industry is the outcome of man's manipulations of these gifts.

Since minerals are strewn in such lavish quantities, mining is an important occupation, the leading one in Arizona. Copper is yet being taken from "workings" bearing the scars and marks of the day when Spaniards conquered and enslaved the Indian, gave him the crude implements of the time and sent him chained into the bowels of the earth to delve for treasure. Later the white man came and conquered and so it is the Mexican miner rather than the Negro or the foreigner of the East, who goes down and up the shaft, in and out the tunnel, down and down into endless pits in quest of minerals.

The vast stretches of grass grown plains give rise to the cattle industry, the greatest pursuit in the State of New Mexico. To all appearances and despite legend—cattle raising is an exclusive white man's trade. Mexican cowboys there are and perhaps in a bygone day, the natives were large cattle owners—but today, one sees only the white cattleman. Occasionally one glimpses a Negro cowboy or rather a Negro who has learned a lot about cattle, quite likely, he has often gone with cattle-trains into Kansas, Nebraska, Old Mexico to punch cattle—to prevent any of the packed cattle lying down, where they would be trodden to death beneath the hoofs of the others—on their long railway journey. But very few black men have ridden beneath the stars, singing cowboy chants to still the restless herds. And in no instance has a black American, plied himself to the task of becoming one of the "big" cattlemen of the Southwest. Maybe, it is due to the side line of cattle rustling; which once upon a time accompanied cattle raising, most profitably, who knows?

In Arizona and New Mexico, man has aptly turned the climate into an industry. We have here the business of dispensing health to the health-seeker. The different chambers of commerce vie one with the other in advertisements of climate.

"Sunshine 365 days in the year," boasts New Mexico.

"Arizona—land of golden sunshine," acclaims Arizona.

Indisputably, these States offer the best in health giving "ozone" and revivifying sun-light. The Sanatorium is the outstanding feature of many towns. But Tucson, in Arizona and Silver City, in New Mexico, are favored spots. Prescott in Arizona and Ft. Bayard in New Mexico, the latter the largest sanatorium of its kind in the country, both Veteran Bureau Hospitals, treat Negro patients. Besides, these, there is no especial provision made for the Negro health-seeker. Several tentative efforts to establish a Negro sanatorium have fallen short. Yet, such an institution is a needed and certainly a humane project for an American Negro.

Again, the scenic wonders of these two States lure the tourist into their midst, while "big game" during the hunting seasons beguile the sportsmen and so the trade of entertaining a traveling public becomes an important one.

Farming, a new and steadily growing project owing to the recently completed dams for the conservation of a bounteous water supply enabling irrigation on larger scales, the climate, the productivity of soil, and the acreage for large crops holds forth a promise of vast reward for the inhabitants of these States. Likewise, farming, more than all its other industries, swings wide its gates and cordially welcomes the Negro.

Cotton as an experiment. Cotton in the Maricopa valley and Mexican peon labor. Cotton in the Mesilla valley and Negro hands from the South. Cotton, a wonderful yield and experiment becomes an established fact. With it all there are many Negroes in Phoenix and some scattered throughout the State. And mayhaps, Mexican peons will eventually return to Mexico. But in the Mesilla valley, Vado, a

Negro town, is born. Jammed against the State's scenic highway, plodding its way to the high road of success.

As industry is dependant upon natural resources, population is dependant upon industry. It is seen, then, that industry in these States has held little promise for the Negro.

The inhabitants here are as striking as the plants and animals of Arizona and New Mexico. They are historically interesting. Consisting of fast dwindling tribes of Indians, living echoes of a by-gone day, remnants of centuries-old civilization. The tatters of the Aztecs, cliff dwellers and the humble dwellers in Pueblos. And the Spanish-American or Mexican native, the first conquerors of Indians, plenteous whites, and essentially, it is the home of the half-breed, the inevitable outcome, where two or more races meet and mingle in an un-accustomed freedom.

While here and there are Negroes, like straggly but tenacious plants growing, nevertheless, though always in the larger towns. Becoming fewer and fewer, until in many or in all of the remoter hamlets and towns they are as sparse as rose bushes upon the prairies.

But all, which the Negro has failed to give to the industry or to the population of Arizona and New Mexico, he has made amends for with the contribution to its history.

It is potent to recall that in 1538, Estevan, the Negro slave in the role of interpreter and guide to the Friar Marcos de Niza, was sent on ahead to spy upon the people and the strange lands they were entering, and send back reports to his peers. Thus, it was that Estevan the Negro, was first to behold the wonders of the seven cities, and though, he, himself was killed, sent back the report:—"Advance, the find is worth it."

Negroes have fought and struggled over all the vast stretches that included the one-time Indian Territory, the Panhandle, New Mexico and Arizona, throughout the years of Indian warfare. Most of the old settlers among Negroes in "these parts" are descended or related to a hoary-haired and fast-passing, honorably discharged, Indian war fighter, who thought wearily upon receiving his discharge, that "here" was as good as "way back there" to settle down and rest after his long arduous campaign.

And mingled with the tales of Indians on warpaths are the stories of heroism performed by avenging whites and all interwoven with these deeds are mingled the deeds of solitary Negroes.

In 1916 Negroes helped patrol the borders in New Mexico and Arizona, safeguarding the doorways through which Villa or a mightier foe might enter. That Villa did enter and raided Columbus, New Mexico, was no fault of theirs. Yet, they it was who rode out into chaparral hard on the trail of the treacherous Villa, to their death in Carrizol.

Among the famous acts of outlawry are knit the acts of black men. Oft'times they have accompanied posses in the capture of dangerous bandits. And a black man was the first to fall before the deadly aim of Billy the Kid, in a gambling hall in Silver City.

Among famous frontier huntsmen are the names of Negroes. One George Parker was the best crack shot and the gamest bear hunter who ever followed a trail. He was also a lucky prospector and amassed a fortune in mines. As did his friend John Young, who still survives; who was at one time the richest Negro and one of the wealthiest mine owners in the territory of New Mexico.

Among the lowly and humble tasks, which likewise make history, are such deeds as this: In Roswell, a town of tree lined streets, it is told that a Negro, an old pioneer, recently deceased, planted the trees which grace the City's streets.

Withal, the Negroes in these States are an isolated lot, yet in nearly all instances they are home owners. In the remote hamlets, if there be blacks at all, they seem a bit hazy concerning their relationship to the great hordes of Negroes beyond their confines. This is not true of the groups in larger towns.

One is almost persuaded to say, that the brains and the brawn of the Negro population is gathered in Alberquerque. Negro enterprise of various sorts are here. Negro doctors and dentists reside here. Two churches are supported. The N.A.A.C.P. is represented—and it is the home of the *Southwest Review,* a Negro publication, edited by S. W. Henry.

Though the greatest outstanding feature of the Negro population is that in New Mexico, there are two exclusively Negro towns: Blackdom, sixteen miles south of Roswell and situated in the Chavis County oil area and Vado, previously mentioned, a score of miles below Las Cruces.

So far, in New Mexico, the Negro has not yet become a bone to gnaw in politics. He is not legislated either pro or con, he is an unconsidered quantity, due to his inconsequential numbers. But what New Mexico may or may not do is evidenced in the fact that the influx of

Negro children to Dona Ana County the center of the cotton activity were not allowed to attend the schools. Separate schools were immediately installed, also Roswell in Chavis County maintains a separate school system.

On the other hand, Arizona has made rigid laws concerning her Negro inhabitants. A rather funny one is eight Negro children in any community is a sufficient quota for instituting a Negro school.

Boiled down to finality—these States are the mecca-land for the seeker after wealth—the land of every man to his own grubstake-and what-I-find-I-keep.

And criss-crossing in and out through the medley of adventure, stalk the few in number black folks. Often, it is only the happy-go-lucky, black gambler, again it is but the lone and weary black prospector—but ever and ever the intrepid, stalwart Negro home seeker forms a small yet valiant army in the land of esperanza.

And over it all the joyous freedom of the West. The unlimited resourcefulness the boundless space—that either bids them stay—or baffles with its vastness—until it sends them scuttling to the North, the South, the East whence-so-ever they have come.

For here prevails for every man be he white or black a hardier philosophy—and a bigger and a better chance, that is not encountered elsewhere in these United States.

Appendix I

Stories by Anita Scott Coleman Not Included in This Volume

"Love's Power." *Half-Century Magazine* May 1919.

"Billy Settles the Question." *Half-Century Magazine* Aug. 1919.

"The Nettleby's New Years." *Half-Century Magazine* Jan. 1920.

"The Hand That Fed." *Competitor* Dec. 1920.

"Remarks Upon Three Things as They Are." Honorable Mention, *Crisis* Awards, 1925.

"Silk Stockings." *Messenger* Aug. 1926.

"Flaming Flame." Honorable Mention, *Crisis* Awards, 1926.

"The Dark Horse." Second Prize, *Opportunity* Awards, 1926.

"White Folks' Nigger." *Messenger* May–June 1928.

"A Deal in Truck." *Black and White Chronicle* 8 Dec. 1928.

"Love Wins." *Black and White Chronicle* 8 Dec. 1928.

"Santa via the Kitchen." *Nashville Clarion* 22 Dec. 1928.

"The Eternal Quest." *Opportunity* Aug. 1931.

"Thursday Off." *Pittsburgh Courier* 13 July 1940.

"Howdy Jesus." *Pittsburgh Courier* 1 Feb. 1941.

"Unofficial Broadcast." *Pittsburgh Courier* 11 Oct. 1941.

"A Child to Keep." *Pittsburgh Courier* 28 Mar. 1942.

"The Poor Are Always With Us." *Pittsburgh Courier* 7 Mar. 1942.

The Family of Anita Scott Coleman: A Genealogical Chart

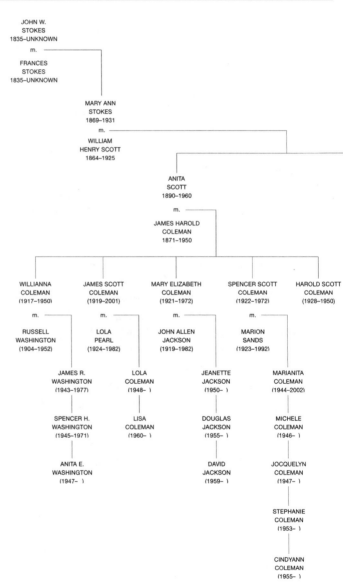

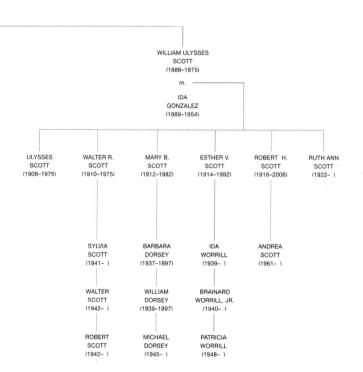

WILLIAM ULYSSES
SCOTT
(1888–1975)

m.

IDA
GONZALEZ
(1889–1954)

ULYSSES
SCOTT
(1908–1975)

WALTER R.
SCOTT
(1910–1975)

MARY B.
SCOTT
(1912–1982)

ESTHER V.
SCOTT
(1914–1992)

ROBERT H.
SCOTT
(1916–2006)

RUTH ANN
SCOTT
(1922–)

SYLVIA
SCOTT
(1941–)

BARBARA
DORSEY
(1937–1997)

IDA
WORRILL
(1939–)

ANDREA
SCOTT
(1961–)

WALTER
SCOTT
(1942–)

WILLIAM
DORSEY
(1939–1997)

BRAINARD
WORRILL, JR.
(1940–)

ROBERT
SCOTT
(1942–)

MICHAEL
DORSEY
(1945–)

PATRICIA
WORRILL
(1948–)

Notes

PREFACE

1. Miller and Coleman won first and second prize, respectively, in the essay division of the 1926 *Crisis* literary contest. During Miller's stint as a journalist with the *California Eagle*, Coleman's husband, James Harold, worked for the newspaper as a printer and photographer.

2. Other members included Frederick Roberts, editor of the *New Age* newspaper for which Coleman's husband worked as a printer; Noah Thompson, husband of writer Eloise Bibb Thompson and later the business manager of *Opportunity*; and Catherine Barr, later secretary of the Urban League. Only Anderson actually published.

3. Other recent anthologies include Elizabeth Ammons, ed., *Short Fiction by Black Women* (1991); Marcy Knopf, *The Sleeper Wakes* (1993); Sondra Kathryn Wilson, ed., *The Crisis Reader* (1999) and *The Messenger Reader* (2000); Tom Lutz and Susanna Ashton, eds., *These "Colored" United States* (1996); Charles H. Nichols and Maureen Honey, *Double-Take: A Revisionist Harlem Renaissance Anthology* (2001); Maureen Honey, ed., *Shadowed Dreams: Women's Poetry of the Harlem Renaissance* (2006); Edgar Roberts and Henry Jacobs, eds., *Literature: An Introduction to Reading and Writing* (2003); and Mary Ford-Grabowsky, ed., *Sacred Voices: Essential Women's Wisdom Through the Ages* (2002).

4. These include *American Women Writers 1900–1945*, edited by Laurie Champion, and Mary Young's "Anita Scott Coleman: A Neglected Harlem Renaissance Writer."

5. Black women writers who, like Coleman, were acclaimed upon publication and subsequently ignored by the canon include Zora Neale Hurston, Dorothy West, Helene Johnson, Pauline Hopkins, Harriet Jacobs, Ann Petry, Marita

291

Bonner, Alice Dunbar-Nelson, Georgia Douglas Johnson, and Nella Larsen. All are now receiving a great deal of critical and commercial interest.

6. Coleman published under the pseudonym Anne Stokes in the *Black and White Chronicle* (Akron, Ohio) and the *Nashville Clarion*, weekly newspapers edited by George S. Schuyler. She submitted pieces to the *Crisis* under the names William Henry, Annie Hawkins, and Elizabeth Stokes.

7. In fact, Elizabeth Stapleton Stokes was born in Saginaw, Michigan, in 1897. She graduated from Smith College, married John Stokes (who was from Georgia), bore three sons, and lived in White Plains, New York, and Stuart, Florida. In addition to *Small Wisdom*, she published in a number of "little" magazines and was active in the post–World War II peace movement. The 1930 census lists Elizabeth, and all of her family members, as white (U.S. Bureau of the Census, 1930, White Plains, Westchester County, New York, roll 1665, page 9A). Several of the poems in *Small Wisdom* had appeared in the Vermont poetry magazine *Driftwind* and in *Bozart-Westminster*, the literary journal of Oglethorpe University in Atlanta; we tracked down copies of these journals and, based on the author biographies, were able to locate Stapleton Stokes's obituary in a Stuart, Florida, newspaper. The obituary includes a photograph of Stapleton Stokes and is in the *Stuart News* (24 Jan. 1974: 8A). Ironically, Stapleton Stokes died in the home state of the Stokes-Scott-Coleman family.

8. Those making this claim include Glasrud and Champion 77; Honey 33; Knopf 268; Patton and Honey 314; Roses and Randolph 1989, 59; Shockley 448–49; Wilson, *Messenger Reader* 409; and Young 271.

9. U.S. Bureau of the Census, 1910, Silver City, Grant County, New Mexico, roll T624-915, page 4B.

10. Scott served at various forts throughout the Southwest.

INTRODUCTION: ANITA SCOTT COLEMAN IN THE SOUTHWEST

1. See also Hutchinson's discussion of the history of African American public health nursing. He notes a widely distributed pamphlet in 1914 titled "Tuberculosis" by Dr. James E. Henderson, in which the author expresses fear that the disease could lead to race extinction.

2. See, for example, DuBois's editorial "Returning Soldiers" in the *Crisis* (May 1919), in which he asserts: "We return. We return from fighting. We return fighting. Make way for Democracy! We saved it in France and we will save it in the United States of America, or know the reason why" (Du Bois, *Writings* 1181).

3. U.S. Bureau of the Census, 1870, Tallahassee, Leon County, Florida, p. 25.

4. The two younger brothers of William and Henry James, Garth Wilkinson (Wilky) and Robertson (Bob) James, were both officers in black units (Wilky was an adjutant in the 54th Massachusetts under Col. Robert Gould Shaw. He was wounded at the battle of Fort Wagner and witnessed the death of Col. Shaw.

Bob served in the 45th Massachusetts and in the Negro 55th and saw action in the siege of Charleston). The brothers were so impressed with the African American soldiers that they purchased a farm near Jacksonville and invited black veterans to join them in a cooperative venture; the project failed due to harassment by local whites. See Gay Wilson Allen's *William James* for more information on the James brothers' experiment in interracial, cooperative farming.

5. For other examples of black women writers who stress the importance of family memories of slavery, see Dorothy West, *The Living Is Easy* and *The Wedding*; Gayl Jones, *Corregidora*; Gloria Naylor, *Mama Day*; and Toni Morrison, *Song of Solomon*.

6. Stokes's mixed race is also confirmed by William Ulysses' memories of visiting Tallahassee cousins who were blonde and blue-eyed (Caffey).

7. A similar image of a loyal, musical, multigenerational family also appears in Coleman's posthumously published children's book, *The Singing Bells*. During the 1940s, Coleman's daughter Willianna served as organist for the Mount Zion Baptist Church Senior Choir, Los Angeles ("Mount" 16).

8. The 1860 census for Tallahassee lists fourteen laundresses, all black or mulatto women (Rogers 157).

9. Florida A & M University (FAMU) would not be founded until 1887, when Thomas Van Rensselaer Gibbs, a black member of the Florida legislature, sponsored a bill establishing the university.

10. Mary was the fifth child. Her siblings were Anthony, James, John, Henry, Frederick, Mildred, and Holland (U.S. Bureau of the Census, 1870 and 1880, Tallahassee, Leon County, Florida, pp. 17 and 25; Florida State Census, 1885, Tallahassee, Leon County, Florida, roll M845-7, p. 9).

11. They married on May 12, 1887 (Caffey; Texas Marriage Collection, 1814–1910, AncestryLibrary.com). Fort Elliott had been built in 1875; the 10th Cavalry had arrived in 1879, and the 9th Cavalry the following year. Between 1881 and 1884, all of the troops at Ft. Elliott were African American. Scott would undoubtedly have seen Lt. Henry O. Flipper, a member of the 10th Cavalry and the first black graduate of West Point.

12. According to Ida Caffey, "'camp follower' was a legal designation for civilians who performed services for the military. The term did not refer to prostitutes, as it did in England. Laundresses were paid and received one meal a day."

13. On his application for a social security number, William U. Scott wrote that he was born May 24, 1888, in Tallahassee, Florida. His granddaughter, Ida Caffey, confirms that "Mary did travel back home to give birth to her first child, William U. I suspect because William H. was in the military at the time."

14. Col. Thomas Wentworth Higginson, commanding officer of the first Civil War black regiment, the 1st South Carolina Volunteers, thought so highly of them that he "used to seriously ponder, during the darker periods of the war, whether I might not end my days as an outlaw—a leader of Maroons" (Higginson 237).

15. A number of young African Americans died of consumption in Silver City, including Hattie Lee, a thirty-five-year-old teacher at a normal school in Houston who was described in her obituary as "highly educated" (*SS* 22 July 1904).

16. Her daughter Willianna died of tuberculosis in September 1950, and her son Harold died of pneumonia in December 1950.

17. All Silver City newspaper and census data courtesy of Pat Bennett, researcher, Silver City Museum.

18. Data from newspapers and census reports at Silver City Museum.

19. Ibid.

20. The soldiers decorated the hall, catered the elaborate buffet supper, and arranged the entertainment, which included solos, group numbers, instrumental pieces, and lessons in the latest dances. A string band provided the music as the senior black soldier opened the dancing with the wife of the commanding officer; everyone then joined in (Kenner 28).

21. In "Pink Franklin" (*Crisis* Feb. 1911), DuBois called the life sentence given a young mulatto in South Carolina for shooting an intruder in his home "an astounding American tragedy" (*Writings* 1132); his letters to Wilson appeared in the *Crisis* in March and September 1913 (*Writings* 1141, 1144).

22. See, for example, Macon Dead in Morrison's *Song of Solomon*, Mutt Thomas in Jones' *Corregidora*, Harpo in Walker's *The Color Purple*, and Bart Judson in West's *The Living Is Easy*.

23. Although Coleman presumably submitted material, she did not win in 1927; prizes went to her contemporaries Marita Bonner, Eulalie Spence, Mae Cowdery, and Ethel M. Caution.

24. Richards reminds A. T. Hannett, the newly elected Democratic governor, that although in 1924 "there are 8,500 Negroes in this state we have not had a place given to us even as janitor at the State House, or guard at the penitentiary." He urges the Governor to appoint a Black Sergeant-at-Arms and offers to provide a list of suitable candidates (Richardson 51).

25. Overton was also the publisher of the *Chicago Bee*, into which he eventually absorbed the *Half-Century Magazine*. The magazine's title referred to the strides made by African Americans in the half-century since emancipation.

26. Coleman's other story published in the *Competitor* is "The Hand That Fed," not included in this book.

27. In the article, DuBois vehemently deplores the "compromising friends" of the Negro who support Washington's accomodationist position: "They want the Negro educated; but the South objects to Negro colleges. Oh, very well, then, high schools; but the South objects to 'literary training' . . . Dear, dear! Then 'industrial training,' but the South objects to training any considerable number of Negroes for industry; it wants them for menial service . . . servants and field hands" (*Writings* 1155).

28. Authored ca. 1861, the full poem reads:

Wild Nights—Wild Nights!
Were I with thee
Wild Nights should be
Our luxury!
Futile—the Winds—
To a Heart in port—
Done with the Compass—
Done with the Chart!
Rowing in Eden—
Ah, the Sea!
Might I but moor—Tonight—
In Thee!
(*Complete Poems* 114)

29. Her granddaughter Anita Green recalls being impressed when she saw the envelope with Serling's return address; Anita Scott Coleman simply shrugged and said, "Well, they turned it down."

30. Coleman's contemporary, the sculptor Augusta Savage (1892–1962), is a possible source for Dora Johns. In 1923 the French government refused to admit Savage to an art program because of her color. The incident received international attention and highlighted discrimination faced by African American artists. Savage later helped to organize the Harlem Arts Guild and in 1937 served as founding director of the Harlem Community Art Center.

31. In a biographical blurb, Coleman wrote that she "attended school in Silver City; am an ex-school teacher; am married; live on a ranch; engaged in raising children and chickens" (*Opportunity* June 1926: 188).

32. She also won awards for "Flaming Flame," "The Dark Horse," and "Remarks Upon Three Things as They Are," which are not included in this volume.

33. Billie is referring to the 5402 Hooper Avenue residence. The house, which is still painted green, is near the corner of Hooper Avenue and East Fifty-fourth Street.

34. Race riots between blacks and whites erupted in various cities in 1919, including Longview, Texas; Elaine, Arkansas; Charleston, South Carolina; and Washington, D.C., in what is now known as the "Red Summer" of 1919. Charlotta Bass's report on the Houston riot in the *Eagle* may have provided source material for "The Brat."

Works Cited

Allen, Carol. *Black Women Intellectuals: Strategies of Nation, Family, and Neigh-borhood in the Works of Pauline Hopkins, Jessie Fauset, and Marita Bonner.* New York: Garland P, 1998.

Allen, Gay Wilson. *William James.* Minneapolis: U of Minnesota P, 1970.

Alexander, Bob. *Six-Guns and Single Jacks.* Silver City: Gila Books, 2006.

Ammons, Elizabeth, ed. *Short Fiction by Black Women, 1900–1920.* New York: Oxford UP, 1991.

Baker, Houston A., Jr. *Singers of Daybreak: Studies in Black American Literature.* Washington: Howard UP, 1974.

Bass, Charlotta. *Forty Years: Memoirs from the Pages of a Newspaper.* Los Angeles: Charlotta Bass, 1960.

"Blacks Played Important Role." *Tallahassee Democrat.* 24 March 1974. Vertical File. State Library of Florida, Tallahassee, FL.

Bond, Max. "The Negro in Los Angeles." Diss. U of Southern California, June 1936.

Bogle, Donald. *Dorothy Dandridge.* New York: Boulevard Books, 1998.

Bordwell, David, Janet Staiger, and Kristin Thompson. *The Classical Hollywood Cinema: Film Style and Mode of Production to 1960.* New York: Columbia UP, 1985.

Bryant, Clora, et al. *Central Avenue Sounds: Jazz in Los Angeles.* Berkeley: U of California P, 1998.

Caffey, Ida. Telephone interviews. 17 and 21 July 2006.

Chesnutt, Charles. *The Wife of His Youth and Other Stories of the Color Line.* 1899. Ann Arbor: U of Michigan P, 1998.

Coleman, Anita Scott. Letter to Spencer Scott Coleman. 10 February 1943.

———. "Prayer." Unpublished journal entry, ca. 1940.

———. *Reason for Singing.* Prairie City: Decker P, 1948.

————. *The Singing Bells*. Nashville: Broadman P, 1961.

Coleman, Willianna. *Billie: An Autobiography*. N.p., 1931.

Cripps, Thomas. "'Race Movies' as Voices of the Black Bourgeoisie: The Scar of Shame." In *Representing Blackness: Issues in Film and Video*. Ed. Valerie Smith. New Brunswick: Rutgers UP, 1997. 47–59.

————. *Slow Fade to Black: The Negro in American Film, 1900–1942*. New York: Oxford UP, 1977.

Dickinson, Emily. *The Complete Poems of Emily Dickinson*. Ed. Thomas H. Johnson. Boston: Little, Brown, 1960.

DuBois, W. E. B. "Postscript." *Crisis* 34.9 (Nov. 1927): 311–12, 322.

————. *The Souls of Black Folk*. 1903. New York: Penguin, 1996.

————. *Writings*. New York: Library of America, 1986.

Dunbar, Paul Laurence. *The Sport of the Gods*. 1903. New York: Signet, 1999.

Dunbar-Nelson, Alice. "Hope Deferred." 1914. Rpt. in Gable 5–11.

Flamming, Douglas. *Bound for Freedom: Black Los Angeles in Jim Crow America*. Berkeley: U of California P, 2005.

Ford-Grabowsky, Mary, ed. *Sacred Voices: Essential Women's Wisdom Through the Ages*. New York: HarperCollins, 2002.

Fultz, Michael. "'The Morning Cometh': African-American Periodicals, Education, and the Black Middle Class, 1900–1930." *Journal of Negro History* 80.3 (Summer 1995): 97–112.

Gable, Craig, ed. *Ebony Rising: Short Fiction of the Greater Harlem Renaissance Era*. Bloomington: Indiana UP, 2004.

Gilbert, Sandra M., and Susan Gubar. Foreword. *Women of the Harlem Renaissance*. By Cheryl A. Wall. Bloomington: Indiana UP, 1995. ix–xi.

Glasrud, Bruce A., and Laurie Champion. "Anita Scott Coleman." *American Women Writers 1900–1945: A Bio-Bibliographic Critical Sourcebook*. Ed. Laurie Champion. Westport: Greenwood P, 2000. 77–81.

————, ed. *The African American West: A Century of Short Stories*. Boulder: UP of Colorado, 2000.

Green, Anita Washington. E-mail interview. 28 July 2006.

Henderson, Cindy, Anita Green, Lisa Coleman, Jeanette Thompson, Douglas Jackson, and David Jackson. Personal interviews, Los Angeles, 30 July 2006.

Higginson, Thomas Wentworth. *Army Life in a Black Regiment*. New York: Collier, 1962.

Himes, Chester. *If He Hollers Let Him Go*. 1945. New York: Thunder's Mouth P, 2002.

————. *The Collected Stories*. New York: Thunder's Mouth P, 1990.

Honey, Maureen, ed. *Shadowed Dreams: Women's Poetry of the Harlem Renaissance*. 2nd ed. New Brunswick: Rutgers UP, 2006.

Hopkins, Pauline Elizabeth. *Contending Forces: A Romance Illustrative of Negro Life North and South*. 1900. New York: Oxford UP, 1988.

————. *Of One Blood. Or, the Hidden Self*. 1902–3. *The Magazine Novels of Pauline Hopkins*. New York: Oxford UP, 1988.

Hurston, Zora Neale. *Their Eyes Were Watching God*. 1937. New York: Harper and Row, 1990.

Humble, Terry. Telephone interview. 10 July 2006.

Hutchinson, George. *In Search of Nella Larsen: A Biography of the Color Line*. Cambridge: Harvard UP, 2006.

Jackson, Douglas. Telephone interview. 15 July 2006.

Jackson, Edward M. *Images of Black Men in Black Women Writers 1950–1990*. Bristol: Wyndham Hall P, 1992.

Johnson, Helene. *This Waiting for Love: Helene Johnson, Poet of the Harlem Renaissance*. Ed. Verner D. Mitchell. Amherst: U of Massachusetts P, 2000.

Johnson, James Weldon. *The Autobiography of an Ex-Colored Man*. 1912. New York: Penguin, 1990.

Jones, Gayl. *Corregidora*. 1975. Boston: Beacon, 1987.

Kenner, Charles L. *Buffalo Soldiers and Officers of the Ninth Cavalry, 1867–1898*. Norman: U of Oklahoma P, 1999.

Knopf, Marcy, ed. *The Sleeper Wakes: Harlem Renaissance Stories by Women*. New Brunswick: Rutgers UP, 1993.

Lutz, Tom, and Susanna Ashton, eds. *These "Colored" United States: African American Essays from the 1920s*. New Brunswick: Rutgers UP, 1996.

Morrison, Toni. *Song of Solomon*. 1977. New York: Vintage, 2004.

"Mount Zion Baptist Church 50th Anniversary Program." May 1942. Department of Special Collections, Young Research Library, UCLA.

Mulroy, Kevin. *Freedom on the Border: The Seminole Maroons in Florida, the Indian Territory, Coahuila, and Texas*. Lubbock: Texas Tech UP, 1993.

Murphy, Beatrice M., ed. *Ebony Rhythm: An Anthology of Contemporary Negro Verse*. New York: Exposition P, 1948.

Naylor, Gloria. *Mama Day*. New York: Vintage, 1988.

Nichols, Charles H., ed. *Arna Bontemps-Langston Hughes Letters: 1925–1967*. New York: Dodd, Mead, 1980.

The Normalite. Vol. XIII, no. 2 (Yearbook of the Senior Class of 1909). Silver City, New Mexico, June 1909.

Patton, Venetria K., and Maureen Honey. *Double-Take: A Revisionist Harlem Renaissance Anthology*. New Brunswick: Rutgers UP, 2001.

Porter, Kenneth W. "Negro Labor in the Western Cattle Industry, 1866–1900." *Labor History* 10.3 (1969): 346–74.

Rampersad, Arnold. *I, Too, Sing America: The Life of Langston Hughes*. Vol. I. New York: Oxford UP, 1986.

———. "Introduction." *The New Negro*. Ed. Alain Locke. 1925. New York: Touchstone, 1999.

Ravage, John W. *Black Pioneers: Images of the Black Experience on the North American Frontier*. Salt Lake City: U of Utah P, 1997.

Richardson, Barbara J. *Black Pioneers of New Mexico: A Documentary and Pictorial History*. Rio Rancho: Panorama P, 1976.

Roberts, Edgar, and Henry Jacobs, eds. *Literature: An Introduction to Reading and Writing*. Upper Saddle River: Prentice Hall, 2003.

Rogers, William Warren. "A Great Stirring in the Land: Tallahassee and Leon County in 1860." *Florida Historical Quarterly* 44.2 (October 1985): 148–60.

Rooks, Noliwe M. *Ladies' Pages: African American Women's Magazines and the Culture That Made Them*. New Brunswick: Rutgers UP, 2004.

Roses, Lorraine Elena, and Ruth Elizabeth Randolph. *Harlem Renaissance and Beyond: Literary Biographies of One Hundred Black Women Writers, 1900–1945*. Cambridge: Harvard UP, 1989.

———, ed. *Harlem's Glory: Black Women Writing, 1900–1950*. Cambridge: Harvard UP, 1996.

Shipley, Lee. "Lee Side O' L.A." *Los Angeles Times* 4 May 1940: A-4.

Shockley, Ann Allen. *Afro-American Women Writers, 1746–1933*. New York: Meridian, 1989.

Singh, Amrijit, and Daniel M. Scott, III, eds. *The Collected Writings of Wallace Thurman*. New Brunswick: Rutgers UP, 2003.

Stokes, Elizabeth Stapleton. *Small Wisdom*. New York: Henry Harrison, 1937.

Thurman, Wallace. "Cordelia the Crude." 1926. Rpt. in Gable 184–87.

———. *The Blacker the Berry*. 1929. New York: Touchstone, 1996.

Tyler, Bruce M. *From Harlem to Hollywood: The Struggle for Racial and Cultural Democracy 1920–1943*. New York: Garland P, 1992.

"An Unfortunate Omission." *Messenger* (May–June 1928): 111.

Vincent, Ted. "The Blacks Who Freed Mexico." *Journal of Negro History* 79.3 (Summer 1994): 257–76.

Walker, Alice. *The Color Purple*. New York: Washington Square P, 1982.

Washington, Booker T. Letter to Miss Elisabeth Nichols. 14 April 1908.

Weems, Robert E., Jr. "Robert A. Cole and The Metropolitan Funeral System Association: A Profile of a Civic-Minded African-American Businessman." *Journal of Negro History* 78.1 (Winter 1993): 1–15.

West, Dorothy. "Hannah Byde." 1926. Rpt. in *Where the Wild Grape Grows: Selected Writings, 1930–1950*. Ed. Verner D. Mitchell and Cynthia Davis. Amherst: U of Massachusetts P, 2005. 79–85.

———. *The Living Is Easy*. 1948. New York: Feminist P, 1982.

———. *The Wedding*. New York: Anchor, 1995.

Wilson, Sondra Kathryn, ed. *The "Crisis" Reader: Stories, Poetry, and Essays from the N.A.A.C.P.'s "Crisis" Magazine*. New York: Modern Library, 1999.

———. *The "Messenger" Reader: Stories, Poetry, and Essays from The "Messenger" Magazine*. New York: Modern Library, 2000.

———. *The "Opportunity" Reader: Stories, Poetry, and Essays from The Urban League's "Opportunity" Magazine*. New York: Modern Library, 1999.

Work Projects Administration. *New Mexico: A Guide to the Colorful State*. New York: Hastings House, 1940.

Young, Mary E. "Anita Scott Coleman: A Neglected Harlem Renaissance Writer." *CLA Journal* 40.3 (March 1997): 271–87.